Brand Licensing

by Steven Ekstract
with Stu Seltzer

Brand Licensing For Dummies®

Published by: **John Wiley & Sons, Inc.**, 111 River Street, Hoboken, NJ 07030-5774, www.wiley.com

Copyright © 2025 by John Wiley & Sons, Inc. All rights reserved, including rights for text and data mining and training of artificial technologies or similar technologies.

Media and software compilation copyright © 2025 by John Wiley & Sons, Inc. All rights reserved, including rights for text and data mining and training of artificial technologies or similar technologies.

Published simultaneously in Canada

No part of this publication may be reproduced, stored in a retrieval system or transmitted in any form or by any means, electronic, mechanical, photocopying, recording, scanning or otherwise, except as permitted under Sections 107 or 108 of the 1976 United States Copyright Act, without the prior written permission of the Publisher. Requests to the Publisher for permission should be addressed to the Permissions Department, John Wiley & Sons, Inc., 111 River Street, Hoboken, NJ 07030, (201) 748-6011, fax (201) 748-6008, or online at http://www.wiley.com/go/permissions.

Trademarks: Wiley, For Dummies, the Dummies Man logo, Dummies.com, Making Everything Easier, and related trade dress are trademarks or registered trademarks of John Wiley & Sons, Inc. and may not be used without written permission. All other trademarks are the property of their respective owners. John Wiley & Sons, Inc. is not associated with any product or vendor mentioned in this book.

LIMIT OF LIABILITY/DISCLAIMER OF WARRANTY: THE PUBLISHER AND THE AUTHOR MAKE NO REPRESENTATIONS OR WARRANTIES WITH RESPECT TO THE ACCURACY OR COMPLETENESS OF THE CONTENTS OF THIS WORK AND SPECIFICALLY DISCLAIM ALL WARRANTIES, INCLUDING WITHOUT LIMITATION WARRANTIES OF FITNESS FOR A PARTICULAR PURPOSE. NO WARRANTY MAY BE CREATED OR EXTENDED BY SALES OR PROMOTIONAL MATERIALS. THE ADVICE AND STRATEGIES CONTAINED HEREIN MAY NOT BE SUITABLE FOR EVERY SITUATION. THIS WORK IS SOLD WITH THE UNDERSTANDING THAT THE PUBLISHER IS NOT ENGAGED IN RENDERING LEGAL, ACCOUNTING, OR OTHER PROFESSIONAL SERVICES. IF PROFESSIONAL ASSISTANCE IS REQUIRED, THE SERVICES OF A COMPETENT PROFESSIONAL PERSON SHOULD BE SOUGHT. NEITHER THE PUBLISHER NOR THE AUTHOR SHALL BE LIABLE FOR DAMAGES ARISING HEREFROM. THE FACT THAT AN ORGANIZATION OR WEBSITE IS REFERRED TO IN THIS WORK AS A CITATION AND/OR A POTENTIAL SOURCE OF FURTHER INFORMATION DOES NOT MEAN THAT THE AUTHOR OR THE PUBLISHER ENDORSES THE INFORMATION THE ORGANIZATION OR WEBSITE MAY PROVIDE OR RECOMMENDATIONS IT MAY MAKE. FURTHER, READERS SHOULD BE AWARE THAT INTERNET WEBSITES LISTED IN THIS WORK MAY HAVE CHANGED OR DISAPPEARED BETWEEN WHEN THIS WORK WAS WRITTEN AND WHEN IT IS READ.

For general information on our other products and services, please contact our Customer Care Department within the U.S. at 877-762-2974, outside the U.S. at 317-572-3993, or fax 317-572-4002. For technical support, please visit https://hub.wiley.com/community/support/dummies.

Wiley publishes in a variety of print and electronic formats and by print-on-demand. Some material included with standard print versions of this book may not be included in e-books or in print-on-demand. If this book refers to media that is not included in the version you purchased, you may download this material at http://booksupport.wiley.com. For more information about Wiley products, visit www.wiley.com.

Library of Congress Control Number: 2025935562

ISBN 978-1-394-29017-8 (pbk); ISBN 978-1-394-29019-2 (ebk); ISBN 978-1-394-29018-5 (ebk)

Printed and bound by CPI Group (UK) Ltd, Croydon, CR0 4YY

C9781394290178_220425

The manufacturer's authorized representative according to the EU General Product Safety Regulation is Wiley-VCH GmbH, Boschstr. 12, 69469 Weinheim, Germany, e-mail: Product_Safety@wiley.com.

Contents at a Glance

Introduction 1

Part 1: Getting Started with Licensing 5
CHAPTER 1: How Brand Licensing Works 7
CHAPTER 2: Probing Branding: Why People Buy. 21
CHAPTER 3: Where on Earth Do Brands Come From? 35
CHAPTER 4: Exploring Licensing Trends and Innovations 47

Part 2: Diving into Licensing 65
CHAPTER 5: Navigating the Licensing Process 67
CHAPTER 6: Negotiating the License Deal 81
CHAPTER 7: Getting Your First Licensed Product Up and Running 97
CHAPTER 8: Developing Retail 113

**Part 3: Forging and Maintaining Strong
Licensing Partnerships** 129
CHAPTER 9: The Key Points in a Successful Partnership 131
CHAPTER 10: Keeping Your End of the Deal. 139

Part 4: Maximizing Sales through Licensing 151
CHAPTER 11: Selling Your Licensed Products. 153
CHAPTER 12: Marketing Tools That Boost Retail Sales. 169
CHAPTER 13: Globalization of Brands 179
CHAPTER 14: The Future of Brand Licensing 189

Part 5: The Part of Tens 201
CHAPTER 15: Ten Do's (and Don'ts) for Licensing 203
CHAPTER 16: Ten Essential Tips for Licensors 211
CHAPTER 17: (Nearly) Ten Brand Licensing Areas. 219

Index 227

Table of Contents

INTRODUCTION 1

About This Book. 1

Foolish Assumptions. 2

Icons Used in This Book 2

Beyond the Book 3

Where to Go from Here 3

PART 1: GETTING STARTED WITH LICENSING 5

CHAPTER 1: **How Brand Licensing Works** 7

Getting a Bird's-Eye View of Brand Licensing 8

Seeing Why So Many Top Companies Love Brand Licensing 9

Licensing as a marketing powerhouse. 9

Brand Licensing 101: How Coca-Cola capitalizes on its brand 10

Exploring the licensing of other brands 11

Deploying a Brand Licensing Strategy 13

Examining the different categories of brand licensing 13

Understanding trademarks, copyrights, and patents 14

Boosting sales through brand licensing. 15

Brand Licensing Includes Products, Services, and Experiences 16

Consumer products: Recognizing the licensing everywhere 16

Experiences: Selling memorable moments 17

Navigating Digital Licensing: The New Frontier. 18

Bringing Together Brand Collaborations 18

CHAPTER 2: **Probing Branding: Why People Buy** 21

Defining Branding 22

Investigating the Ingredients of Branding 22

Breaking Down Why Branding Is Important 23

Trusting in Brands. 23

Why trust matters in branding 24

How brands build trust. 24

Emotional Branding: Creating Connections That Last 25

Branding through pop culture. 26

Considering consumer psychology and brand desire 26

Building Brand Trust with the Purchase Pyramid. 28

Tapping into the Power of Brand Licensing. 29

Noting Three Key Brand Licensing Principles You Can Apply
Right Away 32
    Licensing can make a good product great. 32
    Licensing can be your sustainable competitive advantage. 32
    All licensing is risky; take calculated, manageable risks 33

CHAPTER 3: **Where on Earth Do Brands Come From?** 35
Recognizing Top Brand Licensors 35
    The Walt Disney Company ($62 billion estimated). 36
    Authentic Brands Group ($28 billion estimated) 36
    Dotdash Meredith ($26.4 billion estimated) 37
    Warner Bros./Discovery ($15 billion) 37
    Hasbro ($14.1 billion estimated). 38
    NBC Universal/Universal Products &
    Experiences ($11.5 billion) 38
    The Pokémon Company International ($10.8 billion). 38
    Bluestar Alliance ($8.5 billion estimated). .39
    Mattel ($8.5 billion estimated). 39
    WHP Global ($7.5 billion) 39
Eyeing Entertainment Licensing for Consumer Products and
Experiences 40
Finding Opportunity in Entertainment. 42
Tapping into Brand Licensing for Products of All Kinds. 43
    Getting creative with art and culture licensing 44
    Licensing nonprofits and associations 45
    Expanding licensing with artificial intelligence 45
Bringing a Product Back to Life: Zombie Brands 46

CHAPTER 4: **Exploring Licensing Trends and Innovations** 47
Tracking the Rise of the Brand Collaboration .47
    Breaking down why brands combine. 48
    Understanding what makes a great collab .49
    Drawing on the passion of superfans 49
Digital Licensing: Finding Opportunity Online. 51
    Looking at two examples of online licensing success 53
    Talkin' non-fungible tokens 54
    Understanding phygital products. 56
    Bringing brands to online betting. 57
Seeing How Video Game Brands Are Winning with Licensing 58
    Glimpsing the metaverse through sandbox games. 58
    Discovering brand licensing in the metaverse 59
Growing Opportunity in Cannabis Branding and Licensing 60
Maximizing YouTube Celebrity through Licensing 61
Connecting with a Brand through Experiential Licensing 62

PART 2: DIVING INTO LICENSING 65

CHAPTER 5: **Navigating the Licensing Process**. 67

Knowing Where to Research Licensing Opportunities. 67
Turning to online publications for intel 68
Using AI and the Internet 69
Understanding How to Match Product to License 70
Retail intelligence. 71
Non-exclusive licenses 72
Immersing Yourself in the Licensing Trade 72
Leveraging trade associations. 72
Bringing in a licensing consultant 74
Working important trade shows and conferences. 75
Developing Relationships in the Business. 77
Building trust 78
Crushing the first conversation with would-be partners. 78
Determining your unique selling proposition 79
Translating that trust into a pitch 79
Practicing your pitch 80

CHAPTER 6: **Negotiating the License Deal**. 81

Connecting with the Brand Owner (Licensor). 82
Meeting licensors at a licensing trade show 82
Hitting an industry trade show 83
Turning to social media 84
Leveraging industry directories. 84
Using Your Research to Your Advantage When You
Make Contact. 84
Finding and Hiring an IP Attorney. 86
Crafting and Submitting Your Licensing Proposal 87
Estimating sales and royalties 88
Understanding the guaranteed minimum royalty payment. 89
Advancing to the Next Stage: The Licensing Agreement and
Term Sheet. 90
Negotiating basic terms of your licensing agreement 91
Creating the term sheet 93
Discussing Additional Terms 94
Knowing When to Walk away from a Bad Deal. 95
Finalizing the Long-Form Legal Agreement. 95

CHAPTER 7: **Getting Your First Licensed Product
Up and Running**. 97

Designing Your Product 98
Landing on how it looks 98
Hiring a designer 99
Wait for it: Being patient about product approval 100
Building trust as a new licensee 101

Finding the Right Manufacturer for Your Product 101
  Following a licensor's guidelines 102
  Mass-market manufacturing for retail 103
  Print-on-demand 104
  Considering shipping and duty costs 104
Crafting a Compelling Package that Meets Licensor
Requirements. 105
Developing Your Pricing Strategy 107
Getting the Word Out through Marketing and Public Relations 108
  Maximizing public relations efforts. 108
  Letting the industry know your name: Trade advertising 109
  Advertising to consumers. 109
Tracking Sales and Royalty Reporting 110
Hiring a Licensing Manager to Address Growth 110

CHAPTER 8: **Developing Retail** 113
Understanding What Retailers Want 113
Comparing Wholesale versus Retail 115
Following the Channels of Retail Distribution 115
Finding the Best Retailer for Your Product .116
  Researching potential retail partners 117
  Breaking down who's who at the large retailers 117
  Understanding the three-star process .118
  Getting your products placed at retail .120
  Becoming a preferred vendor 121
Evaluating Brick-and-Mortar and E-Commerce Options 122
  Going for the Goldilocks solution: Hybrid retail 123
  Addressing Amazon's 1P and 3P selling options. 124
Developing Marketing Promotions for Consumers 125
  Utilizing your partner's existing marketing tools 125
  Knowing when to bring in an outside agency 126
  Working with your licensor partner 126

PART 3: FORGING AND MAINTAINING STRONG
LICENSING PARTNERSHIPS 129

CHAPTER 9: **The Key Points in a Successful Partnership** 131
Building Strong Partnership Teams 132
Developing and Maintaining Relationships with Licensors. 133
  Staying connected with your licensor. .134
  Troubleshooting product development obstacles 135
  Embracing ongoing communications. .136
  Respecting the partnership 136

CHAPTER 10: **Keeping Your End of the Deal** 139
    Reporting and Paying Royalties. 139
        Sending your reports as agreed 140
        Paying your royalties on time and in full 141
        Identifying licensors' common complaints 142
    Dealing with an Audit of Royalty Payments. 143
        Understanding why your licensor decides to audit 144
        Going into an audit with the right attitude 144
        Pinpointing common audit issues. 145
        Coping with confrontation when the auditor finds
        accounting errors 148
    Addressing Administrative Tasks in Licensing. 149

PART 4: MAXIMIZING SALES THROUGH LICENSING 151

CHAPTER 11: **Selling Your Licensed Products**. .153
    Peeling Back the Layers of a Licensing Business 153
    Understanding Aspects of Retail Business Development 154
        Recognizing the strength of existing licensed brands 155
        Qualifying your distribution strategy 155
        Preselling licensed products to retail 156
        Embracing marketing assistance from the licensor 157
        Capitalizing on the brand value of your products 158
        Aligning retail distribution and marketing strategy 158
    Setting Up Your License Agreement for Retail Success 161
        Planning an appropriate length of term 161
        Understanding your financial obligations: The minimum
        royalty payment guarantee 162
        Mitigating your risk 162
    Watching Out for Challenges in the Market 163
        Adjusting agreements for timing delays 164
        Playing it safe with franchise classics 164
        Carefully managing celebrity licenses 165

CHAPTER 12: **Marketing Tools That Boost Retail Sales** 169
    Taking Direction from Your Partners 170
        The licensor's investment in your marketing 170
        Tapping into retailers' marketing muscle. 171
    Using Social Media Marketing to Reach Your Target Audience 173
        Embracing social media for product promotion. 174
        Recognizing the scope of social media use 175
    Distinguishing Customers from Fans and Superfans. 176
        Going from consumers to fans: The social media effect 176
        Sliding into superfandom. 176
        Engaging with convention-al fandom. 177

CHAPTER 13: **Globalization of Brands**..............................179
America: Land of the Free, Home of the Brand 179
    Advertising builds brand recognition 180
    Hollywood adds scope 180
    The United States bursts with brand power 181
Setting Your Sights on the Global Market 182
    Responding to global demand for a unique product..........183
    Dissecting the size and scope of the global marketplace 184
Securing Licenses for International Markets.....................185
    Globalization of retail businesses 185
    Sublicensing 186
    Finding global properties 186

CHAPTER 14: **The Future of Brand Licensing** 189
Learning from the Past to Predict the Future 190
Riding the Technology Wave 190
Examining Emerging Tech Shaping Licensing.................192
    AI-generated brands and IP.............................192
    Blockchain and NFTs: The future of digital ownership 192
    Virtual goods and the metaverse: Licensing
    in a digital world 193
    Print-on-demand (POD) 193
    Smartphones and apps: The mobile licensing revolution.......194
Culture Meets Commerce: Seeing How Trends Shape Licensing....194
    Business trends: The changing landscape of licensing 195
    Cultural trends: What consumers want now.................197

PART 5: THE PART OF TENS..................................201

CHAPTER 15: **Ten Do's (and Don'ts) for Licensing**..................203
Do Thorough Research on the Brand Opportunity 203
Do Plan Properly 204
Do Set Realistic Financial Expectations 205
Do Walk Away from Bad Deals 205
Do Leverage the Licensor's Marketing Power..................206
Do Build Strong Relationships...............................207
Do Stay Compliant with Licensing Agreements 207
Do Invest in Quality Legal Support 208
Do Consider Hiring a Licensing Consultant...................208
Do Consider the Risks.....................................209

CHAPTER 16: **Ten Essential Tips for Licensors** 211
Develop a Strategic Licensing Plan 211
Invest in Style Guides and Presentation Materials...............212
Join the Licensing Community...............................213
Ensure Your Trademarks Are Protected 214

       Stay on Top of Tracking and Optimizing Licensing Revenue 214
       Consider Hiring a Licensing Agency 215
       Keep Your Brand Safe and Successful by Managing
       Licensing Risks. 216
       Plan for a Long-Term Investment 216
       Strengthen Your Partnerships by Hosting a Licensing Summit 217
       Expand Your Licensing Program Globally 217

CHAPTER 17: **(Nearly) Ten Brand Licensing Areas** 219
       Entertainment and Character Licensing 219
       Corporate Brand Licensing 220
       Sports Licensing. 221
       Fashion and Apparel Licensing 221
       Celebrity and Influencer Brand Licensing 222
       Music Brand Licensing 223
       Art and Museum Licensing 223
       Nonprofits and Licensing. 224

INDEX 227

Introduction

Brand licensing occurs when one company lets another company use legally protected (trademarked or copyrighted) intellectual property (IP) on products, services, or experiences. As a business, brand licensing has seen significant growth since the beginning of the 2000s. Consumers have transformed into fans of brands, and the Internet has supercharged the business of brand licensing through globalization, speed to market, e-commerce, and new forms of digital engagement.

The fascinating world of brand licensing currently represents $365 billion per year in retail sales of licensed consumer products and experiences and is growing at a rate of 4 percent a year. From cradle to grave, brand licensing reaches into every area of consumer products, services, and experiences. If you're reading this, you're on your way to becoming a licensing insider. The business of IP licensing is still relatively young, and opportunities abound for entrepreneurs looking to cash in on famous brands for their products and services.

In uncertain times, brands have become the trusted anchors for consumers — the one trustworthy constant that keeps them moored in safe harbors. This status is why brand licensing continues to grow. More and more brands are recognizing the power of brand licensing and jumping on board. This growth provides significant opportunities to companies interested in brand licensing.

You can find quite a few books published on the topic, but they tend to be dry and technical. We've written *Brand Licensing For Dummies* to provide an easy-to-understand overview of the licensing business to help you in your journey.

About This Book

Brand Licensing For Dummies is your guide to successfully navigating the world of brand licensing. We've written this book to help you to quickly and easily understand the ins and outs of brand licensing and make your licensing journey smooth and successful. From understanding the requirements necessary to acquire a license to finding a retail partner to sell your licensed products, this book covers it all.

Brand Licensing For Dummies provides you with info on topics like these:

>> Taking advantage of brand licensing to grow your business

>> Finding the right brand for your product

>> Identifying who the major brand players in the business are

>> Recognizing pitfalls to avoid when entering the licensing business

>> Negotiating a licensing deal

>> Getting your licensed product sold at retail

This book guides you through these subjects and plenty of others. We bring you up to speed on how to successfully navigate your brand licensing business journey.

Foolish Assumptions

We've made only one assumption about you, dear reader, while writing: that you're interested in brand licensing and want to find out more, whether you're reading this book to help you develop a brand licensing strategy for your products or simply to discover more about the brand licensing business in general.

Icons Used in This Book

As you go through this book, keep an eye out for the following icons in the margins:

TIP

This icon highlights small pieces of advice that can help you understand key information about brand licensing.

REMEMBER

The Remember icon points out information that's particularly useful. These nuggets will come in handy to you as a new licensee, so pay close attention to them!

WARNING

Look out when you see this icon; it prepares you for potentially detrimental situations to be aware of.

Beyond the Book

You can find even more brand licensing info to delve into online at Dummies.com.

Check out this book's online Cheat Sheet, which includes helpful tips for licensees such as do's and don'ts for licensing deals, questions to ask before signing your licensing contract, and more. Head to www.dummies.com and type **Brand Licensing For Dummies Cheat Sheet** in the search box.

Where to Go from Here

Feel free to skip around to the chapters that contain the information you're most interested in. If you're totally new to brand licensing, you may want to start with good ol' Chapter 1 for an overview. Chapters 5 and 6 help you research and negotiate that first license; after you have it, Part 3 can help you keep it by nurturing lasting relationships with your partners.

When you have the nuts and bolts of licensing down, you're ready to go out and find your first licensing deal. Start by looking into all the different IP available for licensing.

1

Getting Started with Licensing

IN THIS PART . . .

Get a handle on how brand licensing works.

Make the connection between branding and why people buy.

Understand where brands come from.

Get up to speed on licensing trends and innovations.

IN THIS CHAPTER

» Introducing brand licensing

» Showcasing why businesses love brand licensing (and you should too!)

» Looking at the strategy of brand licensing

» Breaking down the major licensing categories

» Collaborating with other brands

Chapter **1**

How Brand Licensing Works

Welcome to the world of brand licensing, and specifically to *Brand Licensing For Dummies.* In the next 16 chapters, we provide you with an easy-to-understand overview of the brand licensing business.

To kick things off, this chapter gives you the big-picture view of why brand licensing can be a game-changer for a product you make (or plan to make). But what exactly is brand licensing, what business practices does it involve, and why do companies do it? We break it all down here; and don't worry, we've got plenty more details throughout the book.

Getting a Bird's-Eye View
of Brand Licensing

Here's how brand licensing works: A company owns intellectual property (IP) — also called *the brand* — that builds a strong positive emotional connection with consumers. Over time, people develop an affinity for the brand. That connection makes licensing a powerful goal for expanding a brand's reach and impact.

Brands license for several key reasons:

>> Boosting consumer engagement by partnering with businesses that can reach a wider audience

>> Tapping into new markets by licensing products that appeal to different demographics and are sold through different marketing channels

>> Driving sales and brand visibility by creating new products or experiences that keep the brand fresh and top of mind

To make brand licensing work, IP owners team up with key players to get their products into the hands of consumers. Each member of the licensing squad has a specific role:

>> **The licensor:** The brand owner who holds the intellectual property and grants the licensee the right to use it.

>> **The licensee:** The manufacturer or service provider who licenses the brand to use on its products or services. In return, it pays the licensor a *royalty* (a percentage of sales).

>> **The sellers:** Retailers, wholesalers, and distributors who help get the licensed products or services into stores, online marketplaces, and ultimately, into customers' hands.

When these three work together, brand licensing becomes a powerful business tool that benefits everyone involved!

Seeing Why So Many Top Companies Love Brand Licensing

The reason so many companies use brand licensing is pretty simple: It's an incredibly powerful marketing tool. When done right, licensing boosts a brand's visibility, strengthens its reputation, and — unlike traditional marketing — actually generates revenue (through royalties paid by licensees) instead of just costing money.

Licensing as a marketing powerhouse

To put licensing's marketing potential in perspective, here's how other common marketing tactics work:

>> **Advertising:** This marketing aspect can include anything from print ads in newspapers and magazines to billboards, TV or radio ads, or even ads online. Companies can spend millions here, but after the money's spent, it's gone.

>> **Social media posts and campaigns:** Platforms such as Instagram, Facebook, and YouTube connect brands with customers, but effectively managing campaigns requires a dedicated social media team to handle the posts.

>> **Email marketing:** Sending emails with special offers and sales to customers to keep the brand fresh in their minds is a great way to encourage repeat buyers. However, developing and maintaining an email database and constantly updating it requires significant time and investment.

>> **Marketing analytics:** Tracking customer behavior helps refine marketing strategies, but it requires specialized software and trained experts to interpret the data.

>> **Search engine optimization (SEO):** Ensuring a brand ranks high in search results helps drive traffic; however, optimizing websites and content requires ongoing work by SEO specialists.

>> **Public relations (PR):** Gaining media attention through press releases and earned media helps maintain visibility, but PR efforts require an in-house team or external agency.

REMEMBER

Unlike these other strategies, licensing allows a brand to expand into new products, reach fresh audiences, and generate revenue at the same time — all while strengthening customer loyalty.

Brand Licensing 101: How Coca-Cola capitalizes on its brand

Ever wonder why you see so many Coca-Cola hoodies, T-shirts, and caps? It's not just fashion; it's smart business! Coca-Cola is a master at brand licensing; the following sections break down how.

Step 1: Spend big to make big

Coca-Cola knows that advertising equals sales. In 2023, the company spent a whopping $5 billion on ads — TV, social media, billboards, you name it. That was 20 percent more than in 2022. But it worked. Its *net operating revenue* (a fancy term for total sales) hit $46 billion that year.

Step 2: Turn fans into free ads

Coca-Cola goes beyond selling drinks by licensing its brand for all kinds of products. Its favorite? Fashion and apparel. Sixty percent of Coca-Cola's licensing business comes from clothing.

Think about it: When someone wears a Coca-Cola hoodie, they're a walking billboard for the brand. But here's the genius part: Instead of paying for the ad, Coca-Cola gets paid!

Step 3: Be selective

Even though Coca-Cola makes billions from licensed products, it doesn't just slap its logo on anything. It carefully chooses licensing partners to protect its brand.

REMEMBER

Too much licensing can flood the market and weaken a brand's image. That's why Coca-Cola sees licensing as a marketing tool first and a money-maker second.

COCA-COLA CHEWING GUM: THE BIRTH OF BRAND LICENSING

Did you know that Coca-Cola was one of the first brands to do licensing? Way back in 1903, Coca-Cola licensed its name to a separate company to produce Coca-Cola–branded chewing gum. This early move set the stage for modern brand licensing.

Fast forward 120-plus years, and Coca-Cola is still one of the most recognizable brands in the world. Licensing has been a key part of its marketing strategy from the very beginning, helping expand its brand far beyond soft drinks. (Flip to the nearby section "Brand Licensing 101: How Coca-Cola capitalizes on its brand" for details.)

Want to dive deeper into Coca-Cola's rich licensing history? Check out The Martin Guide to Coca-Cola Memorabilia's article at www.earlycoke.com/coca-cola-chewing-gum.

Coca-Cola's licensing journey proves that a strong brand can go way beyond its original product and sometimes even create a whole new industry.

Exploring the licensing of other brands

Brand licensing is everywhere. From fashion and publishing to automotive, music, film, and even heavy construction, companies across industries have successfully leveraged licensing to expand their brand reach.

What do all these brands have in common? *Brand equity*, the loyalty and recognition that consumers have for a brand that makes it valuable beyond its core products. Strong brand equity allows companies to license their names into new and exciting product categories, from merchandise and retail experiences to theme parks and even digital content. Licensing is about creating deeper consumer connections and ensuring that a brand stays relevant and visible across different industries.

Table 1-1 provides a look at some of the most famous brands that have thrived through licensing (aside from Coca-Cola, which we cover in the earlier section "Brand Licensing 101: How Coca-Cola capitalizes on its brand"). These brands have successfully turned their names into powerful revenue streams and marketing tools, proving that a well-managed licensing strategy can be a game-changer.

TABLE 1-1   **Famous Successful Brands**

The Brand	How It Started	What It Licenses
Star Wars	Premiered as a film in 1977 and became an instant hit that turned into a franchise.	Toys, collectibles, apparel, home décor, kitchenware, LEGO sets, board games, books, comics, trading cards, video games, and many others
Caterpillar	A manufacturer of construction and mining equipment (becoming the world's leader in the industry); synonymous with rugged durability and quality.	Footwear (work boots), work wear, storage products, tools, and even toys

(continued)

TABLE 1-1 *(continued)*

The Brand	How It Started	What It Licenses
Grateful Dead	Formed in 1965; became one of the most legendary rock bands, with a devoted fan base known as Deadheads.	Apparel, posters, home décor, collectibles, accessories, lifestyle products, and even ice cream. Ben & Jerry's Cherry Garcia flavor is one of the most famous licensed products.
Chevy Corvette	Introduced by the Chevrolet automobile company in 1953 as a boost for sluggish sales; became an icon and developed a fan base worldwide with its iconic designs.	Apparel and accessories, collectibles and diecast toys, jewelry, and car care products.
Keith Haring	Came to fame in the 1980s New York art world as a graffiti artist and died young; art became ubiquitous in the licensing world.	Apparel, accessories, home décor, footwear, and limited-edition collaborations with luxury and streetwear brands.
Pokémon	Released in Japan in 1996; video games (Pokémon Red and Pokémon Green) for the Game Boy expanded into a global franchise.	Trading cards, toys, apparel, accessories, home décor, video games, board games, collectibles, plush figures, stationery, and collaborations with fashion and lifestyle brands.
Dockers	Launched in 1986 by Levi Strauss & Co.; became the go-to brand for casual and business-casual khakis.	Footwear, belts, bags, eyewear, socks, and accessories.
Scotts Miracle-Gro	Founded in 1868; became a trusted name in lawn and garden care.	Lawn mowers, gardening tools, gloves, sheds, hoses, and outdoor power equipment.
Yves Saint Laurent	Founded in 1961; revolutionized high fashion with ready-to-wear collections that merged elegance with modern style.	Fragrances, eyewear, jewelry, shoes, and accessories.
Better Homes & Gardens	Founded in 1924; became the leading magazine for home décor, gardening, and food, shaping American lifestyles for generations.	A direct-to-retail partnership with Walmart featuring over 4,000 products, including bedding, bath, home décor, furniture, paint, wallpaper, and lighting; also licensed for Better Homes & Gardens Real Estate with over 400 offices worldwide.

Each of these brands has successfully expanded far beyond its original product through licensing. Whether it's toys, clothing, gardening equipment, or luxury goods, these companies have tapped into consumer loyalty to create entire new revenue streams while strengthening their brand presence worldwide.

Deploying a Brand Licensing Strategy

If you're new to licensing, the most important concept to grasp is how leveraging a brand's power can boost sales, expand market presence, and strengthen consumer loyalty.

In later chapters, we guide you through the key steps of deploying a brand licensing strategy, including the following:

>> Finding the right licenses (Chapter 5)

>> Developing strong retail relationships (Chapter 8)

>> Creating effective marketing strategies (Chapter 12)

By understanding and applying these principles, you'll be equipped to capitalize on brand licensing opportunities and drive success in the marketplace.

Examining the different categories of brand licensing

Though the most common form of brand licensing involves consumer products, licensing extends into experiences and digital or virtual items as well; we cover those later in the chapter. Many brands license their names, logos, and characters for immersive experiences and digital content.

Here's a quick breakdown of commonly licensed items in all three categories:

>> **Consumer products:** Encompasses nearly every product type, including these:

- Toys and collectibles

- Apparel and accessories

- Food and beverages

- Home décor and furnishings

- Footwear

- Pet products

- Consumer electronics and appliances

- Health and beauty

- >> **Experiences:** Licensing can also bring brands to life through interactive, real-world experiences, such as the following:

  - Stage shows and live events

  - Theme park rides and attractions

  - Branded restaurants

  - Cruises and travel experiences

  - Gaming and lottery partnerships

- >> **Digital and virtual Items:** As technology evolves, brand licensing has expanded into the digital world, including these options (read more about them in Chapter 4):

  - Online video games and in-game content

  - Avatars and skins for characters

  - Online sports betting

  - Non-fungible tokens (NFTs)

By understanding these categories, you can better identify licensing opportunities and strategically expand your brand into new revenue streams.

Understanding trademarks, copyrights, and patents

Before diving into brand licensing, you need a handle on how intellectual property is categorized and protected by law. The three main types of IP — trademarks, copyrights, and patents — help safeguard different aspects of products, brands, and innovations.

This book focuses on trademark licensing, which is the most common form of licensing in branding. However, knowing how copyrights and patents differ is still useful.

With guidance from the U.S. Patent and Trademark Office (USPTO), here's a quick breakdown of each category:

- >> **Trademarks:** *Trademarks* protect brand names, logos, slogans, and symbols that identify and distinguish a product or service. Think of Nike's swoosh logo, the McDonald's golden arches, or the word *Coca-Cola* in its signature font; these are all trademarks. A registered trademark prevents others from using the same or confusingly similar marks.

- >> **Copyrights:** *Copyrights* cover original artistic, literary, or intellectual works, including music, books, paintings, movies, software, and photography. A song by Taylor Swift, a novel by Stephen King, and a movie script are all items protected under copyright law. A copyright owner controls the rights to reproduce, distribute, and display their work.

- >> **Patents:** *Patents* apply to new inventions, processes, or designs like a pharmaceutical drug or device, a unique engine design, or a new type of touchscreen technology. A patent grants the inventor exclusive rights to make, use, or sell the invention for a set period.

TIP

Visit the USPTO website for full descriptions and examples of these IP types: www.uspto.gov/trademarks/basics/trademark-patent-copyright.

REMEMBER

Before entering any licensing agreement, make sure the brand owner has properly registered and protected its IP. If it hasn't, anyone can legally use the brand without permission! (See Chapters 6 and 7 for more.)

Boosting sales through brand licensing

You may be wondering, "How can brand licensing help my business?" The answer is simple: Brand power equals more sales.

If you're selling products, adding a well-known brand to your lineup can instantly boost consumer trust and interest. People are more likely to buy a product with a familiar name because they already recognize and trust the brand behind it.

And as we note earlier in the chapter, it's not just for consumer products. Brand licensing works across many industries. Consider the following:

- >> **Theme parks and attractions:** A Batman-themed ride will attract far more visitors than a generic roller coaster ride.

- >> **Restaurants and hospitality:** A café named after a beloved brand will likely draw in more customers than an unknown name (see the nearby sidebar "How a movie inspired a restaurant empire" for an example).

- >> **Retail and apparel:** A Michael Jordan Chicago Bulls-branded NBA jersey will outsell a generic basketball jersey because of the legendary name associated with it.

No matter what business you're in, strategically using well-known brands can drive sales, increase foot traffic, and give you a competitive edge.

HOW A MOVIE INSPIRED A RESTAURANT EMPIRE

When *Forrest Gump* hit theaters in 1994, it became an instant blockbuster. One of the film's most memorable storylines was Bubba Gump Shrimp Co., the seafood business Forrest started in honor of his friend Bubba.

In 1995, a seafood company licensed the Bubba Gump name to sell frozen shrimp. Soon after, a Monterey, California, restaurant saw the potential and secured a license for a Bubba Gump Shrimp Co. restaurant. The themed dining experience was a hit, catching the attention of Landry's, a major restaurant group, which expanded the brand.

As of this writing, Bubba Gump Shrimp Co. has locations worldwide, making it the first restaurant chain ever inspired by a movie — and a perfect example of how brand licensing can turn fiction into a thriving real-world business.

Brand Licensing Includes Products, Services, and Experiences

In this section, you find a quick overview of key brand licensing segments and how they may fit into your business strategy.

Consumer products: Recognizing the licensing everywhere

The most widespread form of brand licensing is in consumer products. If you want to see brand licensing in action, the best thing you can do is hit the stores! Walk through Walmart, Target, Uniqlo, Zara, GAP, Macy's, Primark, or Hot Topic and take a close look at the products on the shelves. Ask yourself the following:

>> Which ones are licensed?

>> Which ones are *core* (owned by the company itself)?

Chances are you'll be surprised by how many products are either licensed or feature a licensed brand. For those new to licensing, retail research is an eye-opening experience. Most consumers assume that all products come directly from the brand, but after you start looking at packaging details, you realize how deeply licensing is embedded in the marketplace.

Experiences: Selling memorable moments

For Gen Z (born between 1997 and 2012) and Gen Alpha (born between 2010 and 2024), real-world experiences have become an expectation, not just a luxury. These younger generations seek out branded, shareable experiences and love to commemorate them with merchandise.

But experiential licensing is much bigger than just concerts and festivals. Immersive brand experiences such as the following are thriving:

>> **The FRIENDS Experience:** Launched in 2019 for the show's 25th anniversary, this interactive exhibit became a global success with permanent locations and touring exhibits. Fans can explore Central Perk, Monica's apartment, and original props from the show.

>> **The Office Experience:** A touring interactive exhibit where fans can step into Dunder Mifflin, sit at Michael Scott's desk, and relive classic moments from the show.

>> **Titanic: The Exhibition:** A licensed, immersive experience featuring life-size recreations, authentic artifacts, and personal stories from the ship's passengers, offering a deep dive into the history of the legendary vessel. RMS Titanic, Inc. is a company that aims to preserve the legacy of the Titanic's passengers and crew. The company has recovered over 5,500 artifacts from the wreck site since 1987. They have conducted research and recovery expeditions and have also created educational programs and exhibitions.

Branded theme parks and travel, such as the following, are also huge:

>> Universal's Wizarding World of Harry Potter

>> Disney Cruises

Even baby boomers have embraced experiential licensing. Case in point: Margaritaville, the multibillion-dollar lifestyle brand inspired by Jimmy Buffett. Today, it includes restaurants, resorts, and cruises and even retirement communities. The Latitude Margaritaville retirement communities, located in Florida and South Carolina, offer a tropical, laid-back lifestyle for Parrothead fans, complete with live entertainment, beach-themed amenities, and a permanent vacation vibe.

Navigating Digital Licensing: The New Frontier

Brand licensing is going digital at lightning speed. As technology advances, brands are finding new ways to engage consumers in the virtual world, creating massive opportunities for licensing in gaming, AI, and digital fashion:

>> **Video game licensing:** Video games have become one of the largest entertainment industries in the world, with billions of players globally. Brands are partnering with game developers to create exclusive in-game content, including branded weapons, character outfits, vehicles, and even entire game worlds. For example, Batman, Star Wars, and Nike have successfully licensed their IPs in hit games like Fortnite, Call of Duty, and Roblox, allowing players to interact with their favorite brands in a whole new way.

>> **Virtual avatars and branded skins (branded skins are the outfits you can dress your virtual avatars in):** The rise of digital self-expression has driven brands to expand into virtual fashion and accessories. Luxury fashion houses like Gucci, Prada, Louis Vuitton, and Balenciaga have all launched branded skins, clothing, and accessories for avatars in video games and metaverse platforms. (The metaverse is a virtual world accessed online in which users are represented by avatars.) These digital fashion items allow consumers to showcase their style in virtual spaces, and in some cases, they even come with real-world perks, such as access to exclusive events or physical product tie-ins.

>> **AI-generated brand collaborations:** Artificial intelligence (AI) is opening new doors for brand licensing, enabling companies to create AI-generated virtual influencers/brand ambassadors, artwork, and branded content and personalized experiences. For example, AI-driven fashion collections, branded chatbots, and interactive storytelling experiences are becoming new revenue streams for brands looking to tap into digital licensing.

REMEMBER

As digital licensing continues to explode, it's creating endless opportunities for brands to reach consumers in immersive and interactive ways, whether that's through gaming, AI, or virtual fashion.

Bringing Together Brand Collaborations

Brand collaborations happen when distinct brands join forces to create new, innovative products or experiences. These partnerships generate buzz, exclusivity, and high demand, making them one of the fastest-growing areas in licensing.

Consumers love brand collaborations because they're unexpected, fresh, and fun. Following are some examples of brand collaborations; Chapter 4 has more info on collabs:

>> **The Air Jordan sneaker:** The Air Jordan sneaker is the granddaddy of brand collaborations. Nike's partnership with Michael Jordan not only changed the sneaker industry but also paved the way for today's booming footwear collaborations.

>> **Supreme X Louis Vuitton:** In 2017, Supreme and Louis Vuitton redefined luxury streetwear with a groundbreaking collection featuring Supreme's bold red box logo fused with Louis Vuitton's classic monogram. The collab sold out instantly, with resellers flipping items for ten times their retail price., Turns out that high fashion and streetwear can dominate both hype and high-end markets.

>> **Lady Gaga and Oreos:** In January 2021, Oreo released pink and green Lady Gaga-themed cookies inspired by her *Chromatica* album. The collab was a hit; it became Mondelez's top-selling online item and made up one-third of all Oreo sales that month.

>> **Off-White X American Red Cross:** Fashion brand Off-White, founded by Virgil Abloh, partnered with the American Red Cross for a fashion collab featuring hoodies, T-shirts, and hats that blended streetwear with a charitable cause. The collection was a hit, with $710 hoodies at Saks Fifth Avenue selling out quickly, proving that high fashion and philanthropy can drive impact and demand.

IN THIS CHAPTER

» **Starting with an understanding of branding**

» **Looking at the ingredients of branding**

» **Understanding branding's importance**

» **Creating and maintaining trust with brands**

» **Creating connections with emotional branding**

» **Building brand trust with the purchase pyramid**

» **Considering brand licensing to boost your product or business**

Chapter **2**

Probing Branding: Why People Buy

W elcome to the fascinating world of branding! In this chapter, you dive into the collective 50 years of brand knowledge and experience of Professor Stu Seltzer of NYU and me (25-plus years publishing the leading licensing publication). Together, we explore the power of branding and how licensing a brand is one of the best-kept secrets in business.

REMEMBER

Brand licensing's success hinges on the power of branding. Only the strongest of brands can successfully extend into new products, services and experiences. Understanding the essence of what makes a strong brand helps you understand more about brand licensing and begin your journey of finding the right brands to create your success in licensing.

Defining Branding

Branding is the process of creating a unique name, design, and image in a consumer's mind and distinguishing an organization, product, or experience with the aim of creating a lasting impression and developing consumer trust. At its core, branding is about creating an emotional connection with customers through consistent messaging and experiences.

Because you've picked up this book and are reading this chapter, you're already familiar with the concept of a brand. The *For Dummies* series is a perfect example of a well-known and trusted brand. Over more than 30 years, the *For Dummies* brand has helped millions of people simply and easily discover the ins and outs of everything from human anatomy to chess to social media marketing. The *For Dummies* series is so successful as a brand that it has extended its reach into licensed products. How? Because as a brand, *For Dummies* is well-known and trusted. Readers who trust what they've gotten from the *For Dummies* series are naturally attracted to other books branded under the *For Dummies* name. And there are over 1,000 of them!

TIP

By exploring how critical branding is to increasing product sales, you can understand the attributes that separate a brand from simply a product. This distinction is the first step on your licensing journey.

Investigating the Ingredients of Branding

A simple way for you to understand branding is to think of it like cooking a great dish: Both follow a tried-and-true recipe. By using the right combination of ingredients in just the right amounts, products develop into brands. Here's a list of the ingredients that make up successful brands.

>> **Brand identity:** This identity begins with creating strong visual elements. A brand's logo should be simple yet unique in its color and design. Think about Coca-Cola, Apple, and McDonalds; they all have simple, unique logos that utilize design and color to stand out.

>> **Brand promise:** What differentiates a brand from a product? Brands make a promise, whether that's high quality, low prices, innovation, or customer service. Think about Walmart. What makes it so special? Quality products at affordable prices and thousands of convenient locations.

>> **Brand perception:** *Brand perception* is how consumers perceive a brand. If you have an Apple product, you know it's at the forefront of technology and ease of use.

>> **Brand loyalty:** Branding done right leads to consumer brand loyalty. After you've shopped at Walmart, you'll most likely return based on previous experience.

Breaking Down Why Branding Is Important

Branding isn't just about having a cool logo or catchy slogan; it's the heart and soul of your business. It's what makes people recognize you, trust you, and choose you over the competition. Whether you're selling sneakers, software, or sandwiches, strong branding helps your business stand out, build meaningful connections with customers, and create lasting value. Think of it as your business's personality, reputation, and promise — all rolled into one.

Here's why branding is a big deal:

>> **Differentiation:** In a crowded marketplace, a strong brand stands out.

>> **Connection:** It's about creating an emotional bond with your consumer.

>> **Value:** A well-established brand provides a company more leverage in the industry, like getting prime retail shelf space.

>> **Consistency:** Branding builds recognition and trust, helping customers feel more confident in their purchasing choices.

>> **Attraction:** A strong brand keeps loyal customers coming back and also attracts new ones through its reputation and visibility.

REMEMBER

The bottom line is that branding isn't just important; it's essential.

Trusting in Brands

Trust in brands simply means that consumers have confidence and belief in a company's products or services, stemming from the company's perceived reliability, integrity, and competence.

Why trust matters in branding

Trust is the foundation of any strong brand. It's what turns first-time buyers into lifelong customers and casual followers into passionate advocates. When consumers trust a brand, they believe in its products, services, and promises. This confidence comes from a company's perceived reliability, integrity, and competence — qualities that aren't built overnight but are earned through consistent performance and authentic connections.

Here's why trust is a game-changer for brands:

>> **Customer loyalty:** Trust fosters loyalty, encouraging customers to return again and again.

>> **Brand differentiation:** In a crowded marketplace, trust sets a brand apart from the competition.

>> **Tough times:** Trusted brands are more resilient in times of crisis because customers stick with the brands they believe in.

>> **Enhanced brand value:** Trust adds to a brand's overall value, making it not just a product or service but a meaningful part of consumers' lives.

In the end, trust isn't just a nice-to-have; it's a must-have for lasting brand success.

How brands build trust

Trust isn't something brands can buy; it's something they earn over time through consistent actions, authentic connections, and delivering on promises. In a fast-paced, information-rich world, consumers are more discerning than ever. They want to feel confident that the brands they support are reliable, transparent, and genuinely care about their customers. Building trust is about more than just having a great product; it's about creating an experience that reinforces credibility at every touchpoint.

Here are the key ways brands can build and maintain that all-important trust:

>> **Consistency:** Ensure the product experience is the same everywhere — like Magnum ice cream, which looks and tastes the same no matter where you are in the world.

>> **Transparency:** Open communication about business practices cultivates trust. In a world where social media has enabled instant global communication, brands need to be sure they're living up to their customers' expectations.

- **Engagement:** Regular engagement with customers builds relationships and trust. Brands can engage through different forms of marketing from wide (like TV advertising) to narrow (sampling at local retailers, running pop-up stores, or holding other in-person experiences).

- **Delivery on promises:** Every marketing claim a brand makes needs to be backed by real performance. Empty promises erode trust quickly.

- **Authenticity:** Brands that stay true to their values and communicate honestly build trust more easily.

- **Social proof:** Reviews, testimonials, and user-generated content provide powerful validation from real customers.

- **Quality assurance:** Maintaining high standards for product and service quality reinforces a brand's credibility and integrity.

Emotional Branding: Creating Connections That Last

Trust is the foundation of any strong brand, but the emotional connection is what turns loyal customers into passionate brand advocates. *Emotional branding* goes beyond products and services; it taps into feelings, values, and experiences that resonate with consumers on a deeper level. After brands have established trust, they can foster these emotional bonds through powerful storytelling, meaningful user experiences, and authentic engagement. This connection drives sales but also builds lasting relationships that keep customers coming back.

Here's how successful brands create emotional connections:

- **Storytelling:** They create compelling stories that resonate with consumers through marketing such as advertising and PR.

- **User experiences:** They develop enjoyable interactions between consumers and their product (and they then share it through storytelling).

- **Social media engagement:** They build communities and interact directly with consumers. Social media has supercharged brands' ability to build communities and interact with consumers, which in turn has enabled licensing and brand extensions to flourish.

Emotional branding helps nurture deep connections with consumers, but that's just the beginning. The following sections explore how brands successfully integrate with pop culture and consumer psychology to elevate their presence and drive growth.

Branding through pop culture

Brands can amplify their impact by tapping into the power of pop culture. By aligning with cultural trends, celebrities, and media, brands stay relevant but also expand their reach across diverse audiences. For example,

>> **Influence of pop culture:** Brands that successfully integrate with pop culture can majorly enhance their market appeal by developing key consumer demographics such as millennials and Gen Z. For example, Oreo has significantly increased its sales through creative cobranding with such pop-culture icons as Lady Gaga, Post Malone, and Pokémon.

>> **Celebrity endorsements:** The right celebrity endorsement can catapult a brand into the spotlight. The Kardashian/Jenner family is a classic example of this influence in action.

>> **Leveraging content and media:** Incorporating products into movies, shows, or video games can subtly influence consumers' perceptions and desires. This practice is known as *product placement,* and it's now elevated even further through the rise of social media influencers on platforms like TikTok, Instagram, Facebook, and so on.

Considering consumer psychology and brand desire

At the heart of every purchasing decision lies one key factor: consumer psychology. Understanding what drives consumers to choose one brand over another is essential for building brand loyalty and long-term success. The psychological draw to branded products often goes beyond functionality. It's fueled by perceptions of quality, status, and the aspirational values that a brand represents. Brands don't just sell products; they sell experiences, identities, and emotions that resonate with consumers on a deeper level.

Here's how consumer psychology shapes brand desire:

>> **Branded versus generic:** Studies show that consumers are more likely to choose branded products over generic ones because of the brands' perceived reliability and superior quality and the trust that comes with brand recognition.

>> **Influence of reviews and testimonials:** Online reviews and testimonials have become powerful tools in shaping brand perception. Positive feedback from real users reinforces credibility and can significantly influence buying decisions, often outweighing traditional advertising.

REMEMBER

By tapping into these psychological triggers, brands can create strong emotional connections that not only attract customers but also inspire lasting loyalty.

BOB'S COWS: THE FIRST TRADEMARK STORY

Here's a story that I (Stu) use every semester to introduce my NYU students to the concept of branding:

Once upon a time in the olden days, a farmer named Bob was famous in his town for how well he cared for his cows. Bob treated his cows with tender loving care, feeding them only the highest-quality grass. Everyone in town knew Bob's cows were special, and as a result, they sold for higher prices at the market.

To make sure people could distinguish his cows from others, Bob marked his animals with a hot iron brand bearing a unique symbol: "Bob's Cows." This brand became a trusted mark of quality. When buyers at the market saw the brand on the cows, they knew those were Bob's and were worth the extra price.

This branding wasn't just a way to identify Bob's cows; it was the first instance of a trademark. The brand symbolized trust, quality, and care — values that Bob's name and reputation stood for.

So the next time you hear the word *trademark,* remember Bob's cows and how a simple hot iron mark started it all!

Building Brand Trust with the Purchase Pyramid

The *purchase pyramid* outlines the steps a consumer typically takes as they discover, consider, purchase, and ultimately become a loyal customer of your product. Think of it as a journey to build trust and enthusiasm for your brand. Here's how it works:

>> **Step 1: Awareness**

   At the base of the pyramid is *awareness* — the moment a consumer first notices your product. Licensing a popular brand can make this step much easier because consumers are likely already familiar with the brand. This built-in awareness provides a head start!

>> **Step 2: Familiarity**

   After consumers are aware of your product, they begin to recognize your brand and product and learn a bit more about it. This *familiarity* builds comfort, which is crucial for the next step.

>> **Step 3: Consideration**

   When consumers are familiar with your product, they move to *consideration,* the part where they seriously think about purchasing it. They weigh the pros and cons and decide whether your product meets their needs.

>> **Step 4: Purchase**

   The big moment: purchase! Consumers take action and buy your product. This step is essential, but the pyramid doesn't end here. Your goal is to keep these customers coming back.

>> **Step 5: Loyalty**

   At the top of the pyramid is loyalty. These customers not only continue buying your product but also become your brand's biggest advocates — your "apostles." They love the brand and are likely to purchase other products or services associated with it. This stage is the ultimate goal of your brand: to create lifelong fans who trust the brand and keep coming back for more.

This pyramid (see Figure 2-1) explains why brand licensing is such a powerful strategy. Licensed brands have strong awareness and trust from the start, making it easier to guide consumers up the pyramid and convert them into loyal, repeat customers.

FIGURE 2-1:
The purchase pyramid allows brands to build trust with their customers.

Tapping into the Power of Brand Licensing

One of the ways iconic brands continue to grow their influence is through *licensing* — allowing other companies to create products that use their trademarks. Licensing helps these brands expand into new categories and reach more customers while maintaining their core identity. Here are some examples:

» Coca-Cola has turned its instantly recognizable logo into a lifestyle symbol, licensing it for merchandise like T-shirts, hats, and home décor.

» Mickey Mouse, the face of Disney's magic, appears on everything from watches to backpacks, making the character accessible in everyday life.

» Nike extends its influence in sports and fashion with products like branded sunglasses, backpacks, and accessories that carry its signature swoosh.

» BMW, known for luxury cars, licenses its brand for high-end items like driving gloves, luggage, and even bicycles, reinforcing its premium image.

» Yves Saint Laurent (YSL) has gone beyond high fashion, licensing its name for perfumes, sunglasses, and beauty products and making the luxury brand more accessible to a wider audience. (More on YSL in the nearby sidebar "The brand power of Yves Saint Laurent.")

Licensing allows these powerhouse brands to remain relevant, expand their presence, and deepen their connection with consumers across diverse product categories.

REMEMBER

The two biggest benefits of licensing are

>> Increasing your sales

>> Boosting your credibility

Consider this simple yet powerful example of how licensing works: Jacob ran a small business selling basic black T-shirts. Like many entrepreneurs, he was searching for ways to grow his sales. One day, he heard about an upcoming block-buster movie, *Batman.* Curious, Jacob decided to look into licensing the famous Batman logo for his T-shirts.

After doing some research, Jacob struck a licensing deal with Warner Bros., the owner of the Batman brand. He paid a royalty fee for the rights to use the iconic logo on his shirts. When the movie hit theaters, it was a massive success, and fans couldn't get enough Batman merchandise. This surge in popularity led to a huge demand for Jacob's Batman T-shirts, dramatically increasing his sales.

In the end, everyone won. Jacob grew his business by offering a product tied to a popular brand, and Warner Bros. earned royalties from Jacob's sales. By teaming up with a well-known brand, Jacob was able to boost his sales and take his business to the next level.

And here's yet another example of how licensing a well-known brand can help a company enhance its reputation and grow its business: The American Lawn Mower Company makes quality lawn mowers, but it had a challenge in that most people weren't familiar with the brand. It needed a way to stand out and build trust with customers. Enter Scotts, the nation's leading lawn and garden brand. Scotts is widely recognized because it spends $100 million a year on marketing and even ran a Super Bowl commercial featuring celebrities. Consumers trust Scotts for their lawn care needs, so its brand carries significant credibility.

The American Lawn Mower Company decided to license the Scotts brand for its lawn mowers and power tools. By adding the trusted Scotts name to its products, it instantly gained consumer confidence.

The result? A great success! The American Lawn Mower Company boosted its credibility, making selling their products to customers who trust the Scotts brand easier.

THE BRAND POWER OF YVES SAINT LAURENT

Yves Saint Laurent is one of the most iconic fashion designers in history. During his lifetime, he focused on creating breathtaking couture dresses, which sold for $5,000 to $25,000 each. These elegant creations were worn by some of the world's most important and influential women, cementing his status as a fashion legend.

But he didn't stop there. He had the vision to expand his brand's reach beyond couture by using licensing. Licensing allowed him to make his name and designs accessible to a much larger audience while creating lucrative opportunities for his brand. Yves Saint Laurent licensed his iconic brand name and design elements to an array of product categories, including the following:

- **Eyewear:** Licensee Luxottica created sunglasses and prescription glasses with a chic, luxury feel.

- **Jewelry:** Cartier was the licensee creating elegant pieces inspired by his couture designs.

- **Fragrance:** Charles of the Ritz was his fragrance licensee; it sold signature perfumes like Opium and Rive Gauche.

- **Footwear:** Schwartz & Benjamin was his footwear licensee, crafting stylish shoes for both casual and formal occasions.

- **Handbags:** Luc Benoit created coveted accessories that remain timeless fashion staples.

- **Scarves:** Abraham was the licensee that crafted lightweight, elegant scarves that echo YSL's sophisticated style.

YSL even introduced a *ready-to-wear line* — a collection of more affordable women's dresses sold at department stores. This move brought the brand's prestige to a broader audience, allowing women who couldn't afford couture to own a piece of the YSL magic. This line was actually all made by a licensee called Paris Collections.

Today, the company Yves Saint Laurent founded remains a global powerhouse. Through licensing agreements, the brand continues to sell its products worldwide, including its fragrances, accessories, and ready-to-wear collections. Licensing has been key to ensuring that YSL's timeless elegance and influence live on, reaching millions of consumers across the globe.

The lesson here is that licensing doesn't just grow a brand; it helps make legendary designs accessible to everyone.

Noting Three Key Brand Licensing Principles You Can Apply Right Away

Licensing can be a game-changer for your business. The following sections cover three important principles to keep in mind.

By understanding these principles, you can harness the power of licensing to grow your business, enhance your products, and gain a competitive edge.

Licensing can make a good product great

If you already have a good product, adding a powerful licensed brand can elevate it to greatness. This shift can lead to increased sales and stronger customer appeal. Take a look at a few examples:

>> **LEGO and Star Wars:** LEGO was always a popular toy, but when it licensed the *Star Wars* brand, it transformed its products into a must-have line. The combination of LEGO's creativity with *Star Wars'* iconic characters turned simple building blocks into collector's items and skyrocketed sales.

>> **Signature Foods and Breyers:** Signature Foods had a standard line of hot fudge and ice cream toppings. By licensing the Breyers name, it gained instant credibility and consumer trust. Retail buyers and customers embraced the new Breyers-branded toppings, leading to nationwide retail success.

>> **Acme and the American Red Cross:** Acme's products were always good, but when it partnered with the trusted American Red Cross brand, its products became great sellers. Customers associated the brand with quality and reliability, making the products more appealing at retail.

Licensing can be your sustainable competitive advantage

In his famous book *Competitive Advantage* (Free Press), Harvard Business School professor Michael Porter explains that the key to business success is having a competitive advantage, whether it's through innovative or differentiated products. But the real challenge is holding on to that advantage over time.

Here's the good news: Licensing can be your sustainable competitive advantage. By securing the rights to a popular brand, you can create a unique position in the market that's hard for competitors to replicate. Here are some real-world examples:

>> **Unilever and Reese's Ice Cream:** Unilever holds the exclusive license to use the Reese's brand in ice cream products sold under its Breyers, Good Humor, and Klondike brands. This arrangement means no other ice cream company can feature the famous Reese's candy in its products or marketing. The license gives Unilever a powerful competitive advantage, especially because it's a multiyear agreement, making the advantage sustainable.

>> **Topps and Major League Baseball (MLB):** Topps has been producing MLB trading cards since 1951. For over 70 years, the licensing relationship with MLB has provided Topps with a sustainable competitive advantage in the trading card market. The exclusive use of MLB logos, team names, and player images ensured that Topps has been the go-to brand for baseball card collectors.

>> **GUND and Winnie the Pooh:** GUND, a leading maker of stuffed animals (known as plush toys), has been licensing the Winnie the Pooh brand for over 75 years. This partnership allows GUND to create exclusive plush toys featuring one of the world's most beloved characters, giving it a lasting edge in the competitive toy market.

REMEMBER

Licensing doesn't just differentiate your product; it can lock in long-term advantages that competitors can't easily replicate. When you do it strategically, licensing is not just a tool for growth but a powerful way to ensure your business stays ahead of the competition.

All licensing is risky; take calculated, manageable risks

Just like any business venture, licensing comes with its share of risks. But with proper planning and research, you can manage and mitigate these risks effectively. Here's how:

1. **Do your homework.**

   Before jumping into a licensing deal, research the brand thoroughly:

   - Is the brand popular and relevant to your audience?

   - Does it have staying power, or is it a fleeting trend?

   - How does the brand's reputation align with your product?

2. **Run the numbers.**

   Analyze the costs versus the potential revenue. Licensing can be profitable, but only if the deal makes financial sense for your business. Consider the following:

   - Understand the royalty fees, upfront payments, and marketing costs. (We cover royalty fees and upfront payments in Chapter 6.)

   - Project the sales you need to make the licensing agreement worthwhile.

3. **Don't get overwhelmed.**

   When you start exploring licensing opportunities, you may feel like you have too many options to choose from. If you're unsure how to prioritize or evaluate the deals, consider consulting a licensing expert. They can help you find the best opportunities and guide you through the process. (We dive deeper into this topic in Chapter 5.)

4. **Understand the hidden risk of doing nothing.**

   Here's the twist: *Not* licensing can be risky, too. If your competitors are using licensed brands to gain a competitive edge and you're not, it can hurt your business. Sometimes the risk of being left behind is greater than the risk of taking the leap. Licensing isn't foolproof, but by taking calculated, manageable risks and staying informed, you can turn it into a powerful growth strategy for your business.

REMEMBER

Brand licensing allows you to leverage the power of well-known brands to enhance your product or service's marketability. It saves time and resources compared to building brand equity from scratch.

IN THIS CHAPTER

» Noting the big players in licensing

» Getting to know entertainment licensing

» Discovering licensing across industries

» Licensing zombie brands

Chapter **3**

Where on Earth Do Brands Come From?

B rands use licensing as a powerful strategy to expand their reach and generate additional revenue streams. By allowing other companies to use their brand names, logos, and intellectual properties, brands can penetrate new markets and offer a wider range of products. Brands have become part of the culture, and they represent every area of consumer products, experiences, and services.

In this chapter, we show you brands that have mastered the art of licensing and break down why they succeed — and how you can benefit from these lessons in licensing.

Recognizing Top Brand Licensors

In licensing terms, retail sales equal success. And every year since it launched in 1998, *License Global* magazine (the magazine co-author Steven founded) has run down those figures in its annual listing of the top licensors in the world. Many of the brands at the top of the list come from the entertainment world, but brand licensing runs the gamut from A (art) to Z (zoos) and covers everything in between.

The upcoming sections give you a look at the top ten licensors in 2024, their annual retail sales of licensed merchandise, and some important details about the approach that got them onto the list.

REMEMBER

Licensors receive royalties for the use of their intellectual property (IP), which is a fractional percentage of the retail sales. Chapter 6 tells you more about how these agreements work.

One thing these top ten companies have in common is that they understand and value licensing as a critical marketing strategy that not only creates additional revenue streams but also acts as a brand builder that keeps them relevant and top of mind in an ever-changing consumer products marketplace. That knowledge has helped put them in the top ten.

The Walt Disney Company ($62 billion estimated)

Disney leads the pack, and that's no accident. Founder Walt Disney is considered the father of licensing, having begun licensing Mickey Mouse in the 1930s. Today, Disney oversees a vast empire of licensed properties, including classics like Mickey Mouse and Minnie Mouse; Pixar Animated features like *Toy Story*, *Inside Out*, and *The Incredibles*; global smash *Frozen*; the vast Marvel Universe; Lucasfilm productions, including *Star Wars* and *Indiana Jones*; and Twentieth Century Fox's vast library of IP (purchased in 2019), which includes *The Simpsons*, *Family Guy*, *Avatar*, and *Ice Age*, to name just a few licensing juggernauts.

Disney developed its brand IP organically from its inception in 1923 until it acquired the ABC TV network in 1996. In the early 2000s they began a significant third-party acquisition spree, first with Pixar Animation in 2006 and then Marvel in 2009, Lucasfilm in 2012, and Twentieth Century Fox in 2019. Given all this rich IP, Disney is truly a brand management house.

Authentic Brands Group ($28 billion estimated)

Known in the business as ABG, this company was founded in 2010 with the goal of acquiring famous brands and exploiting their brand value through *pure-play licensing*. In other words, the brands it acquires no longer do any of their own manufacturing but are licensed out to third-party licensees, with ABG taking royalties on the sales.

As of this writing, ABG owns and licenses 67 distinct brands, mostly in the fashion, apparel, and lifestyle categories. These include Brooks Brothers, Eddie Bauer, Elvis Presley, Frye, Forever 21, Greg Norman, Jones New York, Izod, Juicy Couture, Lucky Brand, Nautica, *Sports Illustrated*, and so on. What makes Authentic Brands Group so interesting is its focus on buying well-known and loved brands and simply managing them for licensing. As a company, they are a testament to just how successful and ubiquitous licensing has become as a global marketing strategy.

Dotdash Meredith ($26.4 billion estimated)

Dotdash Meredith is a legacy media company that publishes special interest consumer magazines; *Better Homes and Gardens* is its flagship brand. The company developed an online content strategy as the Internet began to overtake print, purchasing famous but financially distressed magazine brands like *People, Food & Wine, Brides, Eating Well, InStyle, Travel + Leisure,* and many more while extending *Better Homes and Gardens.* One of Dotdash Meredith's key licenses is with Better Homes and Gardens at Walmart — a *direct-to-retail* (DTR) deal where Walmart holds an exclusive license to brand housewares and home furnishings, cutting out third-party licensees.

But most of the company's $26.4 billion is based on home sales. Better Homes and Gardens Real Estate LLC is an international real estate company that began operations in July 2008. It franchises independent businesses to operate within its network and has hundreds of offices across the United States and Canada. That's right — Dotdash Meredith licensed the Better Homes and Gardens name to a third-party, no-name real estate company that was looking for a brand name consumers knew and trusted. Their success is based on the power of brand licensing.

Warner Bros./Discovery ($15 billion)

The Hollywood studio Warner Bros. owns such beloved IP as DC Comics (Superman, Batman, Wonder Woman), the Harry Potter franchise, Looney Tunes, Hanna-Barbera, *Friends,* Cartoon Network, Scooby-Doo, *Game of Thrones,* and much more. On the Discovery side of the business, Shark Week and Animal Planet have seen significant licensing.

Warner Bros., like Disney (see the earlier section), created or acquired over many years content that lends itself to consumer products licensing. For a while, Warner was the number-two licensor behind Disney, with its rich library of franchised entertainment. Its move to number four on the list is a direct result of the growth of brand licensing since 2015. Although Warner's numbers haven't fallen, newer players like Authentic Brand Group and Dotdash Meredith, which we cover in the preceding sections, have seen significant increases in growth.

Hasbro ($14.1 billion estimated)

Once simply a toy manufacturer, Hasbro began its transition to full-fledged entertainment company in the early 2000s under visionary president (and later CEO) Brian Goldner. By 2007, Hasbro had released the first *Transformers* movie, which now represents a seven-movie franchise with box office revenue of over $5 billion. Goldner's vision was to identify Hasbro's key brands (Transformers, Monopoly, Magic: The Gathering, Nerf, My Little Pony, Play-Doh, and My Littlest Pet Shop) and use brand extensions and licensing to build them into franchises. He clearly succeeded, and Hasbro has now transitioned from simply a toy company to a bona fide entertainment and brand management company.

NBC Universal/Universal Products & Experiences ($11.5 billion)

Another Hollywood legacy studio — it owns mega-franchises like *Jurassic Park*, *Despicable Me, Fast & Furious, Shrek, Trolls*, Universal Monsters, *Jaws*, and *ET*, to name a few. Like Disney (see the earlier section), Universal has been successful in extending its franchises into theme parks. *Remember:* Both Disney and Universal include their amusement parks as licensed revenue.

Universal, like its rivals Hollywood Studios, Disney, Warner Bros., and Paramount, recognized the important of franchise films as a business model. For more than 25 years, Universal has been working diligently to acquire or develop franchised entertainment. One example of its massive success in this area is the creation of Illumination Entertainment in 2007. The studio has since produced the *Despicable Me/Minions* franchise, Dr. Seuss films, and the *Super Mario* films, proving that animation remains a huge driver for licensed consumer products.

The Pokémon Company International ($10.8 billion)

Originally developed as a video game for Nintendo Game Boy in 1996, Pokémon is now the single largest entertainment franchise of all time, spawning anime, trading cards, films, video games, consumer products, and experiences in every category from fashion to housewares. The company keeps the brand fresh and relevant for new generations with cutting-edge, trendy games like *Pokémon Go*. In 2021 Pokémon celebrated its 25th anniversary, which signals what those in the business call an *evergreen property,* meaning it has maintained its popularity for decades, firmly establishing itself as a proven long-term franchise.

Bluestar Alliance ($8.5 billion estimated)

Like Authentic Brands Group (which we discuss earlier in the chapter), Bluestar Alliance buys up well-known, financially distressed brands, mostly in the fashion industry, and then does pure-play licensing. Bluestar owns such famous fashion brands as Hurley, Scotch & Soda, Kensie, Tahari, Justice, Limited Too, and so on. Similar to Authentic Brands Group, Bluestar Alliance is a relatively new company, founded in 2006 as more companies focused on brand licensing and management saw the opportunity for pure-play licensing.

Mattel ($8.5 billion estimated)

Mattel is famed as the creator of Barbie and Hot Wheels, but — like Hasbro (see the earlier section) — it's transitioning from a traditional toy company to a brand management company that extends its core brands into entertainment as well as licensing for consumer products. The huge success of 2023's *Barbie* movie, which was the highest-grossing film of that year, is a testament to how successful Mattel has been in this endeavor.

Barbie saw Mattel reimagining the Barbie story and brand for a new generation of women and girls. From a brand management perspective, it reinforces just how powerful brand extensions and licensing can be in reinventing and fortifying brands. It's a huge win for Mattel and the Barbie brand. In addition to its many toy brands, Mattel also owns such well-known kids' entertainment brands such as *Barney, Bob the Builder,* and *Monster High.*

WHP Global ($7.5 billion)

A relative newcomer to the licensing world, WHP Global was founded in 2019 as a pure-play brand licensing company. WHP Global buys financially distressed or defunct well-known and loved brands. It specializes in brand management, retail, marketing, e-commerce, sourcing, M&A, and omnichannel retail (simply put, *omnichannel retail* means all types of retail from brick and mortar to e-commerce and social commerce). WHP Global's portfolio includes brands such as Toys"R"Us, Babies"R"Us, Express, Bonobos, Anne Klein, Joe's Jeans, Joseph Abboud, Isaac Mizrahi, Lotto, and William Rast.

Eyeing Entertainment Licensing for Consumer Products and Experiences

Entertainment dominates the list of top licensors; a whopping six of the top ten licensors worldwide in 2024 operated in the entertainment industry. (Check out the full list in the earlier section "Recognizing Top Brand Licensors.") That means the entertainment licensing business is a very rich area that can help you sell more products, experiences, or services.

Wondering why entertainment is so dominant in licensed products and experiences and how you can tap into this side of licensing? Simply put, entertainment properties lend themselves to product extensions. Kids' entertainment has been a driver of toy products for generations and extends into food and beverages, apparel and accessories, footwear, video games, book publishing, and many other consumer products categories.

REMEMBER

One of the major reasons that entertainment companies are so successful in brand licensing is their ability to tell stories. When non-entertainment-based brands look to tell stories, they typically turn to traditional advertising agencies, which then produce short-form video commercials. Entertainment Studios, on the other hand, create 90-minute-to-two-hour films and seasons-long TV series that captivate and engage the viewer, and that makes building them into brand franchises much easier.

The entertainment licensing industry is continually evolving. Digital and interactive experiences, such as augmented reality (AR) and virtual reality (VR), are becoming more prevalent. And the rise of streaming platforms has introduced new, highly popular IPs that are ripe for licensing.

Entertainment licensing is a robust, dynamic industry that brings your favorite characters and stories into everyday life. Whether it's a Spider-Man T-shirt, a Frozen-themed bedspread, or a visit to a Harry Potter theme park, licensed products and experiences are everywhere, creating a world where imagination knows no bounds.

REMEMBER

Popular culture is the driver for consumers in terms of brand extensions and licensing. In a fast-paced world filled with many choices, tapping into established brand equity through licensing enables your products or services to stand out and drive sales.

Consider a licensing juggernaut, Harry Potter. Warner Bros., which owns the film and licensing rights to the book series, has taken a broad licensing strategy that has kept the Harry Potter brand alive and thriving long after the final book and movie were released. Warner Bros. has licensed Harry Potter for a wide range of products and experiences:

>> **Merchandise:** Clothing, toys, video games, accessories, food and beverage, accessories, and even replica wands

>> **Theme parks:** The Wizarding World of Harry Potter with locations in Florida, California, China, and Japan

>> **Events:** Harry Potter-themed escape rooms and live performances

Harry Potter is a perfect example of how a well-loved book series was transformed into a multibillion-dollar brand through natural brand extensions that all have one thing in common: storytelling.

THE LEGACY OF THE MICKEY MOUSE WATCH

In 1929, the Great Depression devastated the American economy, impacting every business. The young Walt Disney was struggling to keep his recently opened studio afloat. He had released his first Mickey Mouse feature, *Steamboat Willie,* in 1928. Audiences weren't that impressed, but Disney knew he had something, and he kept producing Mickey Mouse features. Movies stopped being silent in the early 1930s, and sound technology sent Mickey soaring. Around this time, Disney met a determined and insightful salesperson named Herman "Kay" Kamen, and together they transformed the beloved character of Mickey Mouse into a lucrative enterprise.

Kamen's idea was to get Mickey on as many quality products as possible, making his face synonymous with excellence. On toothpaste tubes that promised smiles as bright as Mickey's and cereal boxes that made breakfast a little more magical, Mickey became a ubiquitous symbol of joy during an economically challenging time. This venture generated millions of dollars, even as the broader economy struggled.

But the big breakthrough came with time — pun 100 percent intended. The Ingersoll-Waterbury Clock Company was teetering on the brink of bankruptcy when Kamen proposed a bold collaboration: a Mickey Mouse wristwatch. Mickey's arms were the watch hands, and a sub-seconds dial displayed three tiny Mickeys in perpetual motion. This design wasn't just a novelty but a stroke of genius.

The watch debuted at Macy's, where it sold an astonishing 11,000 units on the first day. The success of the Mickey Mouse watch was nothing short of extraordinary and helped rescue Ingersoll from financial collapse. It also introduced a new era of licensing, and the world has never turned back.

Finding Opportunity in Entertainment

Anything that holds the attention of large audiences presents opportunity for licensing, and something new always shows up to grab those eyeballs. The following list runs through some of the big ways entertainment can be mined for licensed products.

>> **Movies,** especially film franchises that continue storytelling of the same brand, becoming familiar to (and loved by) generations.

>> **Broadcast and streaming TV,** from classic game shows to YouTube juggernauts, are great fodder.

>> **Animation** draws devotees of all ages.

>> **Comics and graphic novels,** popular for over a century, haven't lost staying power, especially now that they're mined for film content.

>> **Anime and manga** offer a dedicated global fan base.

>> **Sports,** including major leagues, players' associations, collegiate, tournaments, and the state pickleball competition, are a major category.

>> **Video games and e-sports** bring in-game licensing as well as merchandise opportunities, especially as they get made into TV shows and movies.

>> **Music** merch didn't really kick in until the late 1970s but now is a multibillion-dollar industry.

>> **Memes** don't just fly around the Internet; they become licensing opportunities for accessories, apparel, and more.

>> **Characters,** like Hello Kitty (who has surpassed $30 billion in retail sales), can arise inside or outside the entertainment world.

>> **Celebrities and influencers** can represent an extremely broad range of products — think Gwyneth Paltrow's GOOP or any of the gazillion fragrances named after a celebrity.

NOSTALGIA LICENSING: THE FLINTSTONES

2025 marks the 65th Anniversary of the debut of the original *The Flintstones* cartoon and the 57th Anniversary of a classic branded content collaboration with a product. In this case Hanna-Barbera (*The Flintstones'* creator) launched *The Flintstones* vitamins for kids with Miles Laboratories. Their success led to the launch of Fruity Pebbles and Cocoa

Pebbles cereals with Post in 1971. What makes this fact interesting for you as you contemplate your entry into licensing is the historic nature of content collaborating with brand and its longevity in brand extensions.

Prior to 1968, no one had ever created a brand around a media character. Generations of Americans have now grown up with *The Flintstones,* which incidentally was the first made-for-TV cartoon when it premiered on ABC in 1960 in the budding days of television. Originally, it was meant to be a kind of Stone Age *Honeymooners*, and that was reflected in its 8:30 Friday primetime timeslot. Instead it drew a young audience and launched not only sugary cereals but also kids' vitamins that have outsold all the others for 50 years.

Tapping into Brand Licensing for Products of All Kinds

Where brands become popular, licensing opportunity follows. You've most likely seen hotel-branded towels and Harley-Davidson backpacks. These are great examples of product following brand popularity. Here are a bunch more:

>> **Automotive,** where a luxury car brand can become a toy, clothing, or even a condominium tower or posh resort

>> **Food and beverage,** TGI Friday's frozen food, Iron Chef Sauces, Coca-Cola hoodies and KFC Crocs

>> **Household** cleaning and other products

>> **Appliances and hardware**

>> **Hospitality** through hotel and restaurant chains

>> **Outdoor and adventure,** such as fishing, hiking, boating, and other hobbies

>> **Fashion and apparel,** which extends easily into eyewear and fragrances, for example

>> **Luxury brands,** especially sunglasses (which, believe it or not, are all made by the same manufacturer, whether they say Gucci, Burberry, or Versace at the temple)

>> **Footwear and accessories,** which make big money from big names (like, oh, say . . . Air Jordans)

>> **Fragrances and beauty products,** like branded fragrances

FOOD AND BEVERAGE BRAND COLLABS TAKE OFF

Brand collaborations in the grocery aisles had been a growing trend for several years prior to the COVID-19 pandemic, but they saw a marked increase within a year of the pandemic's outbreak as more and more food brands partnered with one another. One of the side effects of the pandemic was that consumers relaxed pre-pandemic healthy eating habits and sought comfort in the sweeter, saltier, less healthy brands they knew as kids. Comfort foods offer consumers something soothing, familiar, and nostalgic at a time when they most need it.

So many of the brands experiencing an uptick in food collaborations are companies whose sales were on the decline prior to the pandemic. Mondelez, for example, doubled the sales of Oreo cookies in 2021 from $1 billion to $2 billion with two unique brand collaborations: Lady Gaga Oreos and Pokémon Oreos. Consumers love seeing their favorite brands collaborate!

Getting creative with art and culture licensing

Not everyone can bring home an Andy Warhol original — unless maybe it's a licensed print or a scarf with the likeness of *Marilyn Monroe.* Licensing art and culture products not only capitalizes on popularity but also makes some of the finer things accessible to those who appreciate but can't necessarily afford the real deal.

Since the 1990's, art and culture licensing has seen significant growth as a result of museums recognizing that licensing is a revenue driver and that through licensing, they can attract more visitors. The fast fashion business has embraced pop artists like Warhol, Basquiat, and Haring, creating major collections at such global mass retail channels as Uniqlo and H&M.

REMEMBER

The beauty of these brand licensing collaborations is that they're not only creating royalty revenue for the artists' estates but also democratizing the art for the masses, creating new audiences for the art and driving interest in the artists' works.

Here are a few of the ways the arts have made their way into licensed products:

>> **Fine art** reproductions or themed clothing and décor

>> **Pop art,** which was practically made to be licensed — and has been for items big, small, and trendy

>> **Museum collections** inside and outside the gift shop

>> **Design,** meaning famous designers with TV or Internet platforms turn their names into products

>> **Non-fungible tokens (NFTs),** which enable digital art and collectibles and other virtual products to be traded in the *metaverse* (virtual worlds like those in VR or AR)

Licensing nonprofits and associations

Nonprofits and associations use licensing to raise funds and awareness. Although this licensing has always been an important area to raise money and brand awareness, it's even more meaningful with today's cause-driven consumers. Some of the more developed areas of nonprofit licensing include the American Red Cross, World Wildlife Fund, Save the Children, and even the beloved Sesame Street. The licensees of these nonprofits have a business motto: "doing good to do well."

But they aren't the only ones, and the list continues to grow. Organizations like AAA, AARP, and others are getting into the act. AARP and AAA both license their brands for credit cards. AARP has a very lucrative licensing deal with United Healthcare on supplemental medical insurance.

Expanding licensing with artificial intelligence

The digital revolution represents a transformative wave that's unlocking a whole new realm of possibilities for brand licensing. Among the most thrilling developments is the rise of artificial intelligence (AI). As AI technology advances, brand licensing is on the brink of a major transformation.

Picture this: It's the not-so-distant future, and you're shopping online. You spot a pair of sneakers adorned with a logo that feels both new and oddly familiar. That's because AI has crafted it specifically for you based on your preferences, mood, and online behavior. This custom blend of branding exists solely within your unique shopping ecosystem.

AI is making brand licensing personal. Fancy a Marvel-themed coffee maker or a Harry Potter-inspired drone? AI has you covered, securing licenses and delivering products faster than you can imagine.

But that's not all. AI may even be able to generate entirely new brands licensed straight from your imagination. Ever dreamed of a fashion line that marries Chanel's elegance with Levi's rugged charm? AI can create it, and your custom brand may just be the next big sensation. Companies could then license these AI-generated brands, blurring the lines between consumer and creator in a vibrant new marketplace.

On the legal front, AI will handle negotiations, manage contracts, and even detect potential infringements before they occur. At the time of this writing, it's still early days with AI and actual licensing contracts, negotiations, and infringement.

Bringing a Product Back to Life: Zombie Brands

A *zombie brand* is a company or product that has experienced a period of decline or near-extinction but later makes a comeback that gives it licensing cache. This resurgence can happen through several means, including the following:

>> **Acquisition:** A new owner buys the brand and revives it.

>> **Redefinition:** The brand is redefined or kept alive in other ways.

>> **Nostalgia:** The brand is brought back as a nostalgic icon.

>> **Fan support:** The brand is sustained by passionate fans.

>> **Trademark revival:** A new company revives an abandoned trademark to capitalize on the brand's goodwill and recognition.

You can find zombie brands in many sectors, including technology, retail, and subscription services. Some examples include Napster, Pan Am, Woolworth's, Mister Donut, Polaroid, and Toys"R"Us.

In almost every case, the company that purchases the zombie brand is taking advantage of that brand's well-known equity and licensing that brand equity to licensees. These companies are pure-play licensing companies that buy the zombie brands and then manage them for licensing.

REMEMBER

The name "zombie" may imply death, but don't discount the power of these brands. Three of the top ten companies in the earlier section "Recognizing Top Brand Licensors" — ABG, Bluestar Alliance, and WHP Global — built their brand management firms using what were once zombie brands.

Chapter **4**

Exploring Licensing Trends and Innovations

L icensing isn't about slapping a logo on a product; it's a dynamic, ever-evolving industry driven by cultural trends, consumer demand, and the latest in technology. This chapter is your roadmap to understanding how brand collaborations, digital licensing, video game intellectual property (IP), and new product categories are reshaping the landscape. Buckle up, because here we cover some of the most innovative and impactful trends in the world of licensing!

Tracking the Rise of the Brand Collaboration

Brand collaborations — when two or more distinct brands come together to create something new — have become a powerhouse in today's licensing business. Typically, when two distinct brands come together to create a new product, they put the letter *X* between their brand names. This styling has become a symbol to distinguish fashion and pop-cultural brand collaborations. Take a look at what Kentucky Fried Chicken did when they collaborated with Crocs (go to `www.crocs. com/KFC.html`).

Another example to whet your appetite: A tasty and very successful brand collaboration between Doritos and Taco Bell arose back in 2012 with Doritos Locos Tacos. Two powerhouse brands joined forces to deliver a product that not only resonated with their shared audience but also became an instant cultural phenomenon.

Blending the bold, recognizable flavors of Doritos with the beloved taco offerings from Taco Bell resulted in more than just a menu item; it was a sensation. The attention-grabbing packaging, paired with an innovative product that consumers couldn't get anywhere else, propelled it to fan-favorite status almost overnight.

The numbers tell the story best: Taco Bell sold nearly a billion units of Doritos Locos Tacos in less than three years, catapulting it to become the fastest consumer product ever to reach the billion mark. This pairing wasn't just a hit; it was brand equity at its peak, an undeniable demonstration of the power that strategic collaborations can wield in today's marketplace. As of this writing, the Doritos/Taco Bell collaboration continues its success.

Brand collaborations stretch into every area of consumer products. An example of a brand collaboration that may seem far-fetched but that has been hugely successful is an unusual partnership the Van Gogh Museum launched for its 50th anniversary. Collaborating with Pokémon to build an exhibition gave the museum a chance to introduce new audiences to Vincent van Gogh's work. The exhibition was popular, but merch was the real star of the show. It attracted so much traffic that it overwhelmed the museum's site.

Breaking down why brands combine

Brand collaborations have become major drivers for today's licensing business, delighting consumers, creating new products and services, and driving more sales. Here's the secret sauce behind their success:

>> **Consumer excitement:** When two beloved brands join forces, it creates a buzz that's hard to ignore. Imagine your favorite sneaker brand teaming up with a popular character like Hello Kitty to create a limited-edition product. Suddenly, that product isn't just a sneaker or a character; it's a must-have item that taps into the psychology of rarity. These collaborations are often limited-time offers, making them even more desirable.

>> **Amplified reach and visibility:** A brand brings its own loyal customer base, and collaboration effectively doubles the audience for each. This practice isn't just bringing two logos together; it's about merging the strengths of each brand to create something unique that resonates with consumers on a deeper level.

» **Innovation:** The best brand collabs think outside the box, bringing together unlikely partners to create products that are new, fresh, and unexpected. When done right, these partnerships can drive significant sales and enhance brand equity for all involved.

Understanding what makes a great collab

Creating great collabs means following some basic tips to increase your chances of success:

» Embracing the popularity of the brands being partnered.

» Bringing brands together that create surprise and excitement for the consumer.

» Creating a new product and/or design that reflects the DNA of both brands.

» Eliciting a positive emotional response from consumers, whether that's wonder, humor, surprise, joy, or (better yet) all of the above.

» Demonstrating a depth of knowledge regarding the retail channel you're looking to sell to (luxury, specialty, or mass, to name a few) and understanding the demographics and *psychographics* (variables such as lifestyle and interests) of those consumers. Chapter 8 tells you more about retail channels.

» Creating a sense of scarcity through limited-edition product — that is, limiting the product's retail distribution.

» Connecting each of the brands' attributes. You're displaying what the combined brands stand for. It can be simply fun or more nuanced feelings that tap into core beliefs.

REMEMBER

Creativity, uniqueness, and scarcity are the attributes you want to strive for in your brand collaborations.

Drawing on the passion of superfans

One of the greatest drivers for brand collaborations has been the rise of the *superfan* — an extremely passionate devotee of a particular hobby, interest, or cultural phenomenon. Subjects for superfans can range from music, sports teams, movies, and fashion to specific products like sneakers. Superfans go beyond typical fans in their dedication, often collecting memorabilia, attending events, and engaging deeply with other fans in the community.

Although the concept of a superfan has existed for decades, the rise of mass media in the 20th century allowed people to connect with cultural icons like musicians, athletes, and actors more intimately through their televisions and radios. Greater exposure tends to feel like connection, and fans have more opportunity to admire their idols, all of which tends to crank up the devotion dial.

The term *superfan* first gained popularity with music and sports. For example, in the 1960s, the Beatles had an incredibly devoted fan base, known as Beatlemaniacs, who were among the first recognized groups of superfans. Similarly, sports teams have long had superfans who are known for their unwavering support and dedication, often attending every game and wearing team colors. These superfans will buy all the branded licensed merchandise with their brand on it, which leads to more licensed merchandise being created and sold.

With the Internet and social media, superfans have become even more visible and influential. They can now connect with other fans worldwide, create online communities, and directly interact with the brands, celebrities, or teams they love. This development has led to superfans playing a significant role in shaping trends, influencing markets, and even impacting the success of cultural products like movies, albums, and sneaker releases.

One particular type of superfan arose in the 1980s, when rappers and basketball stars brought sneakers from the court to the streets. Picture legends like Michael Jordan, Magic Johnson, and Run-DMC rocking their kicks. Companies jumped on board, teaming up with athletes and celebs to create exclusive sneaker lines. Suddenly, those shoes became worth a fortune, leading to a *sneakerhead* culture of people who collect, trade, customize, or admire sneakers as a hobby. They go to great lengths to acquire sneakers, such as camping out or waiting in long lines for exclusive releases.

Nike was just another athletic wear manufacturer when it signed a deal with Michael Jordan in 1985. The deal with Jordan took Nike to the top, making it one of the 100 most valuable companies in the world as we write this. The production of Jordan footwear has grown by about 1,400 percent from its introduction to its current operation. We give you the backstory in the nearby sidebar "A (hefty) fine start for Air Jordans."

REMEMBER

With a history of successful bridges from streetwear to high fashion, music and sports to sneakers, and so on, brand collaborations are now an integral part of brand strategy among every successful business where brand value is key. Here are a few reasons why:

A (HEFTY) FINE START FOR AIR JORDANS

The sneaker market got a big boost in 1985 when Nike released Air Jordans. Michael Jordan, the basketball legend, has one of the most successful brand-celebrity partnerships ever. His Nike Air Jordans turned the brand into a powerhouse, earning him an estimated $2 billion in royalties as of this writing. This collaboration also played a key role in shaping sneaker culture, which has become a huge inspiration for brand partnerships.

Air Jordan shoes weren't an instant bestseller because Michael Jordan wore them on the court. The real buzz started when the NBA banned him from wearing them, claiming they didn't match the team's uniform. But Jordan didn't back down. He kept wearing the shoes for 82 games, racking up a $5,000 fine each time. $410,000 in fines in 1985 was a lot of money! Nike saw the potential in this controversy and covered the fines itself. That turned out to be a genius move. Rather than the $3 million in sales Nike had hoped for over three years, it sold $130 million worth of Air Jordans in just the first year!

Michael Jordan is truly the G.O.A.T. of brand collaborations. As of this writing, his partnership with Nike has been going strong for 40 years, and he continues to earn a 5 percent royalty on every pair of Air Jordans sold.

» Licensing a brand makes a significant difference to grow your business.

» Brand collaborations as you know them are still a young business (only 40 years) but show a successful track record.

» Opportunities abound for brand collabs in every area of consumer products and services. You just have to develop an eye for them.

Digital Licensing: Finding Opportunity Online

The dawn of the Internet in the early 2000s changed the world and has had a major impact on the brand licensing business in so many ways. People now use *Google* as a verb, for instance, and *Amazon* is more likely to bring to mind an online retailer than a rain forest. In a span of just a few years, what was mostly an analog world became a digital one, with so many innovations and changes in consumer behavior that even thinking about it is breathtaking.

COCA-COLA AND OREO SURPRISE AND DELIGHT

As a brand that's been around for 140 years, Coca-Cola knows it needs to stay fresh and connect with today's consumers while also attracting the next generation. Its Creation Division focuses on developing new flavors and collaborating with other brands.

In 2024, that effort produced Coca-Cola OREO Zero Sugar and the OREO Coca-Cola sandwich cookie, leveraging the two brands' tastes and imagery to deliver playfully unexpected innovations. Both sport a sleek, black-and-white packaging design that remains true to the two brands' iconic personalities while embracing creative elements like OREO cookie embossments and stacked Coca-Cola bottles.

The Coca-Cola X Oreo brand collaboration shows what brands are willing to do today to create more excitement and sell more products to consumers. These sorts of brand collaborations were supercharged because of the COVID-19 pandemic of 2020 to 2022. With consumers sheltering in place and in need of whimsical experiences, once-conservative brands that previously only promoted themselves began to think out of the brand box and partner with other brands to excite and delight consumers. And it worked incredibly well. Nowadays, you can walk through any supermarket or convenience store and see brand collaborations in every aisle, increasing consumer awareness and driving greater sales.

In today's world, the Internet is known as *Web3* — think of it as the third big step in how people use the web. This version is all about giving power back to the users rather than big companies. It's designed to be open and accessible to everyone, built from the ground up with *blockchain* technology (which is like a super-secure digital ledger). Web3 also uses something called the *Semantic Web*, which is a fancy way of saying that the data on the Internet will be better connected and more meaningful.

From your perspective today as someone interested in the brand licensing world, Web3 has helped democratize the brand licensing business, making entry into the business much easier and creating a host of new and exciting opportunities in the digital world of brand licensing.

Here are some of the ways Web3 has democratized brand licensing:

>> **Research:** You can now super easily locate brands that do licensing and discover what products they license, how much they do in sales, where the products are sold, and whom to contact to get a license.

>> **Virality:** Through social media and e-commerce, Web3 helps you speed up the marketing process for selling licensed products.

>> **Brand growth:** Web3 has supercharged the spread of brands throughout the globe, seeing brand licensing growth of 260 percent since the introduction of the web.

>> **Novelty:** Web3 created new licensing categories such as social media influencers, sandbox video games, streaming media, esports, digital avatars, NFTs, and online betting. We cover many of these in the following sections and later in the chapter.

Looking at two examples of online licensing success

There's no end to opportunity online. Here are two examples of companies taking a creative approach.

>> **emoji company:** *Emojis,* or icons that represent human emotions, living beings, objects, and so on, have become the phenomenon of the 21st century. The founder of the emoji company, whose background was in the entertainment gaming industry, decided to develop a truly universal lifestyle brand for tangible products; for promotional entertainment services; and for the marketing and advertising industry. Since then, the emoji company has built a gigantic IP and content portfolio available for licensing and merchandising, for promotions and marketing, and for advertising campaigns.

Digital natives regularly use emojis during texting or in social media posts. These symbols have become a part of popular culture, and the emoji company was smart and fast enough to trademark 1,900 of them. From a licensing perspective, if you want to use any of these 1,900 trademarked emoji symbols on products or services, you need a license from the emoji company. In the short amount of time since the company trademarked and has been licensing, it has become one of the top 100 licensors in the world.

>> **The Dodo:** Launched in 2014, The Dodo website featured animal videos and quickly became one of the most popular Facebook publishers, garnering 1 billion video views from the social network in November 2015.

As a result of its popularity online, the brand developed an Animal Planet series, *Dodo Heroes,* in June 2018. The show went on to become the network's top-performing new series and was picked up for a second season in 2019. The Dodo then launched a children's show on YouTube and a Netflix series. It has also worked with Scholastic to publish licensed children's books. What about a podcast? Of course; The Dodo launched *An Animal Saved My Life* in 2020. As of this writing, the company most recently expanded into licensing pet insurance.

As digital-first brands, both the emoji company and The Dodo have been hugely successful because they recognized the branding and licensing opportunities available on Web3 based on consumer demand. Both were companies founded by entrepreneurs with a passion for their subject matter and the vision to brand them and extend the brands into new businesses with licensing.

These two companies are both excellent examples of the opportunities that Web3 provides for creating and building unique brands and licensing. The continued growth of Web3 as well as mobile communications, artificial intelligence, augmented reality, and virtual reality will drive significantly more licensing opportunities for companies and individual entrepreneurs that can find ways to create new physical and digital products and services through licensing.

Talkin' non-fungible tokens

Non-fungible token (NFT) is a fancy term for digital goodies that brands can create and sell. These range from digital art and collectibles to virtual fashion to even virtual real estate in online worlds. Big-name brands like Gucci and Nike are big believers, offering special digital items that your online avatars can wear. As the online universe keeps growing, you're looking at a whole new world where the lines between the real and digital blur, opening tons of new opportunities for creativity. Understanding the licensing side of NFTs is key to knowing what you own, how you can use it, and how everyone involved can keep earning from these digital assets.

REMEMBER

Now, before you jump in, remember that the NFT world has had its difficulties. Back in 2021, NFTs were all the rage, but then the market cooled off. However, don't count them out just yet! In 2024, NFTs began making a comeback, especially in the world of gaming and tying digital tokens to real-world assets. Gaming NFTs are expected to become a billion-dollar industry. So although NFTs face some bumps in the road, their future is looking bright!

Licensing with NFTs is all about who owns what and what you can do with your digital goodies. Here's how it works:

>> **When you buy an NFT, you own the digital token but not always the content (like art or music) it represents.** The original creator usually keeps the rights to the content, so you may not be able to do whatever you want with it.

>> **What you can do with your NFT depends on the rules set by the license.** These rights may include displaying the art, reselling it, or even using it in your business. In online worlds, NFTs can give you rights to use virtual items, like clothes for your avatar.

TIP

Be clear about what buyers can do with these items — whether they can trade them, resell them, or use them across different platforms.

>> **NFTs use *smart contracts*, which are digital agreements that automatically enforce the rules.** For example, they can make sure the original artist gets paid a royalty every time the NFT is resold. These contracts can also set up different rights for different NFTs. One NFT may let you use the artwork commercially, while another may be just for personal enjoyment.

Brands can use NFTs to make sure their digital products are authentic, helping to prevent fakes in the digital world. They simply create a QR code that the buyer can scan to be sure that the product is authentic. Brands can also create special, limited-edition NFTs that offer unique experiences or products both online and in the real world. For example, Gucci offers an NFT that buyers can trade in for an actual Gucci wallet.

One cool thing about NFTs is that creators can keep earning money every time their NFT is resold, unlike traditional sales, where they get paid only once. NFTs can be set up so that multiple people or companies share the money every time the NFT is sold. This business model mirrors the licensing business, where IP owners license their IP and receive royalties for the life of the license.

WARNING

NFTs can be sold anywhere in the world, which makes the legal side tricky. NFTs and blockchain are decentralized, and different countries have different rules about digital stuff, so figuring out the truth, sorting out disputes, and enforcing the rules can be tough, especially when different countries are involved. NFTs are a fast-moving area where the technology is evolving more quickly than the regulatory laws to control it.

NFTs are here to stay, though, and their importance to the digital economy means that regulations will be sorted out. To say it's early days for digital-first products is an understatement, and anyone reading this in 20 years will likely be amazed at how much the business has changed.

FROM NFT SMASH TO UNCERTAIN FUTURE

The Bored Ape Yacht Club (BAYC) was important during the NFT craze of 2021 to 2022. Created by Yuga Labs, these ape-themed digital tokens became super popular, with people lining up at Bored and Hungry — an ape-themed restaurant — and even celebrities getting in on the action. Yuga Labs made millions and was worth $4 billion at its peak. But then, in 2023, the NFT bubble popped, and interest in BAYC started to fade.

(continued)

(continued)

But the hype around BAYC wasn't really about art. Although the artwork mattered, NFTs were more about getting people to buy into cryptocurrency. What started as a fun community of meme lovers was later taken over by finance guys who viewed NFTs as serious investments. This shift made NFTs seem risky and unpredictable.

When the "crypto winter" hit after the NFT boom, many investors were stuck with assets that had lost most of their value. BAYC's price on the OpenSea marketplace dropped by 90 percent from its peak. Increased government scrutiny and doubt from traditional finance also hurt the NFT market.

BAYC is in a tough spot. As we write this, the value of the apes has dropped a lot, and investors are trying to find ways to make money from their tokens. The once-popular Bored and Hungry restaurant now exists only in Korea and the Philippines, and Ape Water is only available in some mini-marts in Nevada. With BAYC's popularity declining, people are starting to look at other NFTs like Bitcoin Ordinals and Runes.

The rise and fall of Bored Ape Yacht Club is a reminder of how risky and unpredictable NFTs can be. BAYC had its moment in the spotlight and caught the attention of the mainstream, but the drop in sales and interest shows how hard it is for NFT projects to stay successful over the long haul.

Understanding phygital products

Phygital products are a mix of physical and digital experiences. Imagine you're shopping for clothes in a store (that's the physical part), but you also have an app on your phone that lets you see assorted colors or styles of the clothes on a virtual model (that's the digital part). Together, they make the shopping experience more fun and interactive — that's a phygital product!

Phygital products make everyday activities, like shopping or playing games, more engaging by blending the real world with the digital one. These products can be tailored just for you. For example, a smart mirror in a store may show you how clothes look on you without your having to try them on. Phygital products open new ways for businesses to connect with customers and create cool experiences that stand out.

REMEMBER

In short, phygital products are all about making things more interactive, personalized, and fun by combining physical and digital elements. They're shaping the future of how people shop, play, and interact with the world around them!

Some of the most active phygital licensing has taken place among luxury designers. Shoppers can purchase designer-branded apparel first as an NFT (see the preceding section) and also as physical apparel for themselves from the designer. Video games are another area where phygital products are active. Players can purchase digital designer clothing for their game avatar and then receive the actual clothing for themselves in real life. This area is a brave new world of licensing and is primed for tremendous growth.

Bringing brands to online betting

With online betting, you don't have to go to a casino or a racetrack to place a bet; you do it on your computer or phone. Online betting has become popular for sports matches, races, or even things like who'll win a TV show. You use real money, and if you guess right, you can win money.

Big names like ESPN and Major League Baseball (MLB) see online betting as an opportunity to make more money. By partnering with betting companies or offering their own platforms, they can reach millions of fans who may want to bet on their favorite teams or sports events.

REMEMBER

For sports brands, online betting is a way to keep fans more engaged. When people have money riding on the game, they're more likely to watch and care about the outcome. Getting big, trusted brands like ESPN or MLB involved helps make online betting seem more legitimate and safer to people who may be unsure about it.

Here's how big brands are getting involved to keep fans engaged and open up new ways to make money:

>> **ESPN,** the big sports channel owned by Disney, works with Penn Sports to add betting options to its shows and website. They show odds, give tips, and even link you directly to places where you can place bets. The licensing deal started in 2023 and pays Disney $1.5 billion over ten years.

>> **Major League Baseball** has teamed up with betting companies, letting them use the MLB name and logo. This partnership means you can find MLB-branded betting options and live game data on these betting sites.

All the major U.S. sports leagues now license their brands for online betting. And many of the teams in these leagues have separate deals to license the team name for online betting. It's a multibillion-dollar business, with teams and leagues raking in the royalties.

Seeing How Video Game Brands Are Winning with Licensing

Video game brands or IPs are extraordinarily successful in licensing in many categories. Video games have huge fan bases, and fans love to buy stuff related to their favorite games. Popular entities like Fortnite and Mario are on T-shirts, hats, toys, and even lunchboxes. Sometimes companies make special-edition game controllers or consoles with game themes.

Game companies license their characters and stories to movie studios and streamers. Many popular video games have become movies or TV shows, like *Pokémon*, *The Witcher*, or *Sonic the Hedgehog*. HBO's *The Last of Us* was the top-rated streaming series in 2023, and Amazon's collaboration with Bethesda Softworks *Fallout* game is considered one of the best-rated game adaptations of all time. These movies and shows bring in new fans who may not have played the game before, which helps sell more games and merchandise.

Taking advantage of the popularity of brand collaborations, video game characters are now showing up in other games or products. For example, you may see Mario in a racing game or a Fortnite character in another popular game. These crossovers get fans excited and help both brands grow.

Some games have spin-off books or comics that explore their stories further. The game companies license their stories and characters to writers and publishers, who create these additional adventures. Popular video games are also turned into board games or card games, letting fans experience their favorite games in a new way.

Glimpsing the metaverse through sandbox games

The *metaverse* is like a giant online world where people can hang out, play games, work, and do pretty much anything they can imagine — all in a virtual space. Think of it as a digital universe where you can create an *avatar* (a character that represents you) and explore different virtual worlds, meet other people, and even buy virtual things like clothes or houses.

The gateway to the metaverse as you probably know it is *sandbox games* — virtual playgrounds where you can build, explore, and create whatever you want. These games have no strict goal or path to follow; you get to decide what to do. Two of the most popular sandbox games are Roblox and Minecraft:

>> **Roblox** is a platform where people can create and play games made by other users. It's not just one game but a collection of millions of different games and experiences that users generate. Roblox lets you be creative: You can make your own games, design virtual items, and even earn money by selling them to other players. Plus, you can explore all kinds of games created by other players, from obstacle courses to role-playing adventures.

>> **Minecraft** is a game where you can build and explore your own world made of blocks. You can gather materials, craft items, and create anything from simple houses to entire cities. Minecraft is like a big box of digital LEGO bricks. You can play in Creative Mode, where you have unlimited resources to build whatever you want, or Survival Mode, where you have to gather resources and fend off monsters.

Sandbox games such as Roblox and Minecraft are like little pieces of the metaverse. In these games, you can create your own worlds, meet other players, and explore endless possibilities. They're like steppingstones to the larger concept of the metaverse, where everything is connected. These games encourage creativity and let you express yourself by building, designing, and creating your own experiences. You can connect with other players, work together on projects, or just hang out in these virtual spaces. Sandbox games are providing a glimpse of what the metaverse will be like — a place where the only limit is your imagination.

TIP

The licensing opportunities here are numerous because players can purchase well-known characters to be their "skins" on their avatars. For example, Hello Kitty is available as an avatar skin in the Minecraft game; SpongeBob SquarePants is an avatar skin in Roblox.

Discovering brand licensing in the metaverse

As we note in the preceding section, people can buy virtual goods to customize their avatars and virtual spaces in the metaverse. Just like in real life, people want their avatars to wear cool clothes, drive fancy cars, or live in stylish homes.

Brands see this desire as a huge opportunity to sell digital versions of their products. *Remember:* Selling virtual goods is a whole new way for brands to make money. Imagine you're in the metaverse and you want your avatar to wear the latest Nike sneakers or carry a Gucci bag. Brands can license these products to be sold in virtual stores. You buy them with virtual currency, and now your avatar is styling in digital designer gear.

Brands can also create exclusive virtual experiences. For example, a car company may let you test drive its newest model in a virtual world, or a fashion brand may host a virtual runway show where you can buy the outfits directly for your avatar.

By offering virtual products, brands can create a deeper connection with customers. If you love a brand in real life, you may also want to represent that brand in the metaverse, whether by putting together your home décor or picking out a bike, motorcycle, or car — or even a plane or spaceship.

REMEMBER

The potential for brand licensing in the metaverse is huge. As more people spend time in virtual worlds, the demand for virtual goods will only grow. Brands that get in early can establish themselves as leaders in this new digital marketplace.

Because the metaverse is so new, opportunities abound for licensing entrepreneurs. The metaverse is full of younger, tech-savvy users who spend a lot of time online. Brands can connect with these users in the metaverse, where traditional advertising may not reach them. The current key demographics of the metaverse are Gen Z (broadly categorized as having been born between 1997 and the early 2010s) and Gen Alpha (born between the early 2010s and 2025). Finding popular IP in the metaverse that you can license into products or experiences provides you with significant opportunities if you do your research. Here are a few approaches:

>> **A plain old Internet search:** The Internet has made conducting research as easy as doing a web search.

>> **AI:** In Chapter 5, we discuss using artificial intelligence (AI) as a tool to assist you in doing deeper research into what brands are becoming popular in the metaverse.

>> **In-person research:** Talk with Gen Zers or Gen Alphas and ask them whether they're hanging out in the metaverse and what IP excites them. By combining real experiences from targeted consumers with research based on popular IP, you discover new IP that has significant licensing opportunities for you.

Growing Opportunity in Cannabis Branding and Licensing

Branding and licensing in the cannabis industry are about creating and promoting specific cannabis products by using recognizable names, logos, and packaging. Just as brands sell soda or snacks, cannabis companies use branding to make their products stand out. Licensing allows these brands to expand by letting other companies use their brand to produce and sell cannabis products in various locations.

Cannabis brands develop unique names, logos, and packaging that make their products easy to recognize. For example, a brand may focus on premium quality, eco-friendliness, or fun and relaxation. This approach helps customers know what to expect when they buy that brand.

Just like with other products, a strong brand creates trust with customers in the cannabis market. If you've tried a cannabis product from a brand and liked it, you're more likely to buy other products from the same brand because you trust the quality and experience. Licensing allows a cannabis brand to grow by letting other companies produce and sell its products in different regions. For example, a popular cannabis brand from California may license its name and products to a company in Colorado. This way, the brand can reach more customers without having to build new facilities in every state.

REMEMBER

Licensing ensures that the product offers the same quality and experience no matter where you buy it. The licensed company follows the brand's guidelines to produce the same product, whether you're buying it in California or Colorado.

Branding and licensing in the cannabis industry help products stand out in a crowded market, build trust with customers, and expand reach across different regions. That leads to more sales and helps cannabis companies grow their business by connecting with more customers.

Opportunities for licensing in cannabis have high growth potential. Though most entrepreneurs may be trying to get the rights to open cannabis dispensaries or farms, the actual branding and licensing part of the business has significant upside. Consider the example of the emoji company in the earlier section "Looking at two examples of online licensing success." In fact, how about a line of cannabis products branded with the smiley face emoji? In licensing, marrying creativity with business savvy is a winning combination.

Maximizing YouTube Celebrity through Licensing

One of the oldest and most established areas of licensing is based around celebrities. More mature readers may remember the 1930s child star Shirley Temple, a very talented and adorable little girl with curly locks who sang and danced her way to stardom in a number of hit movies. She was an early licensing celebrity, with a top-selling Shirley Temple doll and even a nonalcoholic drink (ginger ale and grenadine) named after her.

Ever since Shirely Temple's licensing success, celebrities have been front and center in the licensing business. More recent examples of celebrity licensing juggernauts include the Kardashian-Jenner empire, Rhianna's Fenty, Jessica Alba's Honest Company, Gwyneth Paltrow's GOOP, and Beyonce's Ivy Park. One of the greatest incubators for licensing has been YouTube, which has spawned overnight sensation celebrities, many of whom have licensed their names for products.

Here are a few examples of creators who got big on YouTube and built licensing revenue from it:

>> **MrBeast** is known for his crazy challenges and giving away tons of money. MrBeast has licensed his brand to create things like candy bars, burgers (MrBeast Burger), and even clothing and toys. These products are sold online and in stores.

>> **Blippi** makes educational videos for young kids, teaching them about everything from animals to construction vehicles. Blippi's brand is on all sorts of kids' products, like toys, clothes, books, and backpacks.

>> **Ms. Rachel** makes educational videos for toddlers, focusing on language development, singing, and learning through play. Ms. Rachel's brand is starting to appear on products like educational toys, books, and learning tools for young children.

Fans love buying products from their favorite YouTube stars because it makes them feel connected to the person they watch online. Kids who love Blippi or Ms. Rachel want toys or clothes with their favorite characters on them. Adults and teens who follow MrBeast may want to try his burgers or wear his merch.

Connecting with a Brand through Experiential Licensing

Branded experiences are unique events or activities that companies create to help people connect with their brands in a memorable way. Instead of just seeing an ad, people get to experience the brand firsthand. This can be anything from a pop-up store to a virtual reality game or even an online event where you interact with the brand in a fun and engaging way.

TIP

In a world full of ads, a unique branded experience can help a company stand out. It's more exciting and memorable than just another commercial. When people experience a brand, they're more likely to remember it and feel a connection to it. It's like the difference between reading about a place and visiting it; experiencing it makes a bigger impact. If people enjoy the experience, they're more likely to become loyal customers. They'll associate good feelings with the brand and keep coming back.

Branded experiences have their roots in the COVID-19 pandemic, when people couldn't attend physical events or go to stores easily. Brands had to get creative. They started offering more online experiences, like virtual events, interactive websites, and augmented reality games that you could play at home.

As the pandemic eased, people were eager to reconnect in person. Brands started creating experiences that combined safety with fun, like outdoor events, drive-thru experiences, or small, intimate gatherings. These helped people feel connected again while still being cautious.

REMEMBER

People are more likely to trust and support brands that they've had a positive experience with, especially after a time of uncertainty. A great branded experience can make customers feel valued and understood.

Branded experiences have become more important than ever, especially post-pandemic. They help brands connect with people in meaningful ways, build loyalty, and stand out in a crowded market. Brands have learned to be more flexible, offering both in-person and online experiences. This way, they can reach more people regardless of whether customers prefer to engage from home or in person. These experiences are key to keeping customers engaged and excited about the brand.

2
Diving into Licensing

Research and contact potential licensors.

Put together a deal for your first license.

Beef up your licensing business.

Explore the retail arm of the licensing process.

Chapter **5**

Navigating the Licensing Process

I mmersion into the business of licensing can seem intimidating and over-whelming. With so many brands expanding through licensing and so many products licensed, how does a newcomer to the business choose the license right for their product or service?

In this chapter, you find out how to find the best brands for licensing and how to develop winning relationships with the brands to gain their trust and win the licenses.

Knowing Where to Research Licensing Opportunities

Finding excellent brands that will drive sales of your products requires you to do research to discover the right brands for your products. But here's the good news: Thanks to the Internet, AI, and the insider tips we provide you, finding the right brands for your products has never been easier!

REMEMBER

Licensing is a critical marketing tool in today's highly competitive retail marketplace. Companies use it to extend brands into new areas of products, services, and experiences. The intellectual property (IP) owner licenses the brand to a third party with particular expertise in the designated category, experience, or service for a designated period of time. Licensing reaches into every area of consumer products as well as services and experiences.

Many people in the licensing business mistakenly call it an industry because of its size and scope — estimated to be $360 billion per year in retail sales of licensed products and services in 2025. Instead, think of licensing as a horizontal tool that spans vertical industries such as fashion, sports, home goods, and so on. The scope of licensing crosses into every consumer product and digital category. Although this breadth can seem daunting for developing research on what brands to tap for licensing, you need to focus only on brands that make sense for your product categories.

REMEMBER

Quibbling over the definition of licensing as a business tool versus an industry may seem like semantics, but understanding the difference enables you to explore licensing possibilities in every possible area of consumer products, services, and digital opportunities.

Turning to online publications for intel

You can find several online resources fully focused on brand licensing. Tapping into these resources makes your immersion in the licensing business much easier.

TIP

The largest and best-known of the licensing-specific resources is *License Global,* the publication I (Steven) co-founded in 1998. *License Global* is a free subscription-based business to business daily e-news service that also publishes six print editions of a magazine per year (specifically around large trade fairs). The License Global Daily e-news features breaking news in the form of licenses available and major deals in licensing. It can help you understand the deals being made and the most popular properties that are licensing. Get a free subscription at www.licenseglobal.com.

License Global also publishes an annual listing of the top licensors in the world with their estimated retail sales of licensed merchandise and services. (Check out the 2024 list in Chapter 3.) This list is free to download and provides a bird's-eye view of just how significant licensing is and who the major players in the business are. *License Global* is owned and published by The Global Licensing Group at Informa, which produces the largest licensing trade shows around the globe.

Here are a few more publications to get your research started:

>> The Licensing Letter (`www.thelicensingletter.com`) is available with a paid subscription and is U.S.-based.

>> The U.K. market supports two online licensing publications: `www.licensing source.net` and `licensing.biz`. Both are good information sources with their news tending to skew more heavily toward U.K. brands and retail.

>> Another European licensing business publication called `www.licensing magazine.com` (based in Italy) also covers the global licensing business.

>> The licensing business trade association Licensing International publishes a free newsletter, which you can sign up for here: `https://licensing international.org/news/`.

TIP

Depending on the products or services you sell, you also want to subscribe to online business publications in the specific industries you intend to sell products in. The later section "Working important trade shows and conferences" gives you a thorough list of trade shows and conferences where licensing takes center stage. Most of these have information products or e-newsletters you can subscribe to.

Using AI and the Internet

One of the most exciting developments for doing research in licensing is the advent of artificial intelligence (AI). Simply put, artificial intelligence for research uses key words or phrases to help you find the information you need faster and in a more streamlined way. An AI service can conduct deep searches of brands that are succeeding through licensing by quickly sifting through thousands of bits of data to provide you with the information you need.

We highly recommend you take advantage of AI as a research tool to search for licenses that will drive greater sales of your products. You can also use search engines for your licensing research, but be careful. *Licensing* is an overly broad term, so be specific in your searches. "Brand licensing" narrows your searches to specifically target your business of consumer products licensing. Set up an alert for "brand licensing" and see how many times it gets mentioned. This type of research is a huge help for you as you delve deeper into the brand licensing world.

As we write this book, AI is still in its early stages of development. The current most accessible and easy-to-use AI tool is called ChatGPT. It comes in two versions:

>> **ChatGPT:** This one is free but limits your information. The free version uses information up to Sept 2021.

>> **ChatGPT 4:** ChatGPT 4 is more accurate than the free version, which is based on GPT-3.5. ChatGPT 4 is trained on more than a trillion parameters, which helps it generate more accurate responses. The subscription price is $20 per month (at the time of this writing).

If you're using ChatGPT for your search, use the latest version.

TIP

We recommend using an AI tool versus a simple search engine to help pinpoint accuracy. It saves time, and time is money! For example, say you're interested in licensing the character Winnie the Pooh and want to do research on what Winnie the Pooh licensed products are currently on the market. A simple web search for Winnie the Pooh licensed products brings up a broad range of different websites featuring licensed products for sale. A ChatGPT 4 search lists Winnie the Pooh products and their categories — that is, toys, apparel, home décor, and so on. The ChatGPT 4 search simply makes your search faster, easier, and much more targeted.

Understanding How to Match Product to License

If you're a licensee (manufacturer), you need to find the right licenses that work best with the products you produce. Sounds easy, right? Just get a license for a hot brand or movie and sell more products!

This couldn't be farther from the truth. Your product and the licensed IP you secure to sell it need to align. For example, if your product is geared for a certain age demographic, you need to secure an appropriate license for that demographic. If you make kids' pajamas, for example, Elmo from *Sesame Street* would make a great character license for the pajamas; horror movie legend Chucky wouldn't.

Depending on the products you produce, finding the right brand license to help sell more determines where you do your research. Using ChatGPT (which we cover in the preceding section), you can search the product category you're most interested in acquiring a license for to see which products are bestsellers. Then start asking questions:

>> Are they using a license to sell?

>> Which license are they using?

>> Is there a similar license that perhaps isn't being used for this product category yet?

Doing this easy research really helps you in your license acquisition process because it narrows down what products are successfully selling and what license(s) is/are helping to drive those sales.

WARNING

A license isn't something to rush into. We recommend that any newcomer to licensing spend at least several months doing intensive research before acquiring a license. With so many licenses available in the marketplace, barreling into a licensing agreement without first doing the depth of research necessary to be successful can be tempting. Preparation means doing a deep dive into the DNA of the brand you're licensing: Who are the brand's core customers or fans? Are they the right demographic to purchase the product, service, or experience you're selling? Many well known and loved brands have made the mistake of licensing into product categories where the consumer didn't get the connection — and therefore didn't buy the product!

Retail intelligence

The best research you can do is what's known as *retail intelligence*, meaning that you literally go shopping — but with a purpose. First, define the category of product you plan to sell. Next, think about what type of retailer makes the most sense for your products. Is it mass market like Walmart? A department store like Kohls? An e-commerce giant like Amazon? A specialty retailer like Hot Topic?

Whichever retailer or retail channel you choose to sell into, you need to go to the stores and browse their merchandise. See what's selling in the product category that interests you; is it licensed, or is the retailer more focused on its own store brands? What licenses are they using? Do you see room for more licenses?

TIP

If you're already creating and selling products in the marketplace but are new to licensing, one great resource is to speak with your retail partner/buyer. Retailers are the best barometer for what drives product sales, and they can share with you the licenses that are working in your product category.

Of course, the caveat here is that licensing has become so ubiquitous nowadays that unless you've really immersed yourself in understanding licensing, you may see a licensed product and assume it isn't licensed. This invisibility is the secret to successful licensing: The consumer assumes the product is simply a brand extension versus a license.

TIP

Don't assume that a retailer isn't selling licensed products just because you can't identify those products. These days, brand licensing and collaborations are everywhere and growing stronger every day. In fact, many retailers that never sold licensed products before are now adding them to their product mix to drive greater sales, so don't count anyone out.

Non-exclusive licenses

Licensors often permit the same property to be licensed in the same product category for multiple licensees. This practice is known as a *non-exclusive license.* A non-exclusive license means the licensor isn't restricted to granting the rights to use their intellectual property to only one licensee, allowing them to license it to multiple parties simultaneously.

REMEMBER

Non-exclusive licenses are a double-edged sword. On one hand, you have competitors using the same license to sell products similar to yours, which means either your product quality needs to be significantly better or you need to have a more competitive pricing strategy. In today's licensing world, most popular licensors offer only non-exclusive licenses except in rare cases where your product may be so specialized that you have no competition. On the plus side, the fact that so many non-exclusive licenses are being granted tells you that consumer demand for these products is high and the business is very healthy.

Immersing Yourself in the Licensing Trade

After you understand which licenses work with the products you want to sell (see the earlier section "Understanding How to Match Product to License"), your next step is tracking down those licenses and negotiating to use them. This part may seem daunting, but it doesn't have to be if you've done your homework. The following sections give you a guide to finding those licenses that help you sell more products.

Leveraging trade associations

Every major manufacturing business has a trade association that exists to help companies come to market. *Trade associations,* also known as *industry trade groups, business associations, sector associations,* or *industry bodies,* are organizations that are funded and founded by businesses in a specific industry. They perform a variety of functions, including these:

>> **Setting industry standards:** Trade associations help establish industry standards that protect the public and allow components from different manufacturers to work together.

>> **Representation:** They represent their members before government agencies and legislatures.

>> **Collecting and analyzing data:** They're often the best sources of data and analysis on their industry segment.

>> **Publications:** They often publish trade publications that can help track industry developments, identify competitors, and find industry conferences.

>> **Public relations:** They participate in public relations activities such as advertising, education, and publishing.

>> **Networking:** They offer networking events for their members.

>> **Training:** They provide training and educational materials to members.

>> **Technical advice:** They also offer technical advice to their members.

>> **Conferences:** They produce conferences for members.

>> **Charitable events:** They hold charitable events for their members.

Trade associations can be hugely helpful to you even if you just visit their websites; most of them list resources you can tap into for research and information.

TIP

Because of its importance in all areas of consumer products and services, licensing has its very own trade association called Licensing International. It offers several research reports and tools that help you develop your licensing business. Here you can find valuable resources and research, much of it at little to no cost. Licensing International is also tied closely with trade shows and events that are key to the licensing business.

Licensing-focused trade shows, or *expos,* give licensors a forum to display the brands they have available for licensing. Manufacturers, distributors, and retailers shop the show to see what's available. These expos are an absolute must for newcomers in licensing because they're a window into pop culture and the licenses you can expect to see in the coming years at retail.

In the 1990s, when the licensing business was still relatively new, newbies could easily walk the expos and strike up conversations with the exhibitors to learn about the licenses available. These days, trade fairs are massive events, with some major exhibitors spending hundreds of thousands of dollars on their booths.

TIP

Because the business has become much more sophisticated and grown so quickly, you must preschedule meetings with licensors whose properties you may be interested in licensing. Unfortunately, we've too often seen newcomers without appointments be turned away without ever getting a meeting. That's how competitive and mature licensing has become.

Bringing in a licensing consultant

Licensing agents represent brands for licensing, and *licensing consultants* represent manufacturers and companies seeking licenses. The licensing consultant is your ace in the hole for property recommendations as well as negotiating the licensing agreements on your behalf.

Consultants typically charge a monthly retainer and receive a small percentage of the overall licensing deal. Most consultants represent several different manufacturers, and their primary purpose is to make your job much easier in securing licenses.

TIP

If you're serious about licensing and want to secure top-tier brands for licensing, your best bet is to start off using a consultant. Think of it like this: If you were taking a trip down the Amazon River for the first time, you'd want an experienced guide to show you all the interesting sights and help you avoid the rapids or places where caimans, vipers, and jaguars may gather. A consultant is your very experienced tour guide, well worth their fee for leading you down the licensing river safely and successfully.

Here are some major reasons why a licensing consultant is a good hire when you're new:

>> **Established relationships:** A good consultant has spent years establishing relationships with licensors and agents. They can secure those hard-to-get meetings and help develop the trust necessary to secure a license.

>> **Knowledge:** The licensing consultant's experience has taught them which licenses work best for different product categories. They can steer you toward licenses that have the highest visibility with consumers and the greatest success at retail. They also know how to negotiate a licensing contract, including how much royalty and upfront guarantee payment is fair.

>> **Speed to market:** A licensing consultant speeds up the process of securing licenses as a result of their established relationships and ability to get meetings and negotiate a licensing contract.

After you've successfully navigated the river a few times, you may no longer require the services of the guide, but the licensing consultant is worth their weight in gold for those early forays.

Working important trade shows and conferences

You need to do the important work of shopping for the license. The extensive list that follows covers a wide range of trade shows and conferences where licensing is a central focus, offering vast opportunities for brand extension across diverse industries from books and entertainment to fashion, food, and home goods.

REMEMBER

Licensing is a global business, and many of these trade shows and conferences are global in scope and attendance. If you plan to sell to a limited geographic territory, delve into the local trade fairs specific to the region you're targeting.

» **Licensing-specific trade shows**

- **Licensing Expo (Las Vegas, Nevada, USA):** Global event for licensing and brand extension across industries including entertainment, fashion, sports, and consumer products

- **Brand Licensing Europe (London, England):** Licensing expo for the European market, covering categories like characters, entertainment, and corporate brands

» **Fashion and apparel-related**

- **MAGIC Marketplace (Las Vegas, Nevada, USA):** Fashion and apparel trade show with a focus on licensing apparel, accessories, and footwear, along with lifestyle and retail collaborations

- **Première Vision Paris (Paris, France):** Fashion industry event with licensing discussions around textiles, design, and brand collaborations

» **Toys, games, and entertainment**

- **New York Toy Fair (New York, New York, USA):** Licensing opportunities for toys, games, and entertainment properties, often tied to TV, movies, and video games

- **Gamercon (Dublin, Ireland):** Gaming industry conference with opportunities for licensing in video games, esports, and digital entertainment

- **Comic-Con International (San Diego, California, USA):** Licensing opportunities for comics, movies, TV shows, and fan-driven merchandise

- **New York Comic Con:** Same as San Diego but larger (200,000 attendees)

- **Anime Expo (Los Angeles, California, USA):** Licensing for anime, manga, and pop-culture brands, often expanding into fashion and lifestyle categories

- **Anime Japan (Tokyo, Japan):** Licensing opportunities at the largest and most important trade fair for anime in the world

- **MIPCOM (Cannes, France):** Licensing content for TV, movies, and digital platforms

- **Kidscreen Summit (San Diego, CA USA):** Premier event for the children's entertainment industry, focusing on content licensing, distribution, and brand partnerships in kids' media

- **X Tracks Licensing Summit (New York, New York; Bentonville Arkansas; and Los Angeles, California, USA):** Licensing and branding for entertainment properties, with a focus on cross-media licensing opportunities for content, music, and games; an executive-level licensing conference and networking event focused on new growth areas of IP licensing (three times per year)

>> **Book fairs**

- **Frankfurt Book Fair (Frankfurt, Germany):** Largest global book fair; a major hub for publishing deals and licensing opportunities for books, media, and brand extensions

- **Bologna Children's Book & Licensing Fair (Bologna, Italy):** International children's publishing and licensing fair focused on children's books, multimedia, and entertainment properties

- **London Book Fair (London, England):** Publishing and content licensing for books, digital media, TV, and film rights

- **Beijing International Book Fair (Beijing, China):** Licensing and rights exchange for books and other media content, with an emphasis on the growing Chinese market

- **Sharjah International Book Fair (Sharjah, United Arab Emirates):** Publishing industry event with opportunities for licensing across the Middle East and North Africa (MENA) region

>> **Consumer products and housewares**

- **The Inspired Home Show (formerly International Home + Housewares Show; Chicago, Illinois, USA):** Licensing for home goods, kitchenware, and housewares, often in collaboration with lifestyle brands

- **Outdoor Retailer (Denver, Colorado, USA):** Licensing outdoor goods, sportswear, and equipment for camping, hiking, and outdoor activities

- **Consumer Electronics Show (CES; Las Vegas, Nevada, USA):** Consumer electronics event with opportunities for licensing smart home products, wearables, and entertainment technology

>> **Food and beverage**

- **National Restaurant Association (Chicago, Illinois, USA):** Licensing opportunities for food brands, restaurants, and hospitality products

- **Sweets & Snacks Expo (Chicago, Illinois, USA):** Licensing confectionery, snacks, and food products

- **International Dairy Deli Bakery Association Expo (locations around the United States):** Licensing opportunities in the dairy, deli, and bakery sectors

- **Natural Products Expo (Moves from city to city each year, USA):** Licensing natural and organic food, beverage, and health products

>> **Home, lifestyle, and interior design**

- **High Point Market (High Point, North Carolina, USA):** Home furnishings and interior design event with licensing opportunities for lifestyle and home décor brands

- **NY NOW (New York, New York, USA):** Home, lifestyle, and gift trade show with brand licensing opportunities in décor, fashion, and wellness

- **Maison & Objet (Paris, France):** Interior design, home décor, and lifestyle brands with a focus on licensing home goods and furnishings

>> **Sports and outdoors**

- **Sports Licensing and Tailgate Show (Las Vegas, Nevada, USA):** Licensing for sports teams, leagues, and tailgating products, including merchandise, apparel, and fan experiences

- **ISPO Munich (Munich, Germany):** Licensing sportswear, outdoor, and fitness products, including tech and gear for athletes and active consumers

- **SHOT Show (Las Vegas, Nevada, USA):** Licensing opportunities for shooting, hunting, and outdoor sports products

Though this is a significant list of trade events, it's by no means fully comprehensive to every product category that uses licensing. If you don't see a trade fair for the product categories you're selling, simply do an Internet search for your specific trade.

Developing Relationships in the Business

Like in any business, relationships matter in licensing! Brands are licensing their beloved IP to third-party companies to produce new products and services, which makes the need for trust paramount.

REMEMBER
We aren't just talking about the licensors here, though. Developing relationships with agents, consultants, and retailers is key to succeeding in the licensing business.

Building trust

Throughout the many layers of legal and contractual agreements that need to happen to get a new license, the main consideration on each party's mind is trust. The licensor wonders whether they can trust the licensee to create an excellent product and sell it at retail to the consumer. The licensee wonders whether the licensor will support the product sales with marketing. Each party needs to develop a certain amount of trust for the relationship to be truly successful.

As a new licensee, you need to work especially hard to develop trust. Hiring a well-known and well-liked licensing consultant certainly greases the wheels, but at the end of the day, you need to put in the time to develop a trusting relationship. (Flip to the earlier section "Bringing in a licensing consultant" for more on this role.)

Another surefire way to establish yourself and build trust is to go to as many live events as you can. Whether they're awards presentations or quarterly networking cocktail receptions, showing up at events and talking to as many people as possible builds your relationships.

TIP
If you're uncomfortable in networking situations, a licensing consultant can assist. Tag along with your consultant to as many licensing events as you can, and before long you'll become a fixture in the business.

TIP
The fastest way to build trust is by one-on-one meetings. Typically, somewhere out of the office in a neutral environment works best, whether that's a meal, coffee, or cocktails. The good news for you is that the licensing business is very friendly, and most people understand the importance of developing trusting relationships. As you find companies you want to do business with, start developing these relationships through one-on-one meetings.

Crushing the first conversation with would-be partners

Will Rogers, the noted humorous and social commentator of the early 20th century, famously said, "You never get a second chance to make a good first impression." For you as a potential new licensing partner, making that great first impression is critical. Whether you're using a licensing consultant to secure a license or doing it directly yourself, you need to have done your homework on the IP you're looking to license before you walk into that meeting:

>> Absorb everything you can about the brand: its history, its demographics, and how many licenses it currently has and in what categories.

>> Learn where the core products are sold.

>> Find out where the current licensed products sell and to whom.

>> Get annual sales figures.

>> Project your annual sales for the first year and through the contract.

Go to the meeting overprepared.

Determining your unique selling proposition

Your *unique selling proposition,* or USP, distinguishes your company from your competition. Your ability to identify and highlight it may very well win the license you seek.

For example, if you make kids' pajamas that are 100 percent cotton and made in America using sustainable cotton crops from BIPOC-owned farms, you have an incredible unique selling proposition. Every company has a USP; you simply need to figure out yours and then make it a key point in the presentation you'll show to potential partners. Finding your USP and touting it loudly to your potential licensing partners distinguishes your company and gets you closer to a deal.

Translating that trust into a pitch

The legwork in the preceding sections may sound overwhelming, but remember that licenses generate a lot of competition. If you can stand out through preparation, organization, and pizzaz, you may very well win the license. We've heard many stories over the years about companies that got the license not because they offered the most money but because the licensor trusted and believed in them.

As you build your presentation deck to sell yourself to potential partners, keep the following points in mind:

>> Keep it brief: five to ten slides, which you can present in two minutes.

>> Use graphics and photos to illustrate (rather than a lot of words).

>> Showcase your company's strengths, such as quality products, retail distribution, speed to market, and especially your unique selling proposition (more on that in the preceding section).

>> Illustrate your vision for the product and packaging with the license you're pitching for.

>> Bring in testimonials from happy customers.

Practicing your pitch

Don't go pitch the licensor that has the hot license you know will sell millions of products before you've practiced, practiced, practiced. Bring in the toughest critics in your company or a friend that's brutally honest. Or, if you've hired a licensing consultant, set up a meeting to go over the pitch several times.

No matter how great your presentation is, it always has room for improvement. Getting an honest, knowledgeable, third-party opinion can only help hone the presentation.

REMEMBER

Repetition breeds recognition. The more you rehearse your presentation, the better you sound in that critical meeting.

IN THIS CHAPTER

» **Approaching and contacting brand owners**

» **Bringing in a licensing (IP) attorney**

» **Breaking down the steps of doing a deal**

» **Cutting bait when a potential deal won't work for you**

Chapter **6**

Negotiating the License Deal

L icensing can be a game-changer for your business. It's your ticket to boosting sales and expanding your product's reach by tapping into the built-in brand recognition and loyal audience of an established brand. Sounds amazing, right? But turning that big idea into a signed licensing contract takes more than just enthusiasm; it requires careful planning and savvy negotiation.

In this chapter, we walk you through the key steps to securing a licensing deal that works for you. From making the right connections to hammering out the details, you discover how to navigate the process with confidence and set yourself up for success.

REMEMBER

As a newcomer to licensing, your reputation and future success in licensing will be based on your first deals. Being knowledgeable and fully prepared ensures your success with your first licenses and paves the way for more licensing success in the future.

Connecting with the Brand Owner (Licensor)

Ready to snag your first license? The first step is to connect with the *licensor* — the brand owner you want to partner with. This section provides some tried-and-true methods to help you find the right license and make that crucial first impression.

Choose your approach based on your timeline and budget. For example, if it's July and you're itching to get started, waiting until next May's International Licensing Expo may not be the best idea.

Meeting licensors at a licensing trade show

Attending a licensing trade show is one of the most effective ways to connect with licensors. (See Chapter 5 for a rundown on these events.) It offers a chance to discuss licensing opportunities in a more personal setting. As a newcomer at one of the key licensing trade shows, you get an intensive immersion into the licensing business and a chance to make a whole lot of important connections.

Because you're a new, unknown company entering the market, you must set an appointment ahead of time with a major licensor, or you'll be turned away. Not because companies don't want your business, but because they have very full schedules. Preplanning is crucial.

The best way for you to schedule a meeting is to research the exhibitors in advance of the trade show. For example, Licensing Expo, the annual trade show for licensing, takes place in May. We recommend you visit the expo website (www.licensingexpo.com) in early March to look at the list of exhibiting companies. By March, 90 percent of the exhibitors are signed up, and you can start your outreach for meeting with the licensors you're most interested in talking with.

A few further tips to maximize your Expo time:

>> **Have a list of licenses that may make sense for your product instead of putting all your eggs in one basket.** If you're pursuing a popular license, you may discover in your meeting that the product category is already licensed.

>> **When setting appointments at the Expo, allow yourself a full hour for the meeting.** Most meetings are significantly shorter, but you need to allow for unforeseen delays as well as navigating the show floor.

>> **Map the show floor ahead of time to know where each of your meetings takes place.** Licensing Expo is a large show, and getting from meeting to meeting can take 15 minutes.

>> **Allow yourself several additional hours to just walk the show floor by aisle.** You may discover licenses at the Expo that you hadn't thought of before attending but may be right for your product.

>> **Think outside the show floor.** You can meet important licensors at show-adjacent events and locations, such as at the 5k fun run, bars inside the main hotel, the gym, or other Licensing International events such as their award show.

REMEMBER

The cost to attend a trade show requires airfare, transportation, lodging, and meals. The more you can accomplish, the better the return on your investment. Success is where preparation and opportunity meet, and trade shows provide this opportunity. Being organized and maximizing your meetings can really pay off.

The Global Licensing Group organizes all the major licensing trade fairs. You can register for its trade fairs as well as request meetings with exhibitors at www.thegloballicensinggroup.com/en/home.html. After you register for the licensing expos, Global Licensing Group gives you the ability to set meetings with exhibitors through its web portal and online matchmaking tools. These tools let you send a message and meeting request to some of these hard-to reach licensors. We strongly recommend you use this tool because it's the easiest way to snag that meeting with the busy licensors.

Hitting an industry trade show

Attending industry-specific trade shows where target brands are exhibiting is a great way to seek out brands available for licensing. For instance, if you want to license a fertilizer brand for garden tools, you can find it at hardware industry shows. If you want to license a fashion brand, attend fashion trade events. Think of finding brands for licensing like a farmer seeking ripe fruit to pick. The idea is to go where the brands grow. That's industry trade shows.

REMEMBER

Brands exhibit at industry trade shows to grow their businesses. Be professional in how you approach the brands that interest you for licensing. Like for the licensing trade shows in the preceding section, schedule as many of your appointments ahead of time as you can. This way, you utilize your time wisely and get the most out of your trade show experience.

Even if you don't secure that meeting, making the effort is important. If you approach the company's trade show booth, the representatives may recognize your name from the emails you've sent them.

Turning to social media

What if you've decided you want to get a license, and the next licensing trade show isn't for six months? Social media platforms, particularly LinkedIn, offer another method of connecting with the licensor. Search for licensing or marketing executives in the companies you're targeting and initiate a conversation about potential licensing.

LinkedIn is an amazing business tool that enables you to find and connect with companies you're looking to do business with. As a database alone, it's invaluable, but its social media aspect makes it a great way to learn about and communicate within the licensing business. If you're new to LinkedIn, check out *LinkedIn For Dummies* by Joel Elad (Wiley) to read more about the many ways you can use it for growing your business.

Leveraging industry directories

Licensing industry resources like the Licensing International trade organization or *License Global* magazine offer directories and databases (though some may charge a fee) with contact information for brand owners and their licensing agents. Here you can find listings of leading licensors; top licensees; and service providers like agents, consultants, lawyers, accountants, royalty auditors, design firms, distributors, and more.

Using Your Research to Your Advantage When You Make Contact

Contacting a brand owner presents a big opportunity for you, and you want to be ready to make the most of it. Whether you reach out through email or set up an in-person meeting, your objective is to make a great impression and generate interest while you uncover the information you need. Do as much research as you can about the licensor ahead of time so you know answers to questions like these:

>> What's attractive about the brand that makes you want to license it?

>> Does the brand already do licensing?

>> Is the brand licensing any products similar to yours?

>> Which retailers carry the brand's products?

TIP

The more you know about the brand in advance, the better prepared you are for the first conversation. Having a basic understanding of the licensor before reaching out helps ensure the licensor respects you as a serious business partner.

When you do make contact introduce yourself and briefly explain your interest in licensing the brand for your product. At this point, the brand owner will likely ask you about your experience in product manufacturing and whether you've used licensing before. Be honest. If you don't have previous experience in licensing, that's fine. Many companies are new to licensing, and licensors welcome the opportunity to work with new licensees.

Remember, licensing is a relatively new business model and growing every year. Now is the opportunity in the conversation to show off some of the knowledge you've picked up from your initial research of the brand. We recommend developing a list of questions that help you gain more knowledge about how the brand does licensing while impressing your contact with the research you've done.

TIP

Use your knowledge humbly and inquisitively. For example, pose it in as a question: "I noticed that you've licensed XYZ brand for XYZ product being sold at XYZ retailer; how is that going?" In this way, you can swiftly develop a rapport with the brand owner to move the conversation toward the start of a negotiation.

More than once I (Steven) have been contacted by new potential licensees that wanted a license from an A-level brand but didn't want to pay an upfront royalty. Their "logic" was simple: If the licensed product sells, I'll pay a royalty; if it doesn't, I won't.

WARNING

In terms of licensing etiquette, this approach is a big no! Suggesting this arrangement to a licensor closes the door on ever working with them. A brands, B brands, and C brands have spent millions of dollars and many years building their brand equity. (Head to the later section "Estimating sales and royalties" for more on those brand level distinctions.) They take an enormous amount of pride in their brands. As a result, they exercise discretion and caution in choosing their partners when they license their brands. Ignoring the rules of the licensing game by disrespecting how the business is structured is a surefire way to fail and create a bad reputation for your company. Be humble; remember that licensing is a partnership that requires mutual respect.

Finding and Hiring an IP Attorney

When you're new to licensing, you don't know what you don't know, so tap into the knowledge of professionals who do know. Before negotiation begins, you may want to hire an intellectual property (IP) attorney. The reason you need an IP lawyer who specializes in negotiating the contract is the same reason you'd use a lawyer for any type of contract: You want to be sure it's fair and doesn't contain any hidden or unexplained fees or obligations. The experienced IP lawyer makes sure you understand the details of the licensing agreement and negotiates the best terms on your behalf. You can also work with your attorney to craft the initial licensing agreement proposal (see the following section).

Having an IP attorney on board gives you peace of mind and doesn't cost you a great deal in the long run because they often find ways to save you money through contract negotiations.

You have several options for finding an IP licensing attorney, including the following:

>> If you've joined the industry association (Licensing International), you have access to its directory of service providers. That list contains some IP lawyers you can contact and interview. Be sure you're clear about what their fees are.

>> If you've hired a licensing consultant to help you acquire a license, ask them who they recommend as an attorney. (Flip to Chapter 5 for more on working with a licensing consultant.) The licensing consultant knows the best IP lawyers — and what their fees are — and can work with the attorney to negotiate the best terms on your behalf. *Note:* If you're working with a licensing consultant, they actually may be able to provide you with similar negotiating expertise on the business terms of the agreement.

WARNING

Be sure the lawyer you hire to negotiate your licensing contract specializes in licensing contracts. These contracts are very specific and need a particular expertise. You don't want to hire your cousin who just graduated from law school and took a class in IP law, or even your very experienced and trusted divorce attorney, for this.

When interviewing your potential licensing attorney, ask them what license agreements they've worked on previously. Experience counts! In your initial interview, be very clear that you're new to licensing and are depending on your attorney to advise you closely on specifics in the contract. Ask the attorney how many new companies just getting into licensing they've worked with. Ask them what they see as the common pitfalls of new licensees. These questions help you determine whether a particular IP attorney is right for you.

REMEMBER

Your IP attorney may be crucial to getting you the best negotiated licensing agreement. Be sure you're comfortable with the attorney and trust them to negotiate on your behalf.

Crafting and Submitting Your Licensing Proposal

A solid licensing proposal demonstrates that you understand both the brand and the industry. It also helps the brand owner see how your product and business fit into the brand's overall brand strategy.

After you've advanced the conversation to the point where the licensor asks you to submit a proposal, you're halfway to success. Most major licensors have a template they ask you to fill in with the information they need from you to get the proposal process started. The information they ask for is relatively simple and helps them determine whether you have the business capabilities and financing to be considered as a licensee.

A typical proposal includes the following information:

>> **Part 1: Company Information**

- Company name, address, and key contacts
- Years in business and key personnel
- State of incorporation and annual sales for the past three years
- Size of salesforce, manufacturing capabilities, and distribution channels
- Other licensors you've worked with, plus your top retail accounts

>> **Part 2: Proposal Information**

- Detailed description of the product line you intend to license (include images if possible)
- Sales projections
- Proposed royalty rate, term length, and payment schedule
- Distribution plans (what channels you'll sell through)
- Marketing and promotional support plans

>> **Part 3: References**

  ● Licensor references (if you've worked with licensed brands before)

  ● Retail and bank references

Estimating sales and royalties

The tricky part for many first-time licenses is estimating sales and royalties for the new licensed product. This is where your industry knowledge comes into play. If you already manufacture and sell similar products, use your past sales as a basis for projections. If you're new to the entire process, your experienced attorney and/or licensing consultant can provide guidelines.

REMEMBER

The key to negotiating a successful licensing deal is to know ahead of time how much the retailers you'll be selling the product to are willing to pay you for your product. Your profitability must be based on that figure.

When proposing a royalty rate, here are some general parameters:

>> **Apparel (T-shirts, accessories):** 8 to 14 percent

>> **Hard goods (toys, tools):** 8 to 12 percent

>> **Food products:** 4 to 6 percent

These percentages show the royalty amount you pay the licensors on the wholesale value. As an example, if you're selling T-shirts wholesale for $12 and your agreed-upon royalty rate is 10 percent, each T-shirt sold means the licensor gets a $1.20 royalty payment. If you sell 100,000 T-shirts, your royalty payment is $120,000. See Table 6-1.

TABLE 6-1

Royalty Rates

	Year 1	Year 2	Total
Wholesale Price	$12	$12	N/A
Suggested Retail Price	$24	$24	N/A
Royalty Rate	10%	10%	N/A
Estimated Units Sold	100,000	150,000	250,000
Estimated Wholesale Sales	$1,200,000	$1,800,000	$3,000,000
Projected Royalty Payment	$120,000	$180,000	$300,000

The royalty rate is negotiable, but entering this phase with a realistic proposal is essential. Typically, royalty rates are based on wholesale sales, not the retail price. The reason is that the licensee typically can only track their wholesale sales and can't accurately track the retail sales. The only time a licensee may pay a royalty based on retail sales is when they're the retailer and are selling directly to the customer (which may happen if the licensee operates an online store). You can find out more about wholesale and retail in Chapter 8.

TIP

When you're getting into the licensing business, you hear a lot about A, B, and C properties. Think of them like buying a car:

>> **A properties:** The luxury models — think Mercedes, BMW, Bentley, or Ferrari. They're high prestige and high demand, and they have a hefty price tag.

>> **B properties:** Premium cars like Lexus, Infiniti, Cadillac, or Lincoln. They're still impressive, but they're a bit more affordable than the top tier.

>> **C properties:** Reliable and practical, like Honda, Toyota, Hyundai, or Kia. They're solid choices that get the job done without the luxury price tag.

REMEMBER

All these cars get you to your destination. In licensing, you can still create a successful deal regardless of whether you work with an A, B, or C property. The difference is that the A properties cost more to acquire and often have a bigger demand and brand reputation to match.

An A car is a Mercedes, BMW, or even a Bentley or Ferrari. A B property car is a Lexus, Infiniti, Cadillac, or Lincoln. C property vehicles are Hondas, Toyotas, Hyundais, or Kias. The important thing is that all levels of property get you to your licensing destination. The A's and B's just cost you more to acquire.

Understanding the guaranteed minimum royalty payment

When you're negotiating a licensing contract, you come across something called the *guaranteed minimum royalty payment* (GMRP). It has also been called *minimum guarantee, guaranteed royalty, GM, GMR,* and *MG.*

Including these GMRPs in all licensing agreements is a standard practice. The industry standard GMRP rate as a percentage of projected royalty payments is 50 percent. Therefore, the licensor (the brand owner) requires you to guarantee 50 percent of your estimated royalty payment — whether you hit your sales target or not.

Here's an example: Suppose you expect to sell $2 million worth of your licensed product, and your royalty rate is 10 percent. That means the total royalty due works out like this:

$2,000,000 × 10 percent = $200,000 in royalties

Now, with a 50 percent guaranteed minimum royalty, you're required to commit to paying at least $100,000:

$200,000 × 50 percent = $100,000

Both you and the licensor believe you can hit the $2 million mark, but the $100,000 guarantee ensures they receive a payment of $100,000 if you don't succeed in selling half your projections.

Depending on the licensor and whether the property is A, B, or C (as we outline in the preceding section), the licensor may also expect a minimum upfront payment against the $100,000. Sometimes you can negotiate the payment over a period of months prior to the product release. It really depends on the licensor you're working with, how in-demand the license is, and the relationship you develop with the licensor.

TIP

Many A-list licensors expect you to pay the minimum guarantee upfront when you sign the agreement. (Chapter 3 has a list of 2024's top ten licensors.) The reason is the number of licensees competing to get the A-list properties. A-listers have a long line of licensees in the mix, which means the licensors can demand the most in upfront royalty payments.

The negotiations are another area where a professional licensing consultant can be a game-changer. A good consultant not only gets you in the door but also negotiates the best possible deal on your behalf, including the most minimal of upfront guarantees. The licensing consultant wants you to get the license but also is typically rewarded on the back end in the form of a small percentage (that is, 1 percent) of sales of the licensed product they help secure. So getting the deal done while keeping your risks manageable is in their best interest.

Advancing to the Next Stage: The Licensing Agreement and Term Sheet

Congratulations! The licensor has approved you as a potential licensee. At this point, you're ready to put together the licensing agreement and term sheet, which we discuss in the following sections.

Negotiating basic terms of your licensing agreement

This stage is where both parties — the licensee (you) and the licensor (brand owner) — try to strike a balance that benefits both sides. Table 6-2 shows you the main areas to negotiate.

TABLE 6-2

Points of Negotiation

Key Terms	Licensor Wants	Licensee Wants
Channels of Distribution	Focused coverage	Wider channels
Guaranteed Minimum Royalty Payment	Higher guarantee	Lower guarantee
Territory	Specific rights	Global regions
Advance Payment	Higher upfront	Lower upfront
Auto-Renewals	Restricted	Unrestricted
Sell-Off Period	Short	Long

The considerations for each term in the deal vary by your perspective, which is no surprise. The licensor's interests don't substantially overlap with those of the licensee. Here's a rundown of the terms in Table 6-2 and what they mean for how you proceed:

>> **Channels of distribution** dictate where the product is sold at retail — that is, mass-market discounter, department stores, specialty retail, e-commerce, and so on. In many cases, particularly with A and B properties, the licensors are very specific and limiting about your product's distribution.

- **Wider channels** means as many retailers as possible. This approach is crucial to your success at retail. Getting the widest possible distribution at retail for your products is optimal.

- **Focused coverage** means certain types of retailers, like department store, big-box retail, or discounter. This approach lets the licensee focus its sales and marketing efforts on a specific retail channel of distribution (such as e-commerce or specialty retail) instead of trying to sell to all channels of distribution at once. Typically, licensees have an established focused retail channel where they're a preferred vendor, which you can read more about in Chapter 8.

>> **Guaranteed minimum royalty payment** is the guaranteed amount of money the licensee needs to pay the licensor for use of the license; we cover this item in "Understanding the guaranteed minimum royalty payment" earlier in the chapter. Do your best to negotiate the minimum royalty payment as you're negotiating your contract.

- **Higher guarantee** also means a higher risk to the licensee to sell more. You see a higher guarantee with A-level licensors.

- **Lower guarantee** means the licensee guarantees less to secure the license.

>> **Territory** refers to where you're permitted to sell your products. It may mean only in the United States or in certain international territories. Typically, unless you're a large manufacturer and have global distribution, licenses limit you to your own country for distribution.

>> **Advance payment** is the amount of the guaranteed minimum royalty payment the licensor wants you to pay when you sign the licensing contract. This amount varies based on the brand/property IP you're licensing. An A brand will demand a considerably higher advance payment than a C brand will.

>> **Auto-renewals** let your contract renew without renegotiation. This position is always an excellent one to have because it means the licensor has built a level of trust with you and the products are selling well. Auto-renewals may be restricted or unrestricted.

- **Restricted:** Licensors may allow auto-renewals in a licensing agreement, but they often come with restrictions to ensure both parties stay committed to performance benchmarks. These metrics may include performance requirements (for example, a certain amount of royalty revenue you need to have generated within the past 12 months) and/or limits on the length of the contract renewal (that is, stipulations that the contract won't renew indefinitely without needing renegotiation).

- **Unrestricted:** The licensee would prefer to have an auto-renewal opportunity without the performance requirements and limitations on extension periods.

>> **Sell-off period** refers to the amount of time you have to sell any remaining licensed products in your inventory after your licensing agreement ends. After the contract expires, you're no longer allowed to manufacture new products. However, you can sell off the remaining licensed inventory already produced — until the sell-off period ends. Licensors prefer the shorter sell-off period, which is typically 90 days. Negotiating a longer sell-off period gives licensees more time to clear out inventory, and we've seen agreements with 180 days and even more.

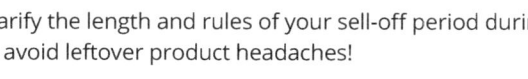

Clarify the length and rules of your sell-off period during contract negotiations to avoid leftover product headaches!

This process of negotiation is the most critical for you as a licensee to try to get as much as you can before you formalize the licensing agreement between you and the licensor. So be sure you're asking for everything you want during this period. The negotiations should move swiftly; as the licensee, you want to keep the ball moving to try to get to the next step in the process, the term sheet, which we cover in the next section.

REMEMBER

The first rule of negotiations is that everything is negotiable! Don't shy away from proposing alternatives that better suit your business. If you're unable to come to terms that suit you, then now is the time to walk away from the deal. If that happens, keep it professional and collegial. Your reputation is important, and you may be negotiating again with the same company for a different license. You can find more about letting unfavorable deals go in the later section "Knowing When to Walk away from a Bad Deal."

Creating the term sheet

After negotiating and agreeing to the basic terms from the preceding section, the licensor drafts a *term sheet* (or *deal memo*), which outlines all the agreed-upon business terms but isn't legally binding. It provides the foundation for the final agreement.

A typical term sheet includes the following:

>> Company information and key contacts

>> Term length, renewal options, and territory

>> Distribution channels (for example, mass-market stores, department stores, and so on)

>> Royalty rates (wholesale, FOB [meaning "free on board," a shipping term], and direct-to-consumer)

>> Minimum guarantees and payment schedules

>> Sales projections and marketing commitments

TIP

At this point, you don't need to bring in your IP attorney, but have them ready for when the final agreement is drafted. We cover working with an IP attorney in the earlier section "Finding and Hiring an IP Attorney."

Discussing Additional Terms

After you agree on the basic terms (which we discuss in the earlier section "Negotiating basic terms of your licensing agreement"), you still have additional details to address. These may include considerations like the following:

TIP

>> **Marketing commitments:** Licensors may require you to spend a percentage of sales on promoting the licensed product. This work may include consumer advertising or retail promotions.

 If your agreement requires marketing commitments, make sure you understand what exactly the licensor will apply toward that obligation. For example, some licensors allow trade show expenditures to count against the marketing commitment, and some don't.

>> **Cross-collateralization:** Some agreements allow you to spread minimum guarantees across multiple years, products, or territories, but many don't.

>> **Common marketing fund percentage:** Some licensors require you to pay them an additional percentage (typically 1 or 2 percent) for them to use to market the overall licensing program.

These additional terms may seem minor but can significantly impact your profitability. For example, if the licensor requires you to spend 10 percent of your sales revenue on advertising, and your profit margin before that request was going to be 20 percent, you're now down to 10 percent profit margin.

The sooner you know exactly the full terms of the deal, the better. We like the analogy of buying a car. The initial negotiation for the purchase of the car goes well until the final negotiations, where the car dealership may add in costs (such as delivery fees or detailing or prep fees) that weren't in the initial discussions. Sometimes these fees are negotiable, and sometimes they aren't. It depends on the car dealership and how badly it wants to sell the car. If the car is in high demand, you may end up having to pay additional fees if you want it.

A similar process happens when you're in final negotiation on your license. The licensor isn't trying to take advantage of you; you may simply have dealt with a salesperson who was eager to get the deal done and assumed you'd know about the additional fees.

TIP

Be sure you know all the terms of the deal before entering into the contract phase. This knowledge and upfront negotiation of all the additional terms of the deal can save you a great deal of time and money.

When you have all the basic and additional contract terms on the table, that's when you need to focus and use accounting principles to determine what you can afford to pay for the license. You have to calculate not just the royalty payment expected from the minimum guarantee you make to the licensor but also all your additional costs in the manufacturing and supply chain process to get your products to retail.

Only then do you know what you can afford to pay for the licensing deal. From attorney fees to accounting and marketing costs, be certain you're aware of all the details and ensure you've left no stones unturned in the agreement.

Knowing When to Walk away from a Bad Deal

For you to be successful in licensing, your licensed product needs to sell at a profit for both you and your retail partner. If you discover during negotiations that the royalty rate the licensor is asking for prevents you from making a profit, and the licensor refuses to negotiate, you need to walk away from the deal. It's like buying a car: If the final price is simply too high for you, visit another dealership.

TIP

Don't get stuck on just one property. Plenty of licensors are willing to collaborate on fair, mutually beneficial terms. Stay focused on finding the right fit for your business.

WARNING

Having a great license and a great product is no guarantee that the combination will sell. Consumers can be fickle and, for a number of reasons unknown ahead of time, they may not see the value in buying your licensed product. Retailers don't have a lot of patience. If products aren't selling well, they replace them quickly.

Finalizing the Long-Form Legal Agreement

After you and the licensor agree on the term sheet (see the earlier section "Creating the term sheet"), you're ready to proceed with drafting and signing the long-form legal agreement. This document codifies all terms and adds legal protections for both parties. At this stage, we strongly advise you to have an IP attorney review the agreement to ensure a fair and reasonable agreement that protects your interests. For details on IP attorneys, check out the earlier section "Finding and Hiring an IP Attorney."

IN THIS CHAPTER

» **Creating a licensor-approved product**

» **Looking for the right manufacturing fit**

» **Pondering package design**

» **Considering all the factors in pricing**

» **Revving up your PR and marketing**

» **Managing sales and royalty monitoring and licensing growth**

Chapter **7**

Getting Your First Licensed Product Up and Running

Securing your first license (which we cover in Chapter 6) doesn't mean you can rest on your laurels. You have real work — and a lot of it — to ensure that you can successfully fulfill the license requirements and get your products manufactured, placed in retail, and marketed to consumers. In other words, you need to establish your licensing business. This chapter covers what you need to know to accomplish this.

WARNING

One of the common (and devastating) mistakes new companies entering the licensing arena make is underestimating the length of time between the initial contract signing for the license to getting the actual product onto a retail shelf.

No easy formula tells you how long the entire process takes. It depends on a number of factors, including the licensor you're working with, the type of product you'll be creating, where you'll manufacture the product, and when the retailer you're working with wants delivery of the product.

TIP

Work closely with your licensor and retail partners from the start. They can help you develop a timeline. Remember, both the licensor and retailer have done this many times before. They understand the process, and both can advise you about a realistic speed to market.

Designing Your Product

The pop-culture marketplace has three broad areas of licensed consumer products:

>> **Physical consumer products:** These are actual physical products sold at retail like toys, apparel, accessories, food and beverages, cosmetics, and so on.

>> **Digital/virtual products:** This category includes virtual products and non-fungible tokens (NFTs) sold online, usually through games or websites. They can also be branded video games or digital skins for gaming characters. (You can read more about many of these products in Chapter 4.)

>> **Experiential:** Any form of product that consumers interact with is experiential. It can be a licensed theme park attraction, a restaurant or hotel, a stage show, or even a branded TV show.

The length of time necessary for designing your product completely depends on how complex the product is. It can be as swift as several weeks (if you're, say, using a logo for a print-on-demand T-shirt) or as long as 18 months (if the product is a complex video game).

WARNING

Don't try to design a product using the licensor's brand without checking in with the company at each stage of the design process. Keeping the brand in the loop not only saves you precious time, money, and resources but also can prevent any misunderstandings or misuse of the brand that may lead the licensor to not approve the product design.

Landing on how it looks

Working with a licensor means you have a framework to follow, and nowhere is this more apparent (and important) than in the product design.

The licensor typically provides you with a style guide that outlines design parameters for using the licensor's logo or brand designs. You're responsible as the licensee for creating the product designs within those parameters. If the style guide says the logo can't be smaller than a half inch, you better believe the brand will reject your design if it includes a quarter-inch logo. Following the style guide to the letter is in your best interest; ignoring it can lead to costly rejections and wasted time for everyone involved.

Hiring a designer

As the licensee, you're responsible for the cost of product design, and the designer you work with is one of your first critical decisions. Quite a few specialized design companies work with the licensing business community, which is great news for a beginning licensee because you gain from their experience. Your licensor partner can recommend designers they've successfully worked with before, making your job easier. Because the designer already has an established relationship with the licensor, the entire process is likely to run more smoothly.

If you've hired a licensing consultant (see Chapter 5), that person also has a go-to list of designers they trust. We highly recommend choosing a designer with proven licensing experience and strong references. But if you find you're truly stuck, check out the list of design resources on the Licensing International website (www.licensinginternational.org) to get you back on track.

Before you hire, interview at least three design firms. The product design process is critical to the success of your finished licensed product, and you want to be sure you're getting not only a great designer but also someone you feel comfortable working with. If none of them is right for you, interview three more. It's a buyer's market for designers, so be sure you're happy with the one you choose. When interviewing, ask the following key questions:

WARNING

>> **How much experience do you have in the licensing business?** Find out just how many licensed products they've successfully designed.

Look for a designer with experience in your product category who also has worked on a number of licensed products. They understand the process of utilizing the licensor's style guide (see the preceding section) and the need for approvals from the licensor.

Make sure you hire a designer who recognizes the need to communicate directly and regularly with the licensor's design team during the process of designing. The brand can approve along the way, saving you from having to (literally) go back to the drawing board if your design doesn't meet its standards. This back-and-forth may seem time-consuming, but it beats having to start from scratch.

>> **Can you provide references from licensors and licensees you've worked for?** You certainly don't want to work with someone who can't connect you with a few people who are willing to vouch for their work. Don't just collect those references; check them!

>> **What's your fee structure?** Due to the nature of product design, a lot of changes may be necessary. Instead of hiring a designer by the hour, structure the fee for the entire project if possible.

>> **Have you ever worked with [insert the name of your specific licensor]? If so, can you provide with an estimated timeline for how long it will take from initial designs to final approval?**

This info can be very valuable for you as the licensee. You may learn that the licensor takes forever to do approvals or that it's a breeze to work with. Either way, forewarned is forearmed.

Wait for it: Being patient about product approval

Product approval, or the final okay on your design from your licensor, may take some steps back and forth, but it's a crucial step in the process of licensing.

WARNING

Without product approval, a project falls apart. We could tell you a number of horror stories where a licensee rushed products to market without first getting product approval and ended up having their contract annulled or becoming the subject of a lawsuit. The following section explains a little more about the consequences of getting ahead of the approval process.

Why would a licensee skip formal approval? Because they're trying to take advantage of pop-culture trends, usually. A trend goes viral, and demand for consumer products for that brand or intellectual property (IP) becomes a feeding frenzy. As the official licensee, they want to take advantage of a hot trend — and, more likely, their retail partners are pressuring them to produce the product quickly to keep their customers. Not wanting to miss a major sales opportunity or let down a major retail partner, a licensee may choose not to wait for final product approval and rush the product to the market.

The potential for millions of dollars in retail sales makes bypassing final approvals very tempting, especially when the approvals process is slow. The larger the licensor, the longer getting approvals can take. Maybe a change in upper management deprioritizes licensing. Maybe a sale or takeover of the company freezes all decision making. Maybe you're just dealing with extremely cautious IP attorneys. No matter the reason, product approvals often get held up.

In our experience, the turnaround time for product approvals is typically ten business days or fewer, so build that into your plans. The larger licensors use online systems to track, process, review, and (hopefully) approve your product submissions. These online systems are efficient and effective for everyone involved because they provide the ability to track your approval through the licensors system.

Building trust as a new licensee

Feeling frustrated and pressured by a major retailer promising big sales numbers may tempt a licensee to follow the adage "It's better to ask for forgiveness than permission." It isn't. It really, really isn't.

WARNING

As a newcomer in the licensing business, you want to strictly maintain each step of the process in the preceding sections to establish your credentials as a trusted licensing partner. At the very least, breaking the rules of the licensing agreement will lead your licensors to not trust you; it also may very well land you in court, unable to sell your licensed products.

REMEMBER

When you're working on your first licenses, being perceived as a trustworthy partner who follows the rules of the business is critical. That's how you build your licensed portfolio! That element of trust is crucial to getting the next license contract, whether that's renewing your existing license or bidding for another license from the licensor.

Finding the Right Manufacturer for Your Product

If you're the manufacturer, you can skip this section. However, if you don't have the capabilities in-house for this licensed product, one of the most important aspects of your new licensing business is the manufacturing of the product. Understanding ahead of time what the costs and timeline are for getting your licensed products to market is essential. This knowledge sets expectations for both you and your licensor partner as to when products can ship to retail for sale as well as the retail pricing strategy you develop.

REMEMBER

Your success in selling licensed products depends on your advanced knowledge of costs to manufacture, ship, warehouse, and distribute at retail.

Depending on the product category you're licensing, finding a quality manufacturer or factory to produce your licensed products may be one of your greatest challenges, particularly if you're new to the manufacturing process.

TIP

The easiest and quickest solution to finding manufacturing partners is either to go directly through your retailer or to hire a licensing consultant, who can help you save time, money, and significant research to find factories to produce your products. We tell you about working with a licensing consultant in Chapter 5.

For many consumer products, manufacturing factories are based overseas. In most cases, manufacturing products outside the United States is less expensive because of lower labor costs and fewer regulations on manufacturing.

Certain countries have specialized factories where certain types of goods are manufactured. For example, most consumer electronics like smartphones have been made in China. Countries like Vietnam and the Philippines are now manufacturing toys and consumer electronics, and countries like India, Pakistan, Bangladesh, and Türkiye are producing more in the way of *softlines* like apparel, accessories, shoes, and home goods and housewares. Mexico has become a major manufacturing center for everything from automobiles to TVs and appliances to food and beverages. As a result of the trade war with China, at the time of this writing Mexico is the United States's number-one trading partner, with $800 billion a year in goods exchanged. On a positive note, there's a significant move as of this writing to bring back more manufacturing to the United States.

TIP

If you're new to manufacturing, educate yourself on the latest trade issues in manufacturing as well as import/export. We highly recommend visiting the Society of Manufacturing Engineers website at www.sme.org for deeper knowledge in these areas.

Following a licensor's guidelines

Your licensing agreement includes the licensor's manufacturing expectations for the product bearing its brand. These factors can include items like approved labor practices, guidelines for materials, and specific energy efficient practices, to name just a few. As an official licensed manufacturer of products being sold using a well-known IP's brand, you're required to follow that brand's parameters and regulations.

What happens if you don't? Just think of past product recalls due to safety issues, harmful materials, or choking hazards. The best way to avoid these issues is to work with a manufacturer that's fully compliant with all the regulations spelled out in your licensing contract. Most major licensors require factory audit documentation before they approve using a particular factory. In fact, some licensors now audit these factories themselves to ensure they adhere to all the guidelines specified in the licensing contract during production. The factories are used to these audits and have audit documents ready because the major U.S. retailers also require factories to meet various standards.

REMEMBER

When a licensor lets you use its brand on your product, it's trusting you with something valuable. It expects the products you create and sell to meet the same high-quality standards the brand is known for, and for good reason! If the product you release is faulty, your reputation isn't the only one on the line; the licensor's brand reputation takes a hit, too. Consumers are buying your product because of the brand you've licensed, so keeping quality top-notch benefits everyone.

Mass-market manufacturing for retail

Most consumer products sold at retail continue to be produced on a *mass-manufacturing* basis, meaning you find a factory that specializes in the product you're producing, and you place an order to produce a certain number of these products.

Typically, licensed products are sold at mass-market retail; you get a commitment (order) from a retailer for a fixed number of products to sell with a specified delivery date. In all cases, the retailer orders the number of products it expects to sell with the caveat that the licensee is responsible for taking back any product that doesn't sell. This arrangement puts the licensee at risk if the product doesn't sell well.

As we mention earlier in the chapter, the retailer you contract with to sell the product has approved manufacturers it recommends you work with. These are factories that the retailer has vetted to ensure that they comply with the strict guidelines and regulations the retailer has set for all products sold at its stores. For example, the factory follows fair labor practices and perhaps adheres to certain environmental and sustainability rules.

Retailers are typically conservative about how much they buy when placing the order through you for the licensed goods. Remember, though, that pop-culture trends and consumer demand can be fickle. At times, retailers sense a feeding frenzy for a pop-culture item and order a lot of products. You may be lucky, get the product to market quickly, and cash in. On the other hand, the fickle consumer may be chasing a new trend by the time the product arrives on the retail shelves.

TIP

A licensee will do their best to reduce their risk by collaborating closely with the retailer to gauge consumer demand for the products being sold. However, even with sophisticated inventory control systems and AI-generated projections of product sales, fast-changing trends and economic circumstances can have an impact on retail sales. As a result, the licensee develops relationships with alternative channels of retail distribution so it can sell the unsold licensed products at a discounted price.

Print-on-demand

One area where the United States excels in manufacturing of licensed consumer products is *print-on-demand* (POD) — a digital manufacturing process that allows manufacturers to create products as orders come in. The technology for POD has been around since the 1990s and began with book publishing, but significant advancements have made it particularly attractive for e-commerce, where consumers order products (often softlines like apparel or accessories) directly from an e-commerce site. POD design quality has increased over the past few years as the business matures.

An example of POD in softline manufacturing is a licensee creating a licensed piece of apparel by printing the logo and designs on a *blank*, or plain item. It's done on everything from T-shirts and sweatshirts to socks to smaller houseware like coffee mugs and decorative items.

POD is revolutionizing the licensing business for several reasons:

FEMEMBER

>> As the name implies, POD means you print only the number of pieces you have orders for, so you have no inventory risk or waste — a major issue for consumer products manufacturers.

>> You can easily and individually change the designs based on the customer's request, creating unique licensed merchandise.

You will need the licensor's permission to customize or change the design of the licensor's logo. Many licensors are becoming much more open to customized POD as they understand it's what consumers want.

>> It lessens licensees' dependence on overseas manufacturing and cuts down production time.

The POD business has grown at an annual rate of 25 percent every year since 2022 and is estimated to be a $43 billion business by 2030, according to a study published online by Vantage Research. By 2035, the advances being made in POD will expand into more product categories and will significantly help with inventory risk and wasted resources.

Considering shipping and duty costs

Shipping and duty costs to import your product back to wherever you intend to sell it affect your pricing and can have ripple effects for your project. You need to figure shipping and duty into your costs of production and distribution prior to deciding how much the product will sell for. Consider the following points carefully:

- » **Shipping:** What does it cost to ship product back to destination where you'll sell it? Do you need to expedite shipping by airplane, or can you ship it by boat? Do your research and figure out costs ahead of time. If you're manufacturing your products overseas, find a reputable shipper that does business in the market where you're manufacturing.

- » **Duty:** You pay customs fees for importing products. The shipping company you hire can help you with calculating the duties you need to pay. This category may be very important because politicians have changed tariffs in select categories greatly in the past.

- » **Warehouse:** Where are you storing products before shipping? Your shipper can give you recommendations for warehouses. Keep in mind that you may need several regional warehouses. Ask your retail partners about their expectations for product delivery.

- » **Domestic shipping:** How much does it cost you to ship the products from the warehouse to the retailer? If you're working with a large retailer with thousands of locations, what are its expectations for you to shipping to individual stores versus regional distribution centers?

Include the royalty cost in your cost of goods sold.

Crafting a Compelling Package that Meets Licensor Requirements

Packaging is a critical part of your marketing strategy. It highlights the brand license and your product together. It's the first impression potential buyers get of your product and needs to represent the brand, your company, and the product itself in an appealing way. The brand license you've acquired for the product is going to be a major selling point on the packaging, so be sure you take full advantage of that. Packaging is your point-of-sale advertising and needs to pop — to stand out on the shelf — so the consumer takes notice. We tell you more about how to make your products stand out in Chapter 8.

REMEMBER

Consumers typically spend about three to seven seconds looking at a product on a retail shelf before making a decision. This brief window emphasizes the importance of eye-catching packaging that quickly communicates the product's value and brand recognition.

Your product designer can double as your package designer if they have that level of experience. Most design firms that specialize in the licensing business have designers who specialize in both product and package design. Flip to the earlier section "Hiring a designer" for more on that topic.

The package design also requires the approval of the licensor. (We cover the approvals process in "Designing Your Product" earlier in the chapter.) As a licensee, you really want to ensure that your package design not only promotes the product to the consumer but also complies with all the licensor's brand requirements. There have been many cases in package design where small details are overlooked, words are misspelled, or brand/product messaging isn't aligned.

WARNING

If the package design has any flaws, the licensor may make you remove the products from retail to fix it. This step is a huge added expense, significantly delays the sale of the product, and may cause the retailer to refuse to stock the product.

WARNING

One simple misprint on packaging for a licensed product can have major repercussions for all the parties concerned and lead to tarnished brands, millions in lost revenue, and potential lawsuits. If it can happen to a giant toy company like Mattel (see the nearby sidebar "When packaging goes wrong"), it can happen to any licensee. Be extra careful that all wording and branding on packaging has been approved and is correct.

WHEN PACKAGING GOES WRONG

In November 2024, Mattel, one of the world's leading toy companies, made an error on the packaging of its much-anticipated licensed dolls for the upcoming Universal Pictures holiday release *Wicked.* As a result, Mattel was forced to recall the dolls from three of the United States's largest retailers — Amazon, Target, and Walmart.

The issue was a misprint on the packaging that listed the wrong web address for the movie and directed consumers to a pornographic website. In addition to generating bad publicity for the movie and for Mattel (the owner of Barbie), the error also negatively impacted the reputations of Amazon, Target, and Walmart and caused significant concern among parents about taking their kids to see the movie. The millions of dollars in lost holiday sales are just the beginning; the costs of negative publicity for the film, the dolls, and the retailers is incalculable. We share this example as a warning that innocent mistakes can create massive headaches!

Developing Your Pricing Strategy

You can't just slap a price on a product and expect the dollars to come pouring in. Landing on the right price — a balance of your profit and what the market will bear — comes down to a lot of careful calculation.

Here are some of the considerations to factor in when you work to determine a price for your product:

- » Design costs
- » Manufacturing costs
- » Shipping and distribution costs
- » Your wholesale product price
- » Your royalty costs (see Chapter 6)
- » Company overhead expenses including salaries and office expenses
- » Travel, entertainment, and any other business costs

Your accountant — and a good accountant is essential — can help you figure out what all your costs will be to successfully bring your product to the market and provide you with an analysis of your potential profit and loss statement. In fact, the pricing strategy may depend on input from a number of other stakeholders as well:

- » The **retailer** tells you what the price of the product should be for its consumer. To get your product placed with a particular retailer, you must conform to the price it sets. Of course, if you happen to have a highly in-demand product with an A-level license, you have some wiggle room with the retailer. (Head to Chapter 6 for more on license levels.) But in a retail marketplace place where a few big-box retailers dominate the retail landscape, you have less room to negotiate because fewer companies are competing to carry your products.

- » Your **licensor partner** specifies what retail channel you can sell your products in.

- » A **licensing consultant** may be able to help with your pricing decisions.

Getting the Word Out through Marketing and Public Relations

To capitalize on your first license, you need to create a buzz within both the licensing trade media and the trade media area where your product is focused — toys, apparel, food, or whatever your category is. You want to let the business community know about your successfully licensed product. Doing so gets your name out and encourages other licensors to think of and approach you with new licensing opportunities.

Getting visibility for your new licensed products and company helps you become known in the industry. After other companies see that you're successful, you'll have more opportunities. You can grow your business by using public relations and marketing to get the word out.

REMEMBER

You may be surprised how many companies in the licensing business overlook the importance of marketing. Because of the amount of competition among companies fighting for popular licenses, a strong marketing strategy can be the deciding factor in whether you get the license. Being visible is key in a marketplace dominated by pop culture!

Maximizing public relations efforts

Public relations (PR) refers to the ways companies develop and maintain a positive relationship with the public through communications like press releases, events, social media, and even internal communications. PR is important for your new licensing venture in communicating your unique position as a licensee in the business.

Depending on your budget, you can develop your PR strategy and program by using a PR agency that works closely with the licensing business. If you understand basic marketing principles like how to write a press release and develop editorial contacts, you can do it on your own.

Your PR strategy should tie in with your overall marketing goals, which also include trade advertising and utilizing social media as a promotional tool. Developing a strong trade marketing strategy that includes PR, advertising, and social media distinguishes your new licensing company and helps you stand out as a new, important player in the business.

TIP

If you decide to use a PR agency, find one that specializes in the trade media you're looking to promote. Here, your licensor partner or licensing consultant can provide suggestions for PR firms that specialize in trade media. Be careful to hire them on a project basis only; some firms look for six-month-to-one-year commitments, which are unnecessary for your needs. Your goal with trade PR is simply to promote your new licensed products within the business community, so you want to get as much visibility in the trade media as possible. A good trade PR firm can develop a social media strategy as well, using LinkedIn and other channels like Instagram, Facebook, and so on.

Letting the industry know your name: Trade advertising

As a new company in the licensing business, you want to spread the word as quickly as possible that you're a player in licensing. Doing so helps you

» Promote your licensed products to retailers who may not yet know your company and may be interested in carrying your products

» Promote your business to other licensors looking for new licenses

» Quickly establish your company name within the licensing community to build credibility

To quickly establish your position as a player in the business, budgeting and planning a trade marketing campaign that includes PR, advertising, and social media gets the attention of the companies you want to work with much quicker and will help drive your success in the marketplace. We recommend reading *Marketing For Dummies,* by Jeanette Maw McMurtry (Wiley), to help you develop your marketing strategy to get visibility for your new licensing company. If you're new to marketing, talk with your licensor partner about marketing support. It can give you guidance in your marketing strategy and suggest marketing consultants who can help you develop your strategy.

Advertising to consumers

Unless you're a major consumer products manufacturer, you most likely don't have a significant budget for consumer advertising. Not to worry: Your license provides you with the built-in brand equity of a famous, recognizable brand. So many companies turn to licensing for a reason: the recognition the licensed brand has with the consumer.

Your licensing contract with the licensor may stipulate its expectations for your marketing spend at the retail and trade level. This work is advertising you do with your retail partners through their in-store circulars or promotions. (See Chapter 12 for more information on this.)

Tracking Sales and Royalty Reporting

As a licensee, you want to stay on top of tracking your sales after you have your products placed at retail. Doing so is simple because most retailers provide you with either monthly or quarterly *point-of-sales figures* (also known as *sell-through numbers*). This monitoring is important for a couple of reasons:

>> **You want to know how well your product is selling.**

>> **It helps you manage inventory.** If your product is selling quickly, you may need to ship more products to the retailer or order more from the factory. If it's moving slowly, on the other hand, you want to speak with your retail partner about shelf placement or perhaps some sort of in-store promotion that can move the product more rapidly. Flip to Chapter 8 to read more about promotion.

Though watching your point-of-sale data is important, remember that you pay the royalty on wholesale sales. This figure is triggered either when you ship or when you invoice the customer.

REMEMBER

As part of your licensing contract, you're responsible for paying royalties on the sales of your licensed products. The industry standard is to pay royalties on a quarterly basis.

WARNING

Don't be late in making your quarterly royalty payments. You may face interest charges and possible late fees. The larger licensors have been very strict with enforcing interest charges for late payments.

Hiring a Licensing Manager to Address Growth

Developing your licensing business and moving through the steps to get your licensed product to market involves a lot of meticulous work. Each step of the product development and marketing process requires supervision, attention to detail, and a dedicated person to manage the details.

When you've reached the stage where you now have a license and are manufacturing multiple licensed products, you may need to hire an experienced *licensing manager.* This person oversees the day-to-day workload, focusing on all the details around developing and selling the licensed product:

>> Manage all the product approvals

>> Interact with the licensor on other contractual obligations

>> Facilitate the factory audit documentation requirements in licensing agreements (more on these audits in the earlier section "Following a licensor's guidelines")

>> Interact with the designer

>> Manage communication with the factory

>> Communicate with the retail partner on orders

>> Track retail sales and royalty payments and submit the royalty reports in a timely fashion

>> Interact with sales and marketing

>> Handle regular communications with your licensing consultant

>> Provide materials and contacts for marketing for promotions

In most cases, your licensing manager also manages the day-to-day established retail relationships and may even be part of the sales team to meet with retail customers.

TIP

You can create your very own e-commerce website to sell your products directly or go through a third-party e-commerce company like Amazon. Chapter 11 gives you the details you need to make that happen.

IN THIS CHAPTER

» **Standing out in a competitive licensing environment**

» **Laying out the differences between wholesale and retail**

» **Mapping channels of distribution**

» **Choosing the right retailer**

» **Getting into physical and e-commerce**

» **Promoting your product with retailer help**

Chapter **8**

Developing Retail

The most important part in your licensing journey is getting your licensed product successfully placed at retail. Although you have an in-demand product with an excellent brand attached, this process is more complex than you may think.

In this chapter, you find out what retailers want, which kinds of retailers will be right for your licensed product, and how to get your product placed at retail. In addition, you discover how to work with your licensing partner in developing retail relationships and how to utilize its marketing to drive sales for your products.

Understanding What Retailers Want

Retailers want three things more than anything else from your products:

>> **That your products sell:** This is paramount.

>> **That your products attract new customers to the store:** Word of mouth is powerful advertising, and consumers who see your product will ask where it comes from. This publicity attracts new customers to the retailer.

>> **That your products are profitable:** Licensed products can sell at a higher price because of the recognizable brand on the product.

Retail is a tough game! Shoppers today have more choices than ever before thanks to e-commerce. With just a quick Internet search, they can find exactly what they need in seconds. This environment makes selling products more competitive than ever and puts the power in the hands of the customer.

So how do you stand out? That's where brand licensing comes in! By teaming up with a well-known brand, your product can grab attention on the shelf (or screen) and rise above the crowd. Plus, a trusted brand may help you — and the retailer — sell at a higher price because people are willing to pay more for names they know and love.

Case in point: Do a search on Amazon for a common consumer product. In most of the consumer products categories you search, you'll find many brands you've never heard of before. They're all remarkably comparable products and close in price. Then you'll see a well-known brand you recognize and trust selling for a premium price. Consumers will pay more for that premium brand based on trust. Even though Amazon guarantees free returns, few shoppers want the hassle of having to send back a product, so they'll pay more for a brand they trust.

That's the power of brand licensing — it builds trust, reduces risk, and drives sales, making your product exactly what retailers want on their shelves.

UPGRADING PAPER WITH JUST A NAME

In 2011, NBC/Universal licensed the name Dunder Mifflin (the fictional office supply company from the hit TV show *The Office*) to Staples (the office supply retailer) for printer paper. The paper was priced at a premium compared to the other paper brands available. The result? A fictional brand turned into real-world sales, proving that a powerful name can transform an ordinary product into a standout success.

Comparing Wholesale versus Retail

As a manufacturer of licensed consumer products, your greatest challenge is to get your products onto retail shelves. If you're selling your products through a third-party retailer (physical or e-commerce), you're *wholesaling* the products to the retailer. You supply the retailer with your products at a wholesale cost. Here's a look at a typical pricing scenario

>> Your cost to manufacture the licensed product is $2.50.

>> The wholesale price you sell the product to the retailer for is $5.00.

>> The retailer sells the product to the consumer for $10.00.

In this scenario, your markup is 100 percent of the cost. However, the cost of production and your wholesale markup will vary based on the products you're manufacturing and the retailer's demands (what its willing to pay). You can't mark all products up by 100 percent.

If you're new to manufacturing and selling products at retail, we highly recommend reading the latest edition of *Supply Chain Management For Dummies,* by Daniel Stanton (Wiley), which goes into much greater detail on the complex logistics necessary to produce products and get them sold at retail. In this chapter, we keep it simple for you.

REMEMBER

As you learn more about the process of supply chain, you'll discover many additional costs involved in the process, including shipping, storage, spoilage, returns, and unsold merchandise. Understanding the complexities involved in the supply chain is critical to your success in selling licensed products.

REMEMBER

As we show you in Chapter 6, the royalty you pay the licensor is based on the wholesale price the retailer is paying you.

Following the Channels of Retail Distribution

Chapter 6 shows you how the licensing contract specifically outlines which retail channel(s) you can sell your licensed products to. Simply put, a *retail channel* is where a consumer can purchase a product. Here are some examples:

>> **Upscale department stores:** Bloomingdale's, Neiman Marcus, Nordstrom

>> **Department stores:** Macy's, Dillard's

- **Mid-tier department stores:** J.C. Penney, Kohl's
- **Specialty stores:** REI, Barnes & Noble, GAP, DICK'S Sporting Goods
- **Mass merchants:** Target, Walmart
- **Do-it-yourself:** Ace Hardware, Lowe's, Home Depot
- **Pharmacy:** CVS, Rite-Aid, Walgreens
- **Grocery:** Kroger, Publix, Stop & Shop
- **Wholesale clubs:** BJ's, Sam's Club, Costco
- **Dollar store:** Dollar General, Family Dollar
- **E-commerce:** Amazon, Fanatics, eBay
- **Social media sites:** TikTok, Facebook, Instagram, Twitch
- **Other:** Amusement parks, home shopping, mail-order catalogs, restaurants

TIP

As a licensee, you likely want to use multiple retail channels based on what your licensor's contract permits.

Retail channels are ever-changing. Although brick-and-mortar retail has experienced downsizing thanks to the growth of e-commerce and social commerce, physical retail's death has been greatly exaggerated (to paraphrase Mark Twain).

The COVID-19 pandemic caused consumers to shelter in place. As a result, the post-pandemic landscape has created new brick-and-mortar retail opportunities in the form of *experiential retail*, where physical retail stores such as Restoration Hardware, Sephora, or even Apple create enjoyable experiences to drive consumer traffic. The convenience of shopping online no doubt has made life easier for consumers, but the pandemic's effects on consumers have created a boom in nostalgia, including a return to the top-tier shopping malls that Gen X and millennials grew up with. The shopping malls experiencing this renaissance are working to add as many forms of immersive, engaging experiential retail as possible.

Finding the Best Retailer for Your Product

A major part of your success in licensing is finding the right retailer(s) for your licensed products, which can be intimidating for beginners.

One of the major details in the licensing contract you sign with the licensor (see Chapter 6) specifies where you can distribute your products at retail. Locating retailers within the parameters of your contract is up to you.

Most new licensees are already product manufacturers and add licensing to help sell more of their products. If this describes you, then you likely already have a retail distribution strategy in place for your product(s). In this case, reach out to your current retail partner to share the idea of adding a license to your current product. In most cases, retailers love carrying well-known brands that consumers trust, and they understand that their customers may be willing to pay a premium for these products. They also know that branded products typically have a higher sell-through than other products, which results in higher sales for the retailers.

Researching potential retail partners

How do you find the right retailer who fits the criteria spelled out in your contract and will do well selling your specific product? In the licensing business, *store checks* refers to going into retail stores to research the merchandise and brands they sell.

Given how consolidated the retail business is and how few major brick-and-mortar retailers still exist, your job is easier than it used to be. Of course, how you go about store checks also depends on what your channel of distribution is. If it's department stores only, then that's where you start your research. If your channel of distribution is wider, then widen your search to include all the major retailers in that channel.

Breaking down who's who at the large retailers

As a licensee selling your products at retail, understanding the organization chart at different retail chains is incredibly helpful when you work toward developing a supplier relationship with them. Here's a typical org chart for a major retail chain:

1. **Chief Merchandising Officer (CMO) or Head of Buying**

   Role: Overall strategy, setting category goals, and aligning buying with the company's objectives

   Responsibilities: Approves all major buying decisions, oversees category budgets, and ensures alignment with market trends and company strategy

2. **Divisional Merchandise Manager (DMM)**

   Role: Oversees a division of related product categories (for example, toys, home goods, or electronics)

   Responsibilities: Manages category-level budgets, monitors product sales and provides strategic guidance to category buyers; reports directly to the CMO

3. **Category Manager**

   Role: Manages the purchasing decisions for a specific category (for example, toys, footwear, or beauty)

   Responsibilities: Selects products, negotiates with vendors and monitors sales and inventory for their category; reports to the DMM

4. **Buyer**

   Role: Manages the purchasing decisions for a specific product (for example, toy action figures, toy collectibles, kids' pajamas)

   Responsibilities: Selects products; assists in data analysis, order processing, vendor communications and promotional planning; provides the category manager with insights and recommendations based on trends

5. **Merchandise Planner**

   Role: Works closely with buyers to determine product quantities and distribution strategies across store locations

   Responsibilities: Uses data to predict demand, allocate inventory, and optimize stock levels to reduce overstock

Major licensors like Disney, Warner Bros., and Universal meet with the CMO, DMM, and even category managers to share upcoming information on new movie properties so that retailers can plan for these programs appropriately. With the rise of streaming, Netflix has taken lessons from these major studios' playbooks and is now meeting with these retailers as well.

Understanding the three-star process

Some of the largest retailers — like Walmart and Target — have fully embraced licensed brands and developed internal processes and committees to decide which ones they'll support (and how). Because retailers are constantly approached by licensors and licensing agents, they need a clear process to evaluate each opportunity. That's where the *three-star process* comes in.

Many major retailers use an internal committee to review and rate licensed properties. Each property is awarded zero, one, two, or three stars. A three-star property represents the retailer's strongest level of support. Think *Star Wars*—a brand that has broad consumer appeal and sells across multiple categories. If you land a licensing deal with a three-star property, retailers are much more likely to buy in (literally).

How the three-star process works

Retailers assign stars based on several key factors that help them evaluate the potential of a licensed property. These factors include the appeal of the property, such as the popularity of the brand, the breadth of its audience (for example, does it appeal to both kids and adults?), and the property's past performance in licensed product sales. Retailers also consider current market trends and their working relationship with the licensor—established licensors like Disney often have an advantage over newer or lesser-known properties in this process.

Once the retailer completes their evaluation and assigns a star rating, they open up opportunities not only for the licensor but, more importantly, for the licensees. A higher star rating often translates into greater shelf space, larger inventory commitments, and increased promotional support, all of which can significantly impact a product's success at retail. Table 8-1 breaks some of these opportunities down for you.

TABLE 8-1   ## The Three-Star Process

	1 Star	2 Stars	3 Stars
Buying Categories	1 to 2 categories (a few), such as Toys and Teen Apparel (T-shirts)	3 to 5 categories (a handful), such as Toys, Teen Apparel, Infant & Toddler Apparel, Stationery, Home Décor	5 to 10 categories (many), including Snacks, Toys, Apparel, Accessories, Food & Beverage, Footwear, Pet Products, Consumer Electronics
Shelf Placement and Endcaps	Good shelf placement	Better shelf placement	Prime shelf placement and high-visibility endcaps
Inventory Commitment	Inventory purchased for select stores	Inventory purchased for all stores	Significant inventory commitment across all stores
Promotional Support (Paid by Licensor)	None required	Limited support, focused on select categories	Broad promotional support across many categories

Why the three-star process matters

A three-star property gets the most retailer support — prime shelf space, broader promotional backing, and bigger inventory buys. It signals that the retailer believes in the brand's sales potential across many product categories.

A one- or two-star property may still get attention, but it's likely to be more limited in scope, both in product categories and store locations.

TIP

Ideally, you want to license a property that your prospective retailer has designated as a three-star brand. These brands are far more likely to gain strong retail support. The tricky part? Retailers usually don't publicize this information. You'll need to do your homework and ask the right questions. Licensors, however, are often happy to share their star status — especially if it helps close the deal!

REMEMBER

Retailers award three stars because they believe in the brand's ability to *sell*. A three-star property typically has high customer demand across multiple categories, making it a lower-risk, high-reward opportunity for everyone involved.

Getting your products placed at retail

Major retailers have buyer teams that buy by category. For example, if your license is for a health and beauty product, the retailer has a specific buyer group for that category. The same goes for toys, hardware, consumer electronics, housewares, food and beverage, and so on.

Most major retailers follow the same process for determining which products they'll buy. Here are the steps you need to go through to get your licensed products placed at a major brick-and-mortar retailer.

1. **Complete the retailer's application to become a supplier.**

2. **Request a meeting or inclusion in the retailer's product line review.**

REMEMBER

   Retailers schedule one week a year to meet with all the manufacturers of a certain category. Being included in that meeting is important if you plan to sell to that retailer.

3. **Negotiate the wholesale price of products to the retailer.**

   This step is critical. If you can't meet the retailer's expectation of price, you won't make a deal.

4. **Commit to a minimum production run.**

   The retailer tells you how many of the product it wants to order. Keep in mind that if the product sells well, the retailer will want to order more, quickly, so you need to be prepared.

5. **Provide the retailer with financial information on your company.**

   The retailer is going to conduct due diligence on your company, including checking your financial stability. It may ask for a letter from your bank to be sure that you're financially able to meet your contractual goals.

6. **Be ready to comply with the retailer requirements.**

   These may include the following:

   - **Factory audits:** As we note in Chapter 7, retailers (or a third-party service they hire) will be interested in manufacturer factory audits. They want to be sure that your facility is in compliance with all of their corporate mandates and values. This includes following child labor laws, which is standard with all U.S. retailers.

   - **Proof of product liability insurance:** If your products are faulty for any reason, the retailer expects you to be responsible to the consumer. Any type of product recall is your financial and legal responsibility as the manufacturer. Because lawsuits can be expensive, retailers require you to have insurance to cover the potential costs involved.

   - **Process for customer complaints:** The retailer expects you to handle any customer complaints about products. Typically, this process requires you to have a toll-free number as well as an active website to manage complaints.

   - **Sustainability requirements:** Most major retailers have been enacting more stringent requirements on the materials you use in your products.

   - **Upfront payment for stocking shelf fees:** Many retailers expect their product suppliers to pay a fee for shelves being stocked. This cost is most common with grocery retailers.

   - **Markdown funds:** If your product isn't selling, the retailer may require you to provide *markdown funds* so it can lower the price while maintaining its margin. Retailers account for these funds on your invoice.

   - **Clearance allowance:** The *clearance allowance* is basically the more extreme version of markdown funds; it allows for deeper discounts as the product is being discontinued and cleared out entirely from the retailer.

   - **Guaranteed sale:** *Guaranteed sale* (or *return privilege*) is when a retailer has the right to return unsold products to the manufacturer. In certain industries, such as publishing, the manufacturer provides a return allowance to the retailers.

   - **Consignment:** The retailer pays for the products only after they're sold, and unsold items can be returned.

Becoming a preferred vendor

After you get placement for your initial licensed products at retail and consumers begin buying the products, you're on the road to becoming what's known as a *preferred vendor*. That means the retailer has fully vetted you based on the quality of your products, pricing, reliability, and delivery times.

Becoming a preferred vendor can take from several months to years. In addition to the parameters of quality, price, reliability, and product sell-through, it also requires you to develop close ties with your buyer. You accomplish this relationship through regular communication with the buyer and their team. Remember, you want your buyer to look good, and the best way to do that is to deliver a successful product.

FEMEMBER

Having a preferred vendor status at a major retailer is a true badge of honor in the licensing business. When you earn that status, the retailer will recommend you to other licensors seeking licensees. That's how licensees build their licensing businesses — through preferred vendor status and word of mouth. It also opens your business up to new retailers. Retailers will seek you out after they see your success with a major retailer.

Evaluating Brick-and-Mortar and E-Commerce Options

The term *brick-and-mortar* simply means a physical retail store rather than an *e-commerce*, or online, retailer. If you're new to both licensing and product manufacturing and getting your products placed at retail seems like a hassle, you may think you're better off avoiding the physical retailer and selling online only. We don't recommend this approach.

Online retail does present some attractive qualities:

>> Creating an online storefront is inexpensive.

>> You can sell your products directly to the consumer without an intermediary.

>> You can charge full retail price for your products — and capture a higher margin for your company

>> E-commerce makes shopping easier for consumers.

But e-commerce has some daunting downsides:

>> You need an advertising and marketing budget to gain visibility for your storefront through social media, online search engines, influencers, and so on.

>> Your inventory risk is much higher. You simply don't know how many products you'll sell.

>> You must manage the financial transactions, shipping, and returns.

>> Technical issues like website glitches or hacking may negatively impact business.

>> Shipping may be expensive. As a result of Amazon's shipping policies, many consumers expect free shipping. Therefore, to match Amazon, your shipping costs may significantly eat into your profit margins.

Going for the Goldilocks solution: Hybrid retail

TIP

Hybrid retail (where you sell both in brick-and-mortar retail and through an online retail channel) works best. If you've invested the time, effort, and money to acquire a license to sell more of your products, you want the widest possible distribution strategy, which means getting your product into as many retail channels as possible. You should ensure you have these rights in your licensing contract.

Typically, if you're selling to a major retailer like Walmart or Macy's, it's going to be offering your product for sale both at physical retail and through its e-commerce operations. These days, most physical retailers have an e-commerce business as well. The exceptions to this rule are the off-price retailers like Burlington (formerly Burlington Coat Factory) and Ross Dress for Less as well as discount grocery stores like Aldi and Lidl. These retailers remain focused on brick-and-mortar and avoid e-commerce solutions.

REMEMBER

We caution you earlier against selling *only* online, but know that e-commerce is such an important retail strategy for you in today's digital marketplace. Every year more consumers are choosing to buy online, so that channel needs to be part of your retail distribution strategy. Understanding the intricacies of selling online is critical to your success.

So much information is necessary for succeeding in e-commerce that you really need to do some research before jumping in. For example,

>> **Does your retail distribution allow you to sell through e-commerce?** As we note earlier, many brick-and-mortar retail channels also exist in e-commerce.

>> **Should you create your e-commerce storefront with a platform such as Shopify?** Shopify is one of the leading e-commerce platforms; it helps sellers set up online stores as well as manage payments and shipping. If you're considering launching your own e-commerce platform to sell your licensed products, Shopify is a smart option to consider.

>> **Should you launch your own sales website?** Many licensees that produce multiple products have their own e-commerce websites. This question will be part of your discussion when developing your licensing contract (see Chapter 6). Selling directly has pros and cons that you need to evaluate with your licensor and retail partners.

>> **Can you sell through social media channels like TikTok, Facebook, Instagram, Twitch, or Snapchat?** *Social commerce* is the fastest growing area of e-commerce. It can be very successful if you're selling a product geared for the Gen Z demographic, which heavily shops through social commerce.

Addressing Amazon's 1P and 3P selling options

TIP

Amazon is the largest online marketplace, and we strongly recommend you sell your licensed products through this important channel. If you're not familiar with selling on Amazon, check out the book *Selling on Amazon For Dummies*, by Deniz Olmez and Joseph Kraynak (Wiley).

As a manufacturer, you have two ways of selling your products on Amazon: first party (1P) or third party (3P). If you want to be a *first-party seller*, you treat Amazon like every other retailer (approach its buyers and sell them the goods). As a *third-party seller*, you control all aspects of the sale and use Amazon as the online platform only. Table 8-2 shows you the differences.

TABLE 8-2

Noting Differences between Seller Types

	First-Party Seller (1P)	Third-Party Seller (3P)
Relationship to Amazon	Supplier to Amazon	Direct seller using Amazon's platform
Inventory ownership	Amazon owns the inventory	You own the inventory
Pricing control	Amazon sets and controls pricing	You set and control pricing
Fulfillment and shipping	Handled entirely by Amazon	You choose between FBA (fulfilled by Amazon) or FBM (fulfilled by merchant [you])
Appears as	"Sold by Amazon"	"Sold by [your company]"
Fees	No fees; you simply sell the product to Amazon at wholesale price	You incur certain fees related to listing on Amazon (and fulfillment by Amazon, if you use it); see Amazon for more info

Both 1P and 3P have their advantages and risks.

» Manufacturers typically choose to be a 1P seller if they want simplicity. The trade-off is that you may earn lower profit margins, but a potential upside is that Amazon can provide marketing to drive significant sales of these 1P products.

» Manufacturers typically choose 3P if they want to have control over pricing, customer relationships, and inventory. Many smaller companies choose 3P to have this control and flexibility.

Developing Marketing Promotions for Consumers

One of the many benefits of brands that do licensing is that most of them understand the power of marketing promotions at retail. A *marketing promotion* is when a retailer comes together with the product manufacturer to create some sort of exclusive offer for the consumer that drives more consumers to the store.

Ever notice how stores explode with themed products when a big movie is about to hit theaters? That's no accident; it's *event-based marketing,* and it's a go-to strategy for Hollywood studios. Here's how it works: When a highly anticipated movie is building buzz, the studio (licensor) teams up with select retailers to create promotional programs that not only help promote the movie but also drive massive sales of licensed merchandise.

Hollywood franchises are some of the most valuable licenses out there because these campaigns move a ton of products off shelves. But it's not just movies; many other brands have caught on and now use similar strategies to boost sales around their own events, such as the 100th anniversary of a product.

The bottom line is that retail promotions equal more buzz, more sales, and more success for everyone involved!

Utilizing your partner's existing marketing tools

Although marketing promotions at retail are huge sales drivers, they aren't everyday events. So how can you as a licensee take advantage of your licensor's brand power at retail to sell more? Through regular communication with your licensor partner, you can discover where it's spending its marketing dollars and find ways to leverage its marketing campaigns.

Speaking with your contacts at the licensor is a great tool in selling more of your products. For example, most major licensors organize licensing summits once or twice a year to update and educate their licensing partners on marketing initiatives and retail developments in the works. At these gatherings, finding other licensees with complementary products is a terrific way to collaborate and help you further develop your retail relationships.

A group of licensees working together with a retailer helps drive greater sales for all of them. This area is where your licensor's retail development manager can play a pivotal role by bringing the licensees together as a unified group to promote the brand at retail.

WARNING

Your licensor partner must approve any use of the licensed property in a marketing program. This includes print ads, sweepstakes ads, social media posts, and so on. Always be sure your licensor partner has approved these elements in writing ahead of time.

Knowing when to bring in an outside agency

Collaborating with other licensees who are selling in the same retailer can pay off (strength in numbers, after all), but sometimes an opportunity arises for you to do your own product promotion at retail. This situation typically happens when your licensed product is in high demand.

For example, say you're a candy product with a license for a spooky character, and Halloween is approaching. You know that naturally you'll sell more candy on the lead-up to the holiday, but creating an in-store promotion will sell even more. This moment is a huge opportunity for your product sales. If you're new to capitalizing on these chances, working with a specialized retail promotions agency that can assist you in creating and executing the promotion may be helpful. Your retail partner can recommend good agencies it has worked with in the past.

Working with your licensor partner

Licensors today are very sophisticated and understand that the only way to succeed in licensing is for every stakeholder (licensor, licensee, and retailer) to be closely aligned. Your licensor partner's retail development person is the best person to help you with retail placement, promotions, and increasing your product sales. Their job is to see that you succeed, so keep them close and communicate often.

REMEMBER

You may be one of hundreds of different companies with the same license, and a brand's retail development person may not have the bandwidth to communicate with you regularly. You need to find ways to stay up to date with all the licensor is doing at retail. Check in regularly with the licensor to see what tools it may have to assist you at retail. Licensees who take initiative and communicate will simply be more successful. Licensing is all about strength through partnerships.

DEEPENING TIES WITH OTHER BRANDS

Your success in selling your product at retail will attract both other retailers who want to carry your product and other brands that also do licensing. In our experience, new licensees who do well at retail with product sales are solicited by many other major licensors to take on their brands. In fact, most successful licensees carry a portfolio of licensed brands for their products. Success breeds success.

All your hard work and effort to secure your license, develop your retail distribution, manufacture your products, and manage the process of royalty reporting will pay off big time. As you grow your licensed portfolio of brands and your retail distribution, your entry into licensing with one brand licensor will establish you as a trusted licensee sought after by many licensors.

3

Forging and Maintaining Strong Licensing Partnerships

Develop a solid relationship with your licensor.

Maintain the licensee/licensor relationship by fulfilling your role in the license agreement.

Chapter **9**

The Key Points in a Successful Partnership

The practice of brand licensing is based on a strong partnership. When a company that has a good product partners with a company that has a strong brand, that partnership potentially leads to great success. In this chapter, you find out how to build and maintain strong partnerships that help build and maintain your licensing business. You also discover the undeniable influence of solid communications on successful brand licensing partnerships.

THINKING OF LICENSING AS A MARRIAGE

Licensing works a lot like a marriage. When two individuals enter a long-term relationship, both (ideally) bring unique strengths to the partnership. The same dynamic applies in the world of licensing.

A brand partners with a licensee because the licensee offers a valuable strength to the brand, such as expertise in product development, manufacturing, or distribution. In turn, the brand provides value to the licensee, like market recognition, trust, and audience appeal.

(continued)

(continued)

Mutual respect is just as important in a licensing agreement as it is in a healthy marriage. Both partners must continue to acknowledge and appreciate each other's contributions for the relationship to thrive.

However, like a marriage, problems can arise when one or both parties lose sight of that original mutual respect. If either partner begins to take the other's contributions for granted, tensions can surface, putting strain on the relationship. The key to long-term success in both cases is to maintain clear communication, mutual respect, and a shared commitment to the partnership's original goals.

Building Strong Partnership Teams

The *brand licensing ecosystem* (the people, functions, and agreements that make up the brand licensing environment) requires a host of specialized individuals — sales professionals, creative talent, accounting personnel, retail development experts, and marketing people — in order to successfully drive your licensed products sales to consumers. On the licensor's team, these roles support the licensee and the retailers. But as a licensee, you also need to staff these positions with the goal of growing your licensed business.

This list outlines key staff areas (and their associated responsibilities) that help you build a strong licensing partnership team:

» **Sales professionals:** This person sells your licensed products into the retail channels specified in your contract. The sales director at your company needs to develop close relationships with your retail partners and communicate directly with them regularly to ensure that the partners deliver on all the commitments outlined in your retail contract.

» **Creative talent:** Your creative director oversees your product design and packaging that represents not only your company but also your licensing partner(s). Your creative staff must work closely with these partners to ensure your products appropriately represent both your own brand specifications (as a licensee) and the licensor's style guides.

» **Accounting personnel:** An important component of licensing is tracking and paying royalties to your licensor partner on a regular basis. This segment of the process requires regular audits that your accountant (probably) oversees. *Remember:* Licensors typically expect royalty payments on a quarterly basis, and sticking to the schedule defined in your agreement is critical for keeping your licensing partner happy and for avoiding any late fees or interest charges.

>> **Retail development experts:** In addition to your sales team members (who sell into retail markets), you may need an expert at your company who specifically develops new retail relationships in order to grow your business. For example, a retail development manager can help locate new retailers (through market research) that are appropriate for offering your products.

>> **Marketing people:** Your marketing director is key to developing retail promotions, collateral sales materials (such as retail sell sheets), public relations (PR) distributions (such as new-product press releases), advertising, and strategies for postings on social media. Marketing experts can also explore new avenues to promote your products, for example through TikTok shops, Instagram, and so on.

>> **Supply chain staff:** In particular, the supply chain manager ensures that your company fabricates your products according to contractual obligations, on time, and on budget. They also control the integral role of shipping and delivery to retail.

REMEMBER

Building a strong team of professionals who successfully execute the responsibilities and contractual obligations of the licensing agreement strengthens your position as a licensee and enables your licensing business to grow.

Developing and Maintaining Relationships with Licensors

Licensing is all about partnership, and as a licensee, your success with licensing situations requires the development and maintenance of strong relationships with your licensor partners. If you look at the licensing arrangement like *an equilateral triangle* (a triangle whose three sides have the same length), you have three partners that represent the equal sides, as depicted in Figure 9-1:

>> **Licensor:** The brand or property that licenses its intellectual property (IP) in an agreement with the licensee

>> **Licensee:** The manufacturer or company (in this case, you) that uses the licensed IP from the licensor for branding a product or service

>> **Retailer:** The outlet that sells the licensed product

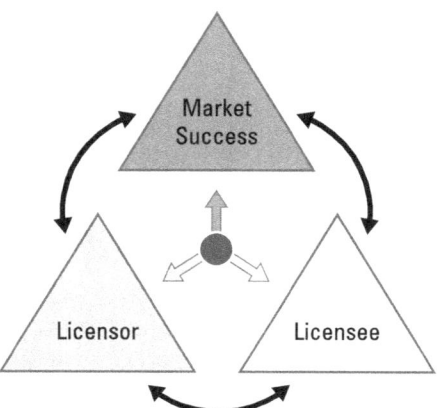

FIGURE 9-1:
The licensing
relationship
triangle.

Staying connected with your licensor

Building a strong communication pipeline with your licensor is essential for a successful licensing partnership. Effective communication ensures both parties stay informed and aligned and can respond quickly to market changes. Here's how you can keep the communication flowing effectively:

TIP

>> **Attend licensing summits.** Many licensors hold annual or semiannual summits where they share brand updates and marketing plans and encourage networking among licensees. These events provide critical insights into the licensor's properties and future plans while offering a prime opportunity to network with their executives.

Use these summits to meet other licensees who may become partners for joint promotions or retail collaborations. Often, licensees discover creative ways to collaborate and approach retailers as a united team.

>> **Schedule quarterly licensing check-ins.** Plan quarterly calls between your licensing leader and the licensor's account executive. These check-ins help clarify royalty reports and address any questions or concerns, ensuring alignment on financial performance.

>> **Set up licensor retail development calls.** Coordinate semiannual calls with the licensor's retail development team to discuss upcoming retail promotions and strategize about how to align efforts for maximizing sales performance.

>> **Offer financial reporting calls.** Submit royalty reports on time and in the required formats and upload into the licensor's systems if required. Proactively offer to explain the reports and answer any questions to maintain transparency and trust.

The old adage that knowledge is power holds true in licensing. Staying connected provides valuable insights, such as the following:

>> **Brand news:** Be the first to know about major developments, like a beverage brand launching a new flavor or a superhero brand announcing a new movie.

>> **Marketing plans:** Access advertising strategies and influencer campaigns early, allowing you to align your product launches for maximum impact.

>> **New licensees:** Understand which other products share the brand space on retail shelves. More licensees often indicate brand strength, which you can leverage for collaborative retail strategies (as we discuss in Chapter 8).

Troubleshooting product development obstacles

Developing close relationships with your licensor partners helps you address issues that may come up along the path as you develop your licensed product before actually getting it to market.

Here are just a sample of issues that you may encounter:

>> **Delayed product approval:** For example, suppose you've submitted your product design to the licensor for approval, but you're concerned it may not respond within the required ten-day window, putting you under a tight timeline. By keeping open lines of communication, you can politely follow up and keep the approval process moving, helping avoid unnecessary delays.

>> **Alterations needed for packaging approvals:** The licensor marks each submission as "Approved," "Not Approved," or "Approved with Changes." With a solid working relationship, you may be able to secure an "Approved with Changes" rather than an outright rejection, keeping your project on track.

>> **Shipping or supply chain delays:** Your product may get stuck in customs at a warehouse. For example, licensed products have sometimes been held up at the U.S. trademark infringement customs department. In such cases, the licensor may be able to provide a letter to expedite the release of your goods.

>> **Retail snafus or cancellations:** As of this writing, the retail landscape is marked by downsizing and bankruptcies, making stability and support at retail crucial for your success in selling licensed products. Developing close relationships with your licensor's retail partner fosters regular communication, ensuring you know exactly where you and your products stand with the

retailer. Occasionally, unforeseen circumstances may lead retailers to cancel an order before delivery. As the saying goes, "Forewarned is forearmed." Staying proactive with your licensor can help mitigate these challenges.

Having the ability to pick up the phone and get a friendly voice at the other end — one that's willing to assist you when problems arise — is worth its weight in gold.

Your close relationship with your licensor pays dividends when the time comes to renew your license. Keep in mind that your licensing agreement has term limitations; if your licensed product is selling well, your competitors will try to negotiate the license away from you for their similar products. This situation happens frequently in the licensing process; many times, competitors try to outbid you to get the licensed spot. But here's where relationships really matter. Most licensors appreciate a profitable, stable, long-term partnership and will do all they can to protect such a partnership.

REMEMBER

Your licensor partner wants you to be successful because if your product — with its brand — sells well, the company looks great. By developing a close relationship, you're helping both you and the licensor.

Embracing ongoing communications

As your relationship with your licensor partner deepens, you discover new opportunities that can help you grow your licensing business. In most cases, licensors represent multiple-brand IP, so your initial success with the brand may be a doorway to additional license agreements. And if you couple brand success with a close working relationship with the licensor (which you achieve by staying in close touch through various communications methods), you can likely expect them to offer you the opportunity to take on licenses for other brand IPs they own. This is how many small licensees have grown into much larger ones: by producing great licensed products while building close alliances with the licensors.

Respecting the partnership

You may face hurdles in the licensing business that can potentially have a negative impact on your relationship with your licensors. Whether you're dealing with a supply chain issue (in which you're unable to meet product demand) or cash flow issues (causing you to delay your royalty payment to the licensor), regular communication and respect for your partner's needs are your keys to getting through to the other side. All businesses go through rough patches, but as long as you're open and honest with your partner about what's happening, in most cases you'll find your partner to be understanding.

PREVENTING COMMUNICATION BREAKDOWN

The best way to prevent a breakdown in communication is by building a strong licensing team within your organization that communicates regularly with the licensors. On the surface, communicating regularly with your licensors partner may no longer seem necessary after the licensing deal is done, approvals have taken place, and product is shipped to retail. (We cover the product development process in Chapter 7).

This couldn't be further from the truth. In Chapter 8, we discuss the importance of working with your licensors to solidify your retail distribution as well as the promotional opportunities at retail that it's organizing. Staying in regular communication with your licensor partner means you're always in the loop on any special promotional it may be planning at retail.

Chapter **10**

Keeping Your End of the Deal

I n Chapter 9, we emphasize the importance of building an effective partnership with your licensor and retail partners. Licensing deals are successful when all the participants involved work together to ensure the licensing processes go smoothly. However, at times, you may experience process hiccups that make the execution *not* go so smoothly for one reason or another.

Partnerships are the essence of brand licensing, but you must realize that you aren't always in control of what your partner does. In this chapter, we focus solely on what you need to do to keep up your end of the deal with your licensor through good administrative practices such as reporting, paying royalties on time, and allowing audits of the accounting figures.

Reporting and Paying Royalties

As you begin your licensing journey, nothing is more important than building a great rapport with your licensor partner. Being a great partner means following the contractual agreements — and royalty reporting and payments are key to doing so.

Your agreements as a licensee involve responsibilities to your licensor partner. A major responsibility is to report and pay your royalties on time. As we explain in Chapter 6, *royalties* are the percentage of the wholesale product value that you agree to pay the licensor for the privilege of using the licensor's brand.

For example, you may have a brand license arrangement in which you've agreed to pay a 10 percent royalty to the licensor on the wholesale value of the products being sold. If you wholesale a product to a retailer for $2 million, you owe the licensor $200,000 in royalties.

Typically, in a licensing contract (like the one outlined in Chapter 6), you agree to a *minimum royalty payment guarantee,* meaning you're going to pay a designated percentage of your estimated royalty payment regardless of whether your sales actually hit that threshold. You pay the licensor the *advance payment,* a certain portion of the minimum royalty payment guarantee, ahead of time — after the contract is signed but before the product is produced.

If you make an advance payment or other payments toward the minimum royalty payment guarantee, you subtract that amount from the total earned royalty you potentially owe. For this example, assume the advance payment is $20,000.

The simplest formula for figuring the royalty you owe looks something like this:

(Value of wholesaled product $\times$ Royalty percentage) – Payments toward your minimum royalty payment guarantee = Royalty you owe

($2,000,000 $\times$ 0.10) – $20,000 = $180,000

REMEMBER

Your royalty payments are tied to your *net sales* (gross sales minus allowed deductions), which your contract will define as either the time of shipment or the time of invoicing. Therefore, you may have an order for $2 million of product from a retailer, but you have no assurance that the retailer will sell all the product it orders and not try to return the leftovers. In this scenario, you must pay the royalty on the full amount shipped and then explore refunds if your actual sales are returned.

The retailer sells your licensed product and pays you at an agreed-upon time — maybe 30 days or 90 days after invoice, for example.

Sending your reports as agreed

As the products are sold and you receive your payments from the retailer, your licensor expects you to send it a royalty report that covers these sales. It wants to know how many units were sold and how much royalty it can expect to receive.

Each licensor has a procedure for when it expects reports, but the industry standard is quarterly.

When you sign a licensing contract for your product, it likely states that you'll pay royalties to the licensor based on your product's net wholesale sales. (See Chapter 6 for more details on typical contract terms.) To calculate these royalties, you'll ideally receive regular sales data from your company so you can prepare the royalty report and pay the royalties you owe your licensor.

Some major licensors have this reporting process fully automated through a royalty tracking system, which involves

>> **The licensor,** who expects you (as a licensee) to use its software tracking system to report on your sales and the royalties owed.

>> **Someone on your licensee team,** who inputs sales data into the tracking system regularly in order to keep up with what royalties you owe.

One of the greatest issues licensors have with licensees happens when the licensees fall behind in reporting royalties. How does this happen? In most cases, it's because of overly busy schedules and lack of attention to detail.

If lagging royalty reporting goes on for too long (say more than six months) your reputation as a licensee risks serious damage. This situation can potentially lead to a licensor demanding an audit of your sales. As a licensee, you want to respect your relationship with the licensor (see Chapter 9 for more on this aspect of partnership) and never place it in jeopardy through late reporting of royalties. The licensor has brought you on board as a partner and trusted you with its brand.

WARNING

These days, many big licensors are charging late fees if you turn in your royalty report late. It's their way of encouraging everyone to stay on track and keep things running smoothly.

Paying your royalties on time and in full

Paying your royalties according to the timeline in your contract is just as important as maintaining your agreed-upon royalty reporting timeline (see the preceding section). You can read more about contract timelines in Chapter 6.

Note: All businesses have a major issue in common — dealing with cash flow — and it can really be disruptive in a licensing business. Remember that the licensor will charge interest on any late payments, even those that are just a few days late. If you don't pay this interest, it can compound and grow into a much larger amount that will appear when you're looking to renew your license.

Here are some ways in which misusing cash flow can potentially affect your licensing business:

>> **If you're growing your licensee business by acquiring new licenses and manufacturing more licensed products, much of your cash flow goes to new product and business development.**

REMEMBER

Many licensees justify paying their royalties late because they're using their cash to chase new licensing. Consistently following this practice is a major mistake that can lead to losing the license(s) that you already have because your royalty payments are late.

>> **If you get into a hole and owe six months of royalty payments (because you used the cash for something else), you may not have the cash flow you need to pay royalties when the licensor demands it.**

>> **If you don't use your cash flow to pay your royalties in a timely manner, the licensor can cancel your use of the brand license.** Your contract *will have* a stipulation that the licensor can cancel if you aren't paying royalties on time. Although cancellation may seem like a rare occurrence, slow and late royalty payments are one of the major complaints that licensors have about licensees. Check out the following section for more about licensor complaints against licensees.

WARNING

Don't get behind in paying royalties. Doing so is the fastest way to lose a lucrative license to your competitor.

Identifying licensors' common complaints

Knowing the common issues that cause licensors headaches with royalty reporting and payment can help save you a lot of trouble. Here are some common licensor complaints regarding royalty-related problems:

>> **Slow or no reporting of royalties:** Believe it or not, this situation occurs more often than you may think. Usually, lagging reporting is simply a mistake that the licensee needs to rectify. Getting behind in your royalty reporting can happen, but don't hope that the licensor won't notice. It will! Flip to the earlier section "Sending your reports as agreed" for details on reporting.

>> **Inconsistencies in reporting:** Reporting discrepancies can happen for a number of reasons, but they'll likely trigger an audit that may end up being costly for you. (We cover audits in the following section.) Your best bet is to check in regularly with your licensor partners to be sure they're satisfied with your royalty reporting.

>> **Not using the licensor's reporting tools:** As we note earlier in the chapter, most of the larger licensors have royalty reporting software they expect their licensees to use. If your licensor is in this camp, be sure you're properly trained on how to use the software, and then use it on a timely basis.

>> **Calculating an incorrect royalty rate:** Be sure both you and your licensor are in full agreement about the amount of royalty due based on net sales after any allowed deductions.

>> **Sublicensing:** As a master licensee in a certain product category, you may sometimes find yourself sublicensing the product manufacturing. A good example involves the manufacture of footwear.

Suppose you have the master license for all footwear for ACME brand, and your factory has the ability to manufacture all types of footwear — except slippers. So you decide to contract with another company to manufacture the ACME brand of slippers. This practice constitutes *sublicensing*. Even though you've sublicensed, reporting and paying the royalties on the sublicensed product is still your responsibility as the master licensee.

Dealing with an Audit of Royalty Payments

After you enter into your licensing journey, you'll inevitably be subject to an audit at some point. Simply put, an *audit* in licensing is an independent examination of a licensee's financial records related to the licensed product they're selling. The licensor calls for an audit to verify the accuracy of the reported sales of licensed products and to discover whether you have any inconsistencies or errors in the reporting.

Especially with major licensors, calling for an audit of a particular licensee may be random — sort of like airport TSA randomly pulling a passenger out of the screening line for a closer look. As a licensee, your random fortune may dictate that the licensor chooses you for an audit. However, in most cases, you trigger an audit due to your poor royalty reporting or slow (or no) royalty payments.

REMEMBER

Your licensor has the right to audit your licensing company. Don't panic; it's standard in the industry, with these typical guidelines:

>> **If an audit finds that your company underpaid royalties by more than 5 percent,** you'll most likely end up footing the bill for the audit. This is a standard industry practice.

>> **If an audit finds a discrepancy of less than 5 percent (or no underpayment at all),** the licensor absorbs the costs.

Understanding why your licensor decides to audit

Here are a few common reasons that a licensor may use when asking for an audit:

» **Suspicion of fraud:** If royalty statements look suspicious (for example, they're consistently lower than expected) or concerning rumors about your company (such as not paying suppliers) start swirling around, the licensor may conduct an audit to verify your reports. Think of this situation as a *trust-but-verify* reaction.

» **Response to sloppy bookkeeping:** Constant errors in calculations or *restated* (corrected) royalty reports may give the licensor reason to believe that your records are unreliable. An audit may be its way of ensuring accuracy. A restated royalty report is defined as one that has been withdrawn and then changed and resubmitted. Too many of these is a red flag.

» **Exercise of a routine practice:** Some licensors audit a certain percentage of licensees annually, especially those whose royalties exceed $1 million. If you're doing well and reporting large royalties, expect to be on the licensor's radar.

Going into an audit with the right attitude

We equate an audit with a visit to the dentist. No one looks forward to it. Your best hope is that the dentist finds no issues with your oral health and you're good for another six months. However, if the dentist does find something amiss, you hope it's small and as easily and painlessly fixed as possible.

As we mention in the preceding section, licensors may conduct an audit on a licensee randomly or because they suspect that royalty payments aren't what they should be. Having a licensor decide to perform an audit of your financials can cause difficulties between you. For a new licensee who is building their licensing business, undergoing an audit

» **Can be stressful and potentially embarrassing if you sense your partner doesn't trust you.** We can categorically say that you have no reason to be embarrassed or stressed due to an audit if you've honestly done nothing wrong. Audits are a naturally occurring process in the licensing ecosystem.

» **Is your responsibility as a dutiful licensee.** You must comply with all requests the auditor may make and provide all financial information pertinent to the sales of the licensed product. By complying with the auditor's requests, you're demonstrating (to your licensor partner) your willingness to make the process go as smoothly as possible.

>> **May uncover inconsistencies in your reporting.** Don't be surprised if this situation happens. Often, the inconsistencies an auditor finds are just honest mistakes. Sometimes a decimal point may be in the wrong place or some other small error may cause the royalty calculations to be inaccurate. And sometimes the auditor may find that you've actually overpaid and are due a refund.

REMEMBER

The most important point when you're going through an audit is that, as a licensee, you remain fully agreeable and cooperative with the auditing process.

Pinpointing common audit issues

If your books are clean and you follow your licensing agreement, you'll likely breeze through an audit. Table 10-1 lists sample aspects of license audit provisions that may accompany licensing agreements; flip to Chapter 6 for more on these agreements.

TABLE 10-1   Sample License Audit Provisions

Area of Agreement	Party Involved	Provision Specifics	Term
Books and records	Licensee	Licensee must maintain adequate books and records relating to compliance with the agreement Books must be available for inspection	Length of agreement plus three years
	Licensor	May call for audit by mutually agreed upon auditor during normal business hours Audit won't unreasonably disrupt licensee's business; 30 days advance notice required	Length of agreement plus three years
Audit rights	Licensee	Agrees to reimburse licensor the amount of any deficiency discovered during the audit Must reimburse licensor for audit expenses if the amount of deficiency is greater than the agreed-upon amount (typically 5 percent) Acknowledges that third-party reports issued regarding this agreement are subject to audit Overpayment discovered will be offset against amounts payable to licensor	Length or termination of agreement plus two years

(continued)

TABLE 10-1 *(continued)*

Area of Agreement	Party Involved	Provision Specifics	Term
	Licensor	Must conduct audits no more frequently than once per calendar year Audits shall be conducted at licensor's sole cost and expense, subject to determination of underpayment by licensee	Length or termination of agreement plus two years
Verifying compliance	Licensee	Will submit to audit verification processes described by licensor Alternatively, will complete self-audit questionnaire relating to products sold under the license agreement	Length of agreement plus one year
	Licensor	May request compliance with verification audits by a recognized accounting firm Will use the information obtained in compliance verification only to enforce its rights related to the terms of the licensing agreement	Length of agreement plus one year
Actions due to audit findings	Licensee	Will pay the full amount of any underpayment revealed by the audit Will pay interest on the amount of underpayment from the due date of the payment Will also pay fees and costs of the audit if the underpayment exceeds a specified percentage (5 percent, for example) Will promptly order sufficient licenses to permit all product usage if unlicensed use of product is found	Length of agreement plus number of years specified in the agreement
	Licensor	Will pay fees and costs of audits unless underpayment in the amount specified in the terms of the agreement is discovered	Length of agreement plus number of years specified in the agreement

For anyone else who isn't quite so squeaky clean, here's a rundown of common areas where problems surface during an audit:

» **Net sales calculations:** Your royalty payments are based on net sales. Common allowed deductions include the following:

- Customer returns (products returned by customers to the store)

- Trade discounts (how much of a discount you offer the retailer on the products)

- Other allowable expenses (capped at a certain percentage — for example, 10 percent)

These items aren't allowable deductions:

- Cash discounts
- Advertising fees
- Slotting fees (fees charged by the retailer to stock their shelves)
- Shrinkage allowances (theft and damage of goods)
- Uncollectible accounts
- Transportation costs

WARNING

Miscalculating royalties by including deductions that aren't allowed is the number one source of audit fines.

» **Product approvals:** As we detail in Chapter 7, the licensor must approve every product sold under a licensing agreement. Selling unapproved products can lead to hefty fines — sometimes up to 100 percent of the product's price. Even if you're using already approved branding artwork or design on a slightly different product (for example, a new size or other variation), that slightly different product still needs approval.

Suppose you have a toy company that sells a licensed toy car in a regular-sized package. Costco asks for a larger packaged version with two cars rather than one. You think, "Same art, same brand — no need for new approval!" So you sell it. The auditor later flags it as unapproved, and you're hit with a significant fine.

» **Approved factories:** Factory compliance is now a standard requirement in licensing agreements. If you use a factory that hasn't passed the licensor's audit or fails to provide documentation, you can face fines as high as 100 percent of the product's sale price. Always ensure that your factories meet the licensor's standards and have documented approval as we outline in Chapter 7.

» **Late payments:** The auditor checks the exact dates on which the licensor received royalty payments. Late payments can lead to compounded interest charges, which can add up if an audit occurs years later. Some licensors also impose flat penalty fees for late payments — sometimes as high as $5,000 per infraction.

TIPS FOR STAYING AUDIT-READY

By keeping accurate records, following the terms of your agreement, and preparing in advance, you can navigate the auditing process with confidence and avoid unnecessary fines. **Remember:** A clean book is a happy book!

Follow this advice:

- **Invest in software.** Use specialized licensing and accounting software to track sales, deductions, and approvals. These tools make complying with your agreement easier.

- **Maintain your own approval records.** Even if the licensor keeps an approval portal, keep a backup. Employees leave, data can change, and systems aren't always perfect.

- **Have a consultant or accountant review your reports.** A second pair of eyes can catch issues before the licensor does.

Coping with confrontation when the auditor finds accounting errors

Accounting errors happen all the time, so don't be embarrassed or ashamed if they happen to your company. You can find many examples in the licensing business where overly eager auditors calculated royalty payments incorrectly, because anyone can make a mistake. When an auditor believes they've found inaccurate royalty calculations, you must be sure that the errors are, in fact, really errors.

Consider these items when responding to an auditor's findings of royalty calculation errors:

>> **If you disagree with the auditor's findings, respond immediately and try to understand where the misunderstanding may be coming from.** The worst thing you can do is to ignore the findings or delay in your response.

>> **Deal with potentially inaccurate audit findings calmly and rationally.** In Chapter 9, we discuss the importance of developing close relationships with your licensor partner. Those relationships pay off in this type of situation. If you believe the auditor has misinterpreted what you owe, pick up the phone and speak with your licensor partner. Go over the details and state your case for why you believe the audit isn't correct.

>> **If the auditor *is* correct about the misreporting of royalties owed, promptly own up.** Work with the licensor to remedy the situation.

REMEMBER

The reason pencils have erasers is that mistakes happen. No one is perfect; as long as the mistakes discovered are honest ones, your licensor partner will likely be understanding. If the licensor has been in the licensing business for a while, you won't be the first, or last, licensee who has experienced a discrepancy in their audit.

Addressing Administrative Tasks in Licensing

In this section we get to the really fun part of the licensing process: administration (just kidding)! Seriously, like any other business, your licensing success demands that you engage in certain administrative tasks that help you keep your end of the deal with your licensor.

Fortunately, several companies (such as Octane 5 and Flowhaven) have created software solutions specific to the licensing business. Much of the licensing software available is *turnkey,* meaning it can assist you throughout the licensing process, from the contract to the royalty reporting phases. Most major licensors utilize a licensing software system or have developed their own.

TIP

Your licensor partner can recommend the best-in-class systems that it or its established licensees are already using. These licensing software solutions can take a lot of stress out of the business. Simply find the right software system for your budget and then get your team trained on how to use it properly.

Because licensing involves partnership, your admin responsibilities aren't just to your own company but to your licensor partner as well. Although royalty tracking, reporting, and payments are critical parts of the administration process, you must share many other administrative tasks with your licensor partner.

In Chapters 6, 7, and 8, we discuss business activities such as product approval, packaging design, retail development, and marketing support. Administrative tasks related to all these activities become a part of the everyday workflow you encounter in your licensing adventure. We include Table 10-2 here as a way to outline the major administrative tasks in the licensing ecosystem, which we mention in this chapter and elsewhere in the book.

REMEMBER

You've entered into an agreement to utilize another company's intellectual property to sell your products. This relationship brings with it the responsibility to work as partners and develop regular reporting processes, which is why your administrative tasks are critical to your licensing success.

TABLE 10-2   Administrative Tasks in Licensing

Task	What It Entails	For More Information
Licensing contract/agreement	Verifying full agreement between the licensee and licensor	Chapter 6
Product design approval	Getting licensor's approval	Chapter 7
Packaging design approval	Getting licensor's approval	Chapter 7
Manufacturing, materials and labor compliance	Getting licensor's approval	Chapter 7
Marketing approvals	Getting licensor's approval	Chapter 7
Retail channel compliance	Getting licensor's approval	Chapter 8
Royalty reporting	Following contractual agreement guidelines	The earlier section "Reporting and Paying Royalties"
Royalty payments	Following contractual agreement guidelines	The earlier section "Reporting and Paying Royalties"

4

Maximizing Sales through Licensing

Succeed at retail when your product hits the market.

Use all the marketing tools at your disposal.

See how globalization affects licensing.

Gaze into your crystal ball to see where brand licensing is headed in the future.

Chapter **11**

Selling Your Licensed Products

A key for a licensing business is that the license itself acts as a marketing tool to help you sell your product. Licensing a famous brand or entertainment property — and coupling it with the right product or service — is proven to increase sales over simply offering a generic product or service. In this chapter, you discover the ins and outs of how to successfully sell your licensed product through various retail channels. And because the ability to develop your retail business is critical to the success of your licensing business, this chapter also covers the inherent characteristics, techniques, and skills that help you develop your retail business.

Peeling Back the Layers of a Licensing Business

Before delving into the intricacies involved in selling at retail, take a look at the business structure that outlines how a brand license involves sales of consumer products in the first place. When I (Steven) started in the licensing business, a veteran of the business explained that licensing was like an onion. The more you peeled the onion, the more layers you discovered.

Keeping with the onion metaphor, here are the layers as explained to me, from outside to core:

>> **A brand's intellectual property (IP):** That valuable resource has immediate recognition with consumers and a history of trust and loyalty. This trust and loyalty are what licensees are after when they look for well-recognized IP to license.

>> **The licensee:** The licensee knows that licensing a well-known brand can help them enhance (and sell more of) their products.

>> **The intermediary (an agent or consultant):** This person acts as the conduit and dealmaker between the licensor and the licensee. They usually have years of experience in understanding how to structure a licensing deal as well as the best way to approach a licensor. Head to Chapter 5 for more on working with a licensing consultant.

>> **The many support services that assist in the success of the licensing process:** These services include IP attorneys who help in the contractual negotiation, accountants, and software providers, for example.

>> **The retailer:** The retailer is the final layer at the heart of the licensing onion. It provides the place you go to sell your finished licensed product. The retail layer is arguably the most critical because it determines whether your licensed product will sell successfully, which leads to success in your licensing business. Or, to borrow a piece of the classic Firestone tire commercial, it's "where the rubber meets the road."

Understanding Aspects of Retail Business Development

An easy description of *retail business development* (as it relates to a licensing business) is this: You focus your business efforts on building the right products and then finding the right retail channels that make sense for you to sell your products.

As a licensee, your job at retail business development may be significantly easier because the brand you're licensing will likely already have other established licensees selling its products at retail. It may even be selling the core licensor's product at retail. Therefore, these established retailers will probably be interested in selling your products as well.

But in addition to the advantage of selling a product that already has established retail channels, you have other business considerations that affect how you focus your efforts on selling your licensed products. We cover these considerations in the following sections.

Recognizing the strength of existing licensed brands

Retailers love a winning brand. When a retailer sees that a licensed product is flying off the shelves, it realizes something important: Customers love that brand! If people are already buying one product with the licensed brand, they're more likely to buy more. That's why successful retailers keep stocking up on licensed products — because they know customers will keep coming back for more.

REMEMBER

For example, the Star Wars brand

>> **Demonstrates success at selling licensed products** starting with the first film released in 1977.

>> **Stays fresh (over the last 50ish years) because it regularly produces** new films, TV, video games, books, toys, apparel, and many other products and experiences.

>> **Has existing retailers who are open to selling new products** that license the Star Wars brand because the brand continues to sell well!

However, classic licensing brands that are a huge success at retail can experience periods of underperformance for one reason or another. The sidebar "The Batman Licensing Lesson" in this chapter takes a look at a classic example of periodic performance issues with the Batman brand.

Qualifying your distribution strategy

From the start of your licensing journey, you determine what products to create and what brand licenses to use as a marketing tool to sell the products. Along with these fundamentals, you must also develop your distribution strategy. In other words, where will you sell the wonderful, licensed products that you're making?

TIP

Figuring out potential retail channels early on in the licensing process is key to your success in selling your products. And having a distribution plan in place upfront makes the sales process much smoother.

Your distribution strategy finds its roots in the licensing contract that you signed with your licensor, which stipulates what retail channels you can sell to. In Chapter 8, we outline retail strategy and discuss the idea of the specific retail distribution that the licensor gives you. For example, if you license a brand to sell your toy product, the licensor may offer the retail/wholesale channel for distribution in your licensing agreement.

Consider the Batman franchise and how Warner Bros. keeps its licensees happy. The Batman brand has multiple licensees that make T-shirts. How can Warner Bros. (owner of the Batman brand) manage this stable so that each licensee doesn't poach sales from the others? They do it by granting each licensee a different distribution channel. One T-shirt company sells to the mass market (such as Walmart), another the mid-tier department stores (such as Kohl's), another upscale department stores (such as Bloomingdale's), and another the comic book specialty stores (such as Midtown Comics).

Preselling licensed products to retail

In Chapter 8, we discuss retail strategy in great detail. One key element of your retail success describes securing your retail strategy in advance of producing your product (a strategy that involves preselling). *Preselling* is defined as meeting with your retail partner/s and having them agree to purchase a certain quantity of your licensed products ahead of time — often before the product is even manufactured. When you do so, you have a solid picture of how many products to manufacture and where to distribute them afterward.

Securing sales before manufacturing your product is a great idea, and here are some aspects of that strategy to keep in mind:

>> **Be sure to get that purchase order.** Suppose you secure distribution for your licensed product with a top U.S. retailer that has both brick-and-mortar and e-commerce sales. Before you place your order at the factory for manufacturing your product, you want to receive that official purchase order from your retailer.

>> **Understand that orders don't translate directly into final sales.** The number of units of your product that a retailer orders doesn't necessarily translate to the number of units sold. If the product doesn't sell, the retailer may expect you to take back unsold inventory.

>> **Know that consumer demand is fickle and that projecting sales involves risk-taking.** As the licensee/manufacturer, you want to both minimize your risk of excess inventory (overproducing) and maximize consumer products sales. You also don't want to disappoint the retailers and potentially damage your hard-earned relationship with them by underproducing. If your partner does in fact sell out of your products and wants to reorder, how quickly will you be able to fulfill that new order?

TIP

Do your best to right-size your product manufacturing. Selling entertainment licensed consumer products is often trend-driven, and being prepared to ride the wave of a trend is critical to your success.

Embracing marketing assistance from the licensor

When you acquire a license for your product or service, in most cases, your licensor partner will want to help you through marketing support. If it's a major licensor, it has deep connections at retail and can open retail doors for you.

TIP

Look for and act on your licensor's deep retail connections so you can benefit by getting distribution of your licensed product with the retailers the licensor is connected with.

Some prime examples of licensors with marketing prowess involve entertainment studios who license their films and TV content. Major studios such as Disney, Warner Bros., Universal, and Paramount all have entertainment franchises that enable them to work closely with major retailers to promote new entertainment releases with products and promotions at retail.

If you have licenses in the entertainment industry, you want to take advantage of your licensor's retail promotion capabilities that let you place products. Figure 11-1 shows a humorous take on how retail sales of licensed products can benefit from marketing promotions.

FIGURE 11-1:
This one's funny because it's true!

Betsy Streeter / Cartoon Stock

Capitalizing on the brand value of your products

The multimillion dollar question that you may be asking yourself is "How do I create consumer demand for my product after it's ready to sell?" The answer is pretty simple. Companies get into the licensing business because they understand the power and value that well-known brands bring to products. *Brand equity* — also known as *brand value* — creates a trust and emotional connection with the consumer that builds up over a period of time.

Consider this example: Imagine that you put $1,000 into a savings account at a fixed interest rate of 5 percent. At the end of the first year you have $1,050. At the end of the second year you have $1,102.50; at the end of the third year, $1,157.63; and so on. Over the years, the interest accumulates and adds to the value of the original deposit, building greater value.

Brand equity increases in the same way. A well-known brand starts out simply as a product or service, but as it builds trust with the consumer over the years, its product (and brand) value also increase. When you license a well-known brand for your product, you're tapping into the brand's value and the consumer demand for both the brand value and the product.

The brand equity from your licensed product is the sales driver at retail. It's the reason the retailer takes your product over your competitor's generic product; the retailer understands the power of brand equity with their customer.

REMEMBER

After you capture this existing brand value and consumer demand — by securing the brand license for your product — the goal becomes finding the best ways to reach the most consumers who will be interested in purchasing your product. And so the discussion returns to retail development strategy. As we suggest in Chapter 8, the best retail distribution strategy is *hybrid*, meaning that you sell your products at brick-and-mortar retailers and online.

Aligning retail distribution and marketing strategy

After you establish your retail distribution strategy, you need to find cost-effective ways to promote the availability of your licensed products. This piece of retail development is part of your marketing strategy. Some straightforward best practices in marketing can help you promote your products. Here are some key ones when working with various parties:

>> **Your licensor:** As we mention in the section "Embracing marketing assistance from the licensor" earlier in the chapter, a licensor will share

what retail promotions it's planning and when. That way, you can take advantage of these opportunities to put your product in the limelight. Your licensor may have strong relationships with key retailers, which can open doors and help you secure important meetings.

>> **Your retail partners:** Often, the retailers themselves create in-store promotions around your particular license. For example if your license is a for a new movie opening soon, retailers may plan special prices or displays to coincide with the premiere. They may also have a seasonal promotion that aligns perfectly with your licensed product, giving you the opportunity to participate and gain prime retail visibility.

>> **Your marketing department or an outside promotions agency:** The professionals — whether inside or outside your company — can create retail promotions that draw attention to your products and assist you in selling more.

THE BATMAN LICENSING LESSON

Here's a story from the licensing world that explains the application of the retail business development function in licensing and shows the ups and downs of managing a successful merchandise program — and what happens when the market doesn't align with expectations.

The *Batman* movie in 1989 (the first) was a huge hit, both at the box office and in merchandise sales. Everyone wanted the iconic black T-shirt with the yellow Bat-Shield logo. It became a fashion statement worn by fashionistas, bike messengers, college students, and kids alike.

What Went Wrong

Retailers were caught off guard by the massive demand and didn't stock enough inventory to satisfy customers. The result? Missed sales opportunities and a lot of disappointed Batman fans.

(Over)correcting the Inventory Problem

Fast forward to the 1992 sequel, *Batman Returns*. This time, retailers weren't going to get caught unprepared for consumer demand. They bulked up on inventory, ordering heavily to meet what they assumed would be another surge in demand. But although the movie and merchandise were a success, the sales didn't meet the huge expectations that the retailers had had based on the way the first film's products had flown off the shelves. Retailers found themselves with excess inventory, and suddenly they weren't as excited about the prospects of selling future Batman merchandise.

(continued)

(continued)

Retailer Hesitation and the Birth of a New Strategy

When *Batman Forever* rolled around in 1995, Warner Bros. faced a big problem. Many retailers still had leftover merchandise from *Batman Returns*, and they were skeptical (and not eager) to take on more Batman-branded goods. Licensees, in turn, hesitated to invest in the new movie's products, citing a lack of retailer interest.

Warner Bros. knew it needed a new strategy to win back retailer confidence and ensure the success of *Batman Forever* merchandise. Enter the retail development team.

How the Retail Development Team Saved the Day

Warner Bros. created a dedicated retail development division with one mission: to work directly with key retailers such as Walmart and Target to build excitement and support for *Batman Forever* products. The new division didn't use a standard sales pitch. It went the extra mile by

- Bringing personal messages from the film's director and actors to meetings with the retailers.
- Highlighting how *Batman Forever* would be fresh, exciting, and different from previous films.

One by one, retailers started coming onboard. Walmart, Target, and others made room for *Batman Forever* products, and with their support, the merchandise program gained momentum.

The Result? A Win for Everyone

Thanks to this new approach by the licensor, *Batman Forever* was both a box-office and merchandising success. Warner Bros. retail development division proved that building strong, direct relationships with key retailers could make or break a licensing program.

The Takeaway

Retailer hesitation can be a tough hurdle to overcome, but as this story shows, communicating proactively and building trust with retail partners can clear the hurdle. This strategy has now become a standard practice in licensing, which ensures that products are backed by strong retail support and that everyone — the licensors, licensees, and retailers — walk away happy.

Now, that's a superhero move!

Setting Up Your License Agreement for Retail Success

Negotiating a licensing agreement with terms that are sensitive to potential sales issues is important. (Check out Chapter 6 for details on licensing agreement negotiation.) When you work with your licensor, make sure you look carefully at the terms and conditions of the license while you keep in mind the factors that impact the timing and extent of sales. You want to be sure you have enough time to design and manufacture the licensed product and deliver it to the retailers when they want it. For example, if your licensed product is seasonally driven (by Christmas season, for example) you want to be certain you have enough time to deliver by early fall.

Planning an appropriate length of term

In Chapter 6, we discuss the length and terms of your licensing agreement as well as the renewal options. When you're initially signing a licensing deal, think through the factors that may impact your ability to sell your licensed merchandise in a timely fashion. Try to anticipate outcomes that can

>> **Delay your ability to market and sell your licensed products.** For example, in the entertainment industry, release dates can change and impact the intended sales timeline for your licensing business. Ensure you have a clause in your contract that protects your business in case of a delay in the release of the branded property that you're licensing.

  When a movie release date gets changed, the whole process of creating, marketing, and selling related products is disrupted, with these results:

  - Retailers may cancel or postpone their orders.

  - Products already in production can end up stuck in warehouses.

  - Without the movie to generate buzz, selling movie-themed merchandise is incredibly challenging to do. Flip to the section "Adjusting agreements for timing delays" later in the chapter for more about damages caused by release delays.

>> **Negatively affect the timeline and conditions for contract renewals.** A delay in the release of the branded property can mess up your contract renewal timeline as well. Make sure your agreement gives you extra time to sell your product so you can hit your royalty targets — even if the licensor's launch gets pushed back.

Understanding your financial obligations: The minimum royalty payment guarantee

When you sign the contract with a licensor, you face a particularly important financial obligation: the *minimum royalty payment guarantee,* which is an amount of your projected royalties you agree to pay regardless of whether your actual sales hit that mark. If you're licensing an *A property* (a heavily sought-after brand, as we discuss in Chapter 6), the licensor asks for a significant amount as a guarantee of royalties that you must pay. You also may be obligated to pay a portion of it, the *advance,* right after signing the contract.

For example, suppose you sign a licensing agreement to sell lunchboxes for the next Batman movie, and the licensor (Warner Bros.) expects you'll sell $5 million wholesale in lunchboxes at a royalty rate of 15 percent. Your royalties on $5 million would be $750,000. The licensor may expect a minimum royalty payment guarantee of half of that amount ($375,000). In addition, your advance may be 25 percent ($93,750), and that's due when you sign the agreement.

In this situation, you're out of pocket approximately $93,750 before you've even manufactured one lunchbox.

What happens if no one wants to buy your Batman lunchbox (or whatever licensed product you're selling)? What if some other market situation affects the timing and amount of your sales?

TIP

Always determine how much of a licensed product you need to sell in order to (at least) break even after paying the upfront guaranteed amount to your licensor. As a licensee, understanding all the risks when you sign a license agreement is critical. The most important question for you as a licensee is "How many of the licensed items do I need to sell to meet my minimum royalty payment guarantee?"

Mitigating your risk

As a licensee, minimizing the risk you take on the license agreement you sign and the product you manufacture is paramount. You have a number of ways to do so:

>> **Do your homework on the license you're taking.** Find out how well other products with the same license sell and how long they've been selling (well or otherwise). Head to Chapter 5 for more about doing the upfront research for your licensing deals.

>> **Check out the distribution channel the licensor assigns you in the agreement.** Determine whether the channel is wide or narrow (see Chapter 8) and estimate the scope of potential sales.

>> **Determine how negotiable your licensor will be regarding** *product sell-through* **(products selling at retail).** For example, ask whether the licensor will provide you with financial relief — and how much — if all the products don't sell through at retail. (Chapter 6 has more information on negotiating licensing deals.)

>> **Find out the most effective way to set the quantity and timing of manufacturing efforts.** You can lessen your risk by working closely with your retail partner to understand the manufacturing deadlines required to move the right amount of appropriately priced product through the sales cycles. Chapter 7 includes information on manufacturing and marketing issues.

Watching Out for Challenges in the Market

As a licensee, you may run into situations that impact the market for your licensed products. Most times, they're outside of your control. (Take a look at the nearby sidebar "Pandemics, shutdowns, strikes, and delays" for an example.) When conditions occur that adversely affect marketing and sales opportunities, take advice from other licensees who have had to deal with them, as we outline in the following sections.

PANDEMICS, SHUTDOWNS, STRIKES, AND DELAYS

The COVID-19 pandemic of 2020 to 2022 had a major negative impact on the Hollywood film industry. It virtually shut down movie theaters and caused Hollywood studios to delay anticipated blockbuster releases. In turn, these shutdowns and delays impacted companies that had related licensed products to sell.

Then both the Writers Guild of America (which includes screenwriters) and SAG-AFTRA (the actors' union) went on strike, halting any films that were in development. These dual strikes essentially shut down movie and TV productions from April to November of 2023. As of this writing, the industry is still feeling the impact of movie and TV delays and losses estimated between $5 and 6 billion dollars.

For licensees, these occurrences provide a cautionary tale for the industry segment that makes up a significant part of the licensing business — entertainment licensing represents $150 billion a year in retail sales. And the result impacts the sales of products and services that directly tie to film and TV releases.

Adjusting agreements for timing delays

Many license agreements that rely on the completion of a creative or technological property (for example, movie-related licenses) constitute a long game. As a licensee, you probably sign your agreement 12 to 18 months before the scheduled release date of the entertainment property. That gives you enough time to

>> **Develop the licensed product,** complete with branded attributes and manufacturing details.

>> **Pitch and sell it to retailers** within the channels assigned by your licensing agreement to gauge interest and better know how much inventory to build.

>> **Ship it to warehouses or stores** where your retailers have access to the product for selling it to the consumer.

All these activities hinge on one major assumption: The creative or technological property you licensed will hit the market as planned.

When delays in creative properties (such as movie releases) happen, many licensors understand the challenges and work with licensees to minimize the financial impact. One common solution for licensors involves granting relief on the minimum guaranteed sales outlined in the licensing agreement.

The *relief* may mean that the licensor adjusts the payment terms or reduces the minimum-guarantee requirement to help the licensee weather the disruption. Another common licensor response is to simply extend the term of the agreement without any additional financial obligation. Licensors make these concessions because they want to maintain strong relationships with their licensees and ensure the success of the licensing program in the long run.

REMEMBER

When you consider certain licensing situations, specifically movie licenses, timing is everything. But when delays occur (and they do), clear communication with your licensor and retailer partners is essential for navigating the related challenges. After all, even in the licensing world, flexibility is key!

Playing it safe with franchise classics

Every time a studio releases a new film in a long-running franchise, it creates a new logo for the new film to differentiate it from the classic original brand.

The studio uses the new logo in advertising and promotion and licenses it for many product categories. Many longtime licensees who've seen the delays (and sometimes flops) of new entries in a franchise avoid taking on the license for new logos or designs and stick to the classic logos of the original brand. Picking up a new logo for licensing is a definite gamble, and these licensees understand that the classic IP and logo are less of a risk.

This same type of situation happens when any brand makes changes to its logo. For example, the car brand Jaguar changed both the lettering and fonts in its name as well as the jaguar in its logo (it became a leaping jaguar). The reasoning was that the company was rebranding for a new generation, but the change was poorly received by both consumers and the marketing community.

Carefully managing celebrity licenses

One category of licensing that continues to see extensive growth in this pop-culture/social-media-dominated world involves celebrities and influencers. A cursory look at any major brick-and-mortar retail store — such as Walmart or Target — shows you a plethora of licensed influencers and celebrity brands being sold. Notice how many top-selling fashion and beauty brands for women have built their brands through licensing the associated celebrity into many products. Here are just a few examples:

- Beyonce's Ivy Park
- Drew Barrymore's Flower
- Gwyneth Paltrow's GOOP
- Jessica Alba's Honest Company
- The Kardashian-Jenner empire
- Kate Hudson's Fabletics
- Meghan Markle's American Riviera Orchard
- Rhianna's Fenty
- Selena Gomez's Rare Beauty

A couple of other common licensing areas that involve celebrities and influencers include these:

- **Food and beverage industry:** These partnerships include such pairings as Miley Cyrus and a Chipotle burrito; Lady Gaga and Oreos; McDonald's and the Travis Scott burger; and Dolly Parton and Duncan Hines. The list of licensed celebrity food and beverage brands is long and gets longer every year.

>> **Kids category:** Toys, accessories, and apparel — as well as food and beverages — have linked up with YouTube stars such as Ryan of Ryan's World (toy and other product reviews), Ms. Rachel (learning videos), and Blippi (learning adventure tours).

REMEMBER

Make sure to choose your celebrity partners wisely. As the following sections explain, their fame *and* infamy both reflect on your product.

Invoking a morality clause

WARNING

Celebrity/influencer licensing can be a double-edged sword. You've licensed a celebrity brand, and everything's going great — until the celebrity does something that lands them in hot water, tarnishing their image and, by extension, the brand you've licensed.

Unfortunately, situations in which a celebrity taints their reputation (and that of their associated brands) happen. That's why many savvy licensees now include a morality clause in licensing agreements with celebrities. A *morality clause* is an industry-standard provision that protects you (the licensee) if the celebrity engages in immoral or unethical behavior that damages their brand's reputation.

Here's how a morality clause typically works: If the celebrity's actions tarnish their brand, you may be granted relief; that may include eliminating or reducing the contractual minimum guarantees. In some cases, it may even allow you to terminate the agreement entirely (as we explain in the following section).

REMEMBER

Licensing a celebrity always comes with some level of risk. After all, their personal actions can directly impact the perception of the brand you've invested in. A morality clause helps minimize that risk and gives you an exit strategy if things go south.

A TALE OF CELEBRITY LICENSING THAT IMPLODED

In 2022, Kanye West (also known as Ye) was arguably one of the most popular and wealthiest hip-hop superstars, with 30 million Twitter followers. Then he found himself banned from both Twitter (now X) and Instagram for making blatant anti-Semitic remarks. Ye was no stranger to controversy; he'd spent the better part of two decades building a following through music and lyrics that became more and more controversial, as well as his well-publicized marriage and split from another big-name licensing celebrity, Kim Kardashian.

Despite his previous controversial statements about slavery and COVID-19, Ye had continued to find success in brand extensions and licensing until that fateful fall of 2022, when he publicly made those terrible anti-Jewish hate statements. At that point, his longtime luxury brand collaborator, Balenciaga, broke ties with him; his GAP deal died; and his largest deal of all — with Adidas — fell apart when the company cut all ties with him. Even his talent agency (CAA) and his music distributor (Def Jam) both dropped him.

A cursory look at Ye's licensing deals shows just how lucrative they could've been for him. In 2013, West signed a more successful contract to make his Yeezy brand sneakers with Adidas AG. The agreement was hugely profitable for both Ye and Adidas and was supposed to extend to 2026. But because of his anti-Semitic comments, Adidas canceled the deal in October 2022. Adidas was projected to lose an estimated $250 million that year because of the terminated deal, but the company found a way to offload the Yeezy sneakers, bringing in over $400 million in sales and donating much of the profit to anti-hate groups.

Canceling a licensing agreement for cause

When you have to invoke a morality clause (see the preceding section) and cancel a celebrity licensing agreement, do so with cause. Canceling a high-profile licensing agreement is complicated, and you should contact your company's legal team if you think cutting ties is necessary. Your legal team can offer the best advice in exactly how to go about doing this.

High-profile celebrities from various industries have endured canceled licensing agreements and lost out on lucrative returns. In the food business alone, high profile chef Paula Deen had both of her shows on Food Network canceled and lost profitable licensing deals with Walmart, Target, Home Depot, QVC, JCPenney, and Smithfield Foods — all for having used racial slurs. And Mario Batali had his TV shows and his licensing deals with Target canceled after sexual misconduct allegations. The nearby sidebar "A Tale of celebrity licensing that imploded" offers another high-profile example of celebrity licensing deals that went sour.

Chapter **12**

Marketing Tools That Boost Retail Sales

I n the ever-changing retail landscape, having marketing tools to help you with selling your licensed products is essential. Consider that more than 20,000 new products hit the market every year. That number sounds impressive, right? Here's the reality check: Only about 5 percent of those products actually succeed by achieving the sales goals they need to support their continued production.

REMEMBER

Licensing a well-known brand can make a huge (positive) difference in your chances of introducing a successful product. When you attach a trusted brand name to your product, you tap into built-in consumer trust. People already recognize the brand, trust its quality, and are more likely to trust your licensed product — even if it's new to the shelves.

By licensing a recognizable brand, you start out with a marketing edge. The brand's reputation does some of the heavy lifting and gives you a head start in the marketplace. Although licensing gives you a great foundation, however, you still need to use other marketing tools to maximize your product's success.

In this chapter, we explore the tools and techniques you need to accompany the marketing boost you get with a licensed brand. We also provide you with the knowledge necessary to implement the best, most cost-effective marketing strategy to sell your licensed products at retail.

YOUR FIRST MARKETING TOOL?
THE LICENSE ITSELF

Your licensing agreement is more than just a legal document; it's a built-in marketing tool! The whole point of licensing a well-known brand is to tap into its existing brand equity; consumers already recognize and trust it.

Here are two key factors to consider:

- **Your licensing agreement:** Your contract with the licensor outlines what you can and can't do. For example, if you have a Coca-Cola socks license, you can team up with other Coca-Cola licensees (like T-shirts and hats) to create a coordinated collection that makes a bigger splash at retail.

- **Your retail agreement:** After your licensing deal is in place, you negotiate with retail partners to get your product in stores. When doing so, align your marketing efforts with their planned promotions for the brand to help you maximize exposure and increase sales.

Remember: Licensing gives you a leg up, but combining the built-in advantages with smart marketing strategies can give your product the best shot at being really successful.

Taking Direction from Your Partners

The great thing for you as a licensee is that you're in a partnership with two powerful allies: your licensor partner and the retailers in your distribution channel. Building relationships with both of these allies makes your marketing efforts so much easier and reinforces — for the licensor and retailers — your desire to be successful.

The licensor's investment in your marketing

Your licensor partner has spent years building a formidable brand that you now have the opportunity to use on your product. Your licensor partner can be a huge help to you by

>> Providing marketing assets in the form of logos and graphics.

>> Sharing information about what other licensees are doing to market their licensed products.

>> Acting as a conduit to bringing you together with other licensees to collaborate on *earned placement* (being featured without a related fee) and paid social media ads, as well as share in the costs of these.

Most importantly, your licensor partner lives and breathes the brand, so it understands what the brand's fans want and what drives them to buy the branded products. As a licensee, you can count on your licensor to keep the brand in the spotlight by continuing to drive brand popularity through the following:

>> **New content releases:** These include movies, TV shows, games, books, and other products (for entertainment-based brands) that keep the brand fresh. Consider Barbie-branded Krispy Kreme donuts, the *Squid Game* mobile video game, or *Wicked* dolls from Mattel.

>> **Core product releases:** For corporate brands like Procter & Gamble, music brands, fashion brands, and technology brands, continued product launches help maintain visibility. For example, Procter & Gamble's Mr. Clean brand has licensed a significant number of products, such as Mr. Clean buckets, mops, and brooms, that keep the brand expanding, fresh, and enticing for consumers.

>> **Promotional campaigns**: Especially with major retailers, licensors create campaigns that licensees can participate in. The *Barbie* film from 2023 makes a great example: Warner Bros. (the film's distributor) and Mattel (the company that makes Barbie dolls) worked together to create massive promotions with some of the biggest names in retail: Walmart, Target, Gap, Primark, Hot Topic, Spirit Halloween, Bloomingdale's, and many more.

Tapping into retailers' marketing muscle

When planning your marketing strategy, don't overlook the promotional power of your retail partners! Retailers often invest in marketing efforts that can complement your brand's campaigns, giving you extra visibility at no additional cost.

For example, suppose a brand is celebrating its 50th anniversary with a big marketing push. The licensor may be rolling out ads, social media buzz, and in-store signage. A retailer that carries the licensed brand may decide to join the celebration by featuring it on a special *endcap* display (that prime real estate at the ends of store aisles) or running *free-standing inserts* (FSIs) in newspapers to highlight the milestone.

By aligning your marketing efforts with your retail partners' promotions, you can amplify your brand's reach and maximize impact — without spending a dime of your own budget.

As a licensee, you may have the chance to join in these kinds of promotions, often for a fee. But here's why the opportunity is worth considering even with a fee:

>> Your products get prime retail placement that increases their visibility on the retail floor.

>> You can not only tag along with but also expand on the licensor promotions and enjoy an additional marketing boost.

REMEMBER

Participating in these licensor/retailer promotions and programs is a very cost-efficient way to cut through the retail clutter. These promotional programs can be game-changers for driving sales; don't miss out on the chance to participate!

When it comes to placing your products on their shelves, retailers' goals are pretty straightforward. They want the following:

>> **Products that sell well:** Retailers need items that move quickly and meet their customers' needs.

>> **Reliable manufacturing partners:** They expect partners who can deliver on time and in the right format to keep shelves stocked.

>> **Customer alignment:** Retailers have a deep understanding of their shoppers: what they love, how much they spend, and which price points work best. By adding a licensed brand to your product, you gain an instant edge with built-in recognition and trust. Consumers are more likely to choose a product featuring a brand they already know and love, making it easier for retailers to sell.

TIP

Make sure your retail partners have reason to trust your role in the licensing arrangements. A trusted brand name helps get attention for your products, but strong product quality, appropriate pricing, and timely delivery are the aspects of a licensing partnership that still matter most to the retailers. That's why most licensors prefer to work with licensees who have well-established and proven retail relationships.

LICENSEE MARKETING FUNDS

When I (Stu) worked at a major fashion brand, all licensees were required to contribute a small percentage of their sales into a common marketing fund. This shared pool of money was specifically set aside to promote the entire licensing program and the licensed products under the brand.

Here's how the arrangement worked:

- Every licensee contributed a set percentage of their sales to the fund.
- As the licensor, our job was to spend these funds effectively to support the success of the licensed products.

The fashion brand decided to keep its marketing approach simple and highly focused by allocating 100 percent of the licensee-contributed funds to a single key fashion magazine. The entire budget went toward purchasing as many magazine ad pages as possible.

This straightforward strategy not only maximized brand visibility but also provided complete transparency for the licensees. They could clearly see where the brand licensor spent their marketing contributions. This openness helped build trust between the licensees and the licensor, fostering a stronger partnership. The results were consistently positive, and the strategy was successfully repeated for many years. By keeping the marketing strategy focused and transparent, both the brand and the licensees benefited from consistent, high-impact visibility.

Using Social Media Marketing to Reach Your Target Audience

In today's marketplace, the fastest, easiest, and most cost–effective way to reach your consumer is through social media marketing. Social media advertising takes a couple of forms:

>> **Paid social media:** Paying platforms (such as Facebook, Instagram, LinkedIn, TikTok, and so on) to promote content, display ads, or boost posts to reach a targeted audience

>> **Earned social media:** *Organic* (unpaid) exposure gained through shares, mentions, reviews, user-generated content, and word-of-mouth

How you use these promotional structures depends on your marketing strategy and budget. The most successful marketers tend to use a hybrid model that includes both paid and earned social media marketing.

Both paid and earned marketing tools are extremely effective in today's online world, where consumers spend hours engaging with social media. Consumers' tastes create *algorithms* (a set of rules used to determine which content appears most prominently in a specific customer's feed), which is a significant benefit for marketing. Social media platforms use artificial intelligence (AI) tools to pick up the customer preferences (from their web searches and post interactions) and then feed ads for similar products and services back to the consumer.

REMEMBER

This AI-based form of online targeted marketing has revolutionized identifying consumers preferences; it enables sellers to reach buyers without wasting a lot of money and time placing unwanted and unseen ads.

Embracing social media for product promotion

Licensees looking to promote their licensed products nowadays turn to social media to boost visibility and drive sales. The key marketing opportunity when working with a licensed brand is to tie into the activity of the licensor's social media presence. You can see this trend across platforms such as Instagram, YouTube, X (formerly Twitter), Facebook, and TikTok.

Here's how this shared social media presence works:

>> **Licensees can tag the licensor's official account in their posts.** Doing so helps align the licensee's marketing efforts with the core brand's audience.

>> **Licensors can actively repost or share content that features their licensees' products.** This move can be a huge marketing boost and is something you should discuss upfront during contract negotiations (see Chapter 6). Keep the following in mind:

- **Some licensing agreements now include a commitment from the licensor to share or repost the licensee's content.** This provision allows for a more seamless integration into the licensor's broader marketing campaigns by maximizing visibility and promotional impact for the licensed products.

- **Larger licensors with multiple licensees may not include these commitments in their agreements.** These licensors may not be able to repost content from every partner due to the sheer volume of collaborations.

TIP

Aligning with the licensor's social media agency can be a highly effective strategy for licensees. By working with the same agency as the licensor, licensees can increase the chances of retweets, shares, and reposts, ensuring their content reaches a wider audience. This collaboration also helps maintain consistent messaging and visual alignment with the core brand, creating a more unified brand presence across platforms.

Recognizing the scope of social media use

As of this writing, these are the most popular social media platforms based on monthly active users (MSUs):

>> **Facebook:** 3 billion MSU

>> **Instagram:** 2 billion MSU

>> **Snapchat:** 800 million MSU

>> **Telegram:** 900 million MSU

>> **TikTok:** 1.5 billion MSU

>> **YouTube:** 2.5 billion MSU

>> **WeChat:** 1.3 billion MSU

>> **WhatsApp:** 2 billion MSU

A significant benefit for you as a licensee in today's social media world is that consumer interests create algorithms (as we explain earlier in the chapter). Each of the platforms we list in this section uses algorithms that filter and feed appropriate content to individual users based on their preferences and tastes. Using social media platforms (and their algorithms) for your marketing efforts allows you to target consumers who are likely to be interested in your products. This targeted marketing can lead to significant results through increased sales.

REMEMBER

As of this writing, the average consumer spends 2 hours and 23 minutes per day on social media. Promoting your licensed product through social media is a winning strategy!

You may be wondering which social media platform is the best choice for reaching your target audience. Choosing where to place your messaging also depends on the audience demographics your product appeals to. For a more detailed understanding of this amazing marketing tool, we recommend *Social Media Marketing For Dummies,* by Shiv Singh and Stephanie Diamond (Wiley), which can provide details for how to promote and sell your licensed products through social media.

Distinguishing Customers from Fans and Superfans

In marketing parlance, consumers are often referred to as *fans* — particularly when you're dealing with brands. The term *fan* used to refer specifically to someone who followed a certain sports team or celebrity. However, the advent of social media as a major source of mass communications and information has shifted the definition. Nowadays, a *fan* can be someone who favors a certain brand.

For example, Tide laundry detergent has fans, and so do Pillsbury products, Coca-Cola, and McDonalds. These fans consist simply of consumers whose preferences are specific to certain brands. If you're a Coca-Cola fan, you likely order Coke over Pepsi in a restaurant. A McDonalds fan will choose the McDonalds establishment over Burger King. This seemingly simplified way to refer to a consumer's brand preferences is actually a powerful reinforcement in the merchandising of licensed products.

Going from consumers to fans: The social media effect

In the world of pop culture, fandom has become obligatory. If you're passionate about a brand, you're a fan or superfan.

What shifted consumers to become fans? Social media! Social media has supercharged branding and, as a result, licensing. After consumers began communicating on social media, they found new friends and groups that they immediately related to because of their likes. These like-minded individuals formed groups open to other like-minded individuals to share their fandom with one another. This feature of social media democratized the business of branding and enabled everyday consumers to interact with and discuss their experiences with brands.

REMEMBER

After ordinary customers become fans of a brand, they're most likely to buy your licensed product with the brand on it, whether that's a Batman lunchbox, a New York Yankees jersey, or a Pillsbury Doughboy Halloween costume.

Sliding into superfandom

An even greater fan known as the *superfan* exists. Consumers with this moniker have very strong emotional ties to (and possibly obsessive admiration for) certain brands, to the point where they join brand fan groups. For example, did you know that the Pillsbury Doughboy has a significant fan club of superfans?

What's great for you as a marketer of licensed products is that these superfans belong to social media fan groups where you can post directly about your licensed products. The nature of the superfan suggests that they're also influencers for other superfans. And if they like your licensed product, they'll share this enthusiasm with other superfans.

Engaging with convention-al fandom

What was once a niche market for superfans — consumer fan conventions (*cons* for short) — has exploded since the early 2000s as a direct result of social media as a marketing tool.

The original fan convention for comic books was a small affair in NYC in 1964. In 1970, the San Diego Comic-Con was launched; by the early 2000s, it had become a pop-culture phenomenon with more than 150,000 attendees over 4 days. With the huge success of San Diego Comic-Con, more fan conventions began springing up across the United States and around the world.

This growth happened as a result of social media communications. Live events, festivals, and conventions continue to see significant growth as a direct result of both fandom and the post COVID-19 pandemic world, which embraces experiences over all else. Of course, along with that experience, fans need to have *merch* (merchandise) to *flex* (show off) their attendance.

TIP

Social media — combined with a celebration of fandom and a generation of consumer fans who celebrate experiences — means that you (as a licensee) have a major opportunity. Staying in step with the cons through savvy social media marketing of your licensed products increases your opportunity for sales and success.

Chapter **13**

Globalization of Brands

You can thank the advent of mass media and communications for the growth of brand licensing from its humble beginnings a century ago to its lofty status today. As brands learned to use advertising in print, radio, and then television, they began building the emotional connection between consumers and brands. The blossoming of motion pictures and the Internet (with its visual media components) further expanded the reach of branding into the multibillion-dollar business that it is now. Of course, the Internet also brought with it the revolution of brands going global.

In this chapter, we examine the opportunities of licensing into the global marketplace. You pick up a bit about the history of licensing in business dealings, discover some of the brands recognized worldwide, find out how to take advantage of international sales opportunities, and explore how to get help for recognizing trends that may make for global licensing opportunities.

America: Land of the Free, Home of the Brand

The concept of licensing in business dealings has a long history in the United States. The recipient of the first U.S. patent (Samuel Hopkins in 1790) also launched the first patent licensing program, in which he received acknowledgment and payment for use of his new process for making *potash* (a key ingredient in fertilizer).

But two very American industries took off at the start of the 20th century and are responsible for the huge success that brand licensing now enjoys more than 100 years later: the advertising business and Hollywood. A brief history of these two industries provides a better understanding of how the globalization of brand licensing has grown into today's $350 billion annual retail global licensing business.

Advertising builds brand recognition

The golden age of advertising began in the late 1800s, with an emphasis on branding products to appeal to consumers' emotions. This emphasis marked the beginning of *advertising agencies*, companies formed to create images and copy that would sell more products through brand recognition and consumer loyalty. Here are some factors that helped these ad agencies deliver the sought-after consumer attention:

» **Many new technological innovations became available to the masses.** Examples include electricity and the light bulb, the phonograph, the telephone, the automobile, the airplane, and moving pictures.

» **Disposable income became a reality.** Industrialization combined with fair labor practices through labor unions helped build a solid middle class. For the first time in history, these millions of consumers had disposable income to spend on branded goods.

» **Mass-media channels brought branded advertising to the consumers.** The radio in the 1920s and then TV in the 1950s were incredible tools that helped develop mass-media distribution, which in turn helped capture the imaginations and attention of consumers.

Hollywood adds scope

Disney's licensing of Mickey Mouse was really the start of today's multibillion-dollar-a-year entertainment brand licensing business. Since that little mouse, Hollywood has created an incredible ecosystem of movies, TV, music, video games, consumer products, experiences (such as brand extensions of Broadway plays like *Wicked* and restaurants like Bubba Gump), and retail. Think of how much entertainment started in the United States and transmitted globally: jazz, the blues, rock and roll. . . .

The United States bursts with brand power

With the expansion of the Internet in the early 21st century, globalization of pop culture happened at the press of a few keys. Fast forward to social media platforms and massive multiplayer video games, and the world gets much smaller. Fans from all over the world can use the Internet to share their fandom with one another; as a result, consumer appreciation for brands and entertainment spread.

Although most of today's massively licensed intellectual properties (IP) have their base in U.S. companies, some of the most highly licensed IP in the world are from Japan (Pokémon, Hello Kitty, and Super Mario), the United Kingdom (Paddington Bear and the Beatles), Australia (Bluey), and Mexico (Corona).

Based on information from *License Global* magazine (`www.licenseglobal.com`), 25 of the top 30 brand licensing companies as of February 2025 are U.S.-based. The 25 from the United States are

Authentic Brands Group	National Hockey League
Ford Motor Company	Nickelodeon (ViacomCBS)
General Motors	PGA Tour
Hasbro	Procter & Gamble
The Hershey Company (U.S.)	PVH Corp.
Iconix Brand Group (U.S.)	Ralph Lauren
Learfield IMG College (U.S.)	Sequential Brands Group
Major League Baseball (U.S.)	Stanley Black & Decker
Mattel (U.S.)	Sunkist Growers
Dotdash Meredith Corporation (U.S.)	Universal Brand Development
National Basketball Association	The Walt Disney Company
National Football League	WarnerMedia
	WWE

The remaining five of these largest licensors (not from the United States) are

BBC Worldwide (U.K.)	The Pokémon Company International (Japan)
Electrolux (Sweden)	Sanrio (Japan)
Ferrari (Italy)	

Setting Your Sights on the Global Market

Brands have truly gone global. As a licensee, you have the opportunity to take advantage of this globalization by finding great brands that translate to whatever market you're selling (or hoping to sell) your products in. If your product happens to be a big hit and you have exclusivity in your product category, you may very well end up selling your products globally.

Demand for your unique product may become so great that your retail partner asks to buy your products for its stores located outside the United States. Because of e-commerce, consumers from many markets can find and order your products online, even if you're not expecting consumers from that market. Here are some points to examine when faced with selling to a global market:

>> **Shipping internationally can be extremely costly and may not be practical for you.** However, if demand in certain markets is strong — for example, the United Kingdom and the European Union — you may have the opportunity to work with an overseas distributor or major retailer(s) in the markets that want your products. These partners can help manage the logistics and share the shipping-cost burden, making international expansion more feasible.

>> **If you're limited to selling in your domestic market but the international demand for your product is strong, you can negotiate additional distribution rights in these markets with your licensor.** Because licensors typically earn royalties from sales, they're often motivated to support you in expanding your distribution channels to maximize revenue.

COSTCO'S GLOBAL GROWTH LESSON

Costco operates more than 800 locations worldwide, with more than 250 of them outside the United States. This global footprint opens up huge opportunities for brands that perform well in U.S. stores.

Take the case of the Miracle-Gro garden tool toy set for kids. It was a hit in U.S. Costco locations, flying off the shelves. Seeing its success, Costco wanted to roll it out globally.

Here's the catch: The licensee, Red Toolbox, had only the U.S. rights to the Miracle-Gro brand. To meet Costco's demand, Red Toolbox had to secure global licensing rights, proving how a single retailer's international reach can drive major business decisions.

The takeaway is that if your licensed product performs well in the United States, be ready to think bigger. Global licensing success may be just around the corner!

Responding to global demand for a unique product

As a result of globalization of brands, the demand for licensed products continues to grow. If you have a unique licensed product, you may find that viral social media marketing has created global demand for it.

The issue you face in this situation is that your licensing contract stipulates your areas for geographic distribution. You can resolve this issue with an amendment to your contract. This conversation should be straightforward, especially if your product is unique. After all, the licensor has the same goal as you: to keep consumers happy and see the licensed business flourish. However, if you're selling common products such as socks or backpacks, attempting to secure the license for international markets won't be so easy because the local markets may already have a licensee in place.

An example of a unique licensed product line that went global is ZURU Toys (see the nearby sidebar, "Tiny toys, huge impact").

REMEMBER

Entering international markets introduces challenges like language barriers and government regulations on ingredients and packaging. If you're new to global sales, understanding these differences and preparing accordingly is crucial.

TINY TOYS, HUGE IMPACT

ZURU, a dynamic toy company, created a unique product line called Mini Brands — tiny, detailed replicas of popular household items like Dove soap, Breyers ice cream, and Campbell's soup. To produce these miniature marvels, ZURU secured global licensing agreements with major companies, ensuring each mini was an authentic replica of the real product.

The result? Mini Brands became a global sensation, captivating collectors and enthusiasts worldwide. The craze took TikTok by storm, with over 5 billion posts showcasing creative unboxing, trading, and customization of these collectible toys. This social media buzz significantly contributed to the toys' global popularity and catapulted ZURU into the ranks of the top ten toy companies globally, showcasing the power of innovative products combined with strategic licensing. By blending creativity with authentic branding, ZURU demonstrated how unique concepts can achieve international acclaim through effective global licensing.

Dissecting the size and scope of the global marketplace

Imagining your business going global can certainly be attractive, and understanding the markets you'll be selling into is important. As more and more emerging countries experience economic growth, disposable income in these markets also continues to grow. When you combine this fact with the popularity of Western brands and culture in the marketplace, the opportunities for expanding the sales of your licensed products outside the United States have never been greater.

According to the most recent research from global trade association Licensing International (www.licensinginternational.org), in 2023, the global licensing market was estimated to make up $337.61 billion in retail dollars with a *compound annual growth rate* (CAGR, the rate of return needed to grow from beginning to ending balances) of 4.3 percent. This growth rate, if sustained, can increase the global licensing market to be worth $511.89 billion in retail dollars by 2032.

Here are the major geographic markets and their current and projected market shares that make up the global licensing market as of this writing:

>> **North America** held the major market share with more than 40 percent of the global retail licensing revenue and is expected to grow at a CAGR of 2.7 percent from 2024 to 2032.

>> **Europe** accounted for a market share of more than 30 percent of the global retail licensing revenue with a predicted 3.65 percent CAGR from 2024 to 2032.

>> **Asia Pacific** held a market share of around 23 percent of the global retail licensing revenue in 2023 and is expected to grow at a CAGR of 6.5 percent from 2024 to 2032.

>> **Latin America** had a market share of more than 5 percent of the global revenue in 2023 and is predicted to grow at a compound annual growth rate (CAGR) of 3.9 percent from 2024 to 2032.

>> **Middle East and Africa** had a market share of around 2 percent of the global licensing revenue and is projected to grow at a CAGR of 4.2 percent from 2024 to 2032.

Securing Licenses for International Markets

Given the growth rate of the global brand licensing market (see the preceding section), a significant opportunity clearly exists for you as a licensee to expand beyond your U.S. distribution and grow your licensed products into new global markets.

But to accomplish international expansion, you need to have certain business instruments in place. For example, you must

>> Establish your licensing business and show success in your domestic market.

>> Have strong retail relationships with global retailers that can expand your distribution globally.

>> Have global distributors ready to sell your products in your new international territories.

REMEMBER

Retail relationships are critical for selling licensed products. If you can secure a relationship with major global retailers that want you to expand your distribution globally, this external interest can be a compelling factor in convincing your licensor to grant you these additional territory rights.

Globalization of retail businesses

As a result of globalization, retail business has consolidated product distribution with such global retailers as Walmart, Amazon, Ikea, Alibaba, Tesco, Uniqlo, Zara, H&M — the list goes on.

All these retailers have one thing in common: They sell licensed merchandise. This global status means that if your licensed product sells well at Walmart in the United States, for example, the company may want to extend your contract to sell the product to Walmart establishments in Canada, Mexico and Latin America, China, and the United Kingdom. This path is one way in which licensees can go global. And remember, all these physical retailers have online presences where they sell your products as well.

SUBLICENSING IN ACTION: HASBRO AND STAR WARS

Hasbro holds the *master* toy license for the Star Wars franchise, allowing the company to produce a wide range of Star Wars-themed toys and games. However, for specialized products that fall outside its core manufacturing capabilities, such as a unique toy robot, Hasbro has the option to sublicense these rights to other companies. By doing so, Hasbro ensures that a diverse array of Star Wars merchandise reaches the market, catering to even niche or specialized consumer interests while maintaining brand consistency.

Remember: When Hasbro grants a sublicense, it remains fully responsible for all contractual obligations outlined in its original agreement with the licensor.

Sublicensing

REMEMBER

When negotiating your licensing agreement (see Chapter 6), ensuring it addresses your ability to *sublicense* — to grant your licensed rights to another company — can be particularly advantageous if you encounter opportunities to sell your product in markets where you don't currently have distribution channels.

By sublicensing to a local distributor, you can effectively expand your reach without directly managing operations in those regions. However, confirming that your original licensing agreement permits sublicensing and carefully structuring any sublicensing agreements are crucial to protect your interests and comply with the terms set by the original licensor.

The nearby sidebar, "Sublicensing in action: Hasbro and Star Wars," is a great example of how Hasbro, the master toy licensee for Star Wars, was able to sublicense Star Wars for a unique toy robot.

Finding global properties

In the section "The United States bursts with brand power" earlier in the chapter, we point out that 25 of the top 30 licensors in the world are from the United States. As a licensee, you can run into a lot of competition with other licensees to secure licenses with these major U.S. licensors.

Looking at a global IP phenomenon

Some intellectual properties (IPs) come from international markets and also become huge global hits, like Pokémon or Hello Kitty from Japan. Before 1996, no one had ever heard of Pokémon, which started its life that year as a trading card game in Japan. Then Pokémon came to the United States in 1998, and today, the Pokémon franchise is the highest-grossing media franchise in the world — and its licensed merchandise is a major contributor to its success.

In 2023, the Pokémon Company generated $10.8 billion from licensed goods, which brought the franchise's lifetime revenue from merchandising alone to $102.9 billion. Suppose you were the young new licensee that had taken a chance on Pokémon in 1998; what a coup that would've been!

TIP

So how do you discover promising IP? Table 13-1, which gives you a look at the all-time earnings achieved by leading media franchises, is a great start.

TABLE 13-1   **Licensing Revenue for Media Franchises**

Media Franchise	Total Estimated Revenue	Merchandise Revenue
Pokémon	$147.0 billion	$102.9 billion
Hello Kitty	$89.0 billion	$88.5 billion
Winnie the Pooh	$76.0 billion	$76.2 billion
Mickey Mouse & Friends	$74.0 billion	$73.4 billion
Star Wars	$70.0 billion	$42.2 billion
Anpanman	$56.0 billion	$56.4 billion
Disney Princess	$46.0 billion	$46.3 billion
Jump Comics (Shōnen Jump)	$40.0 billion	-
Mario	$38.0 billion	$4.3 billion
Marvel Cinematic Universe (MCU)	$35.0 billion	$12.5 billion
Harry Potter	$32.0 billion	$12.3 billion
Transformers	$30.0 billion	$12.2 billion
Spider-Man	$29.0 billion	$15.9 billion
Batman	$28.0 billion	$21.3 billion
Dragon Ball	$27.0 billion	$7.7 billion
Gundam	$26.9 billion	$26.4 billion
Barbie*	$24.7 billion	$22.7 billion

*Barbie revenue doesn't include revenue from the 2023 movie, Barbie. Table condensed from information found at www.visualcapitalist.com/the-worlds-top-media-franchises-by-all-time-revenue/

Recognizing popular trends related to IP

Being a strategically inclined licensee that understands the global marketplace can help differentiate you from your competitors. No matter what brands you're licensing — whether they're entertainment, food and beverage, automotive, fashion, art, or whatever — staying up to date on what's trending in popular culture is critical.

TIP

Licensed products can do well based on trends in pop culture. Much of your success in licensing will be based on your ability to understand trends before they become *mainstream* (that is, regarded as normal or conventional).

As a savvy licensee, you need to have someone on your team who can be your trend hunter. If you have time and are steeped in all things pop culture, great. As a new licensee launching your licensing business, though, you likely won't have the time to stay tuned in to all popular trends. But you can onboard a consultant that specializes in trend spotting, and (as we discuss in Chapters 5 and 6) a licensing consultant can offer fabulous assistance as you grow your business.

REMEMBER

Even with an exceptional consultant, predicting the next pop-culture phenomenon remains challenging. Although future advancements in artificial intelligence may reduce uncertainty, trend-spotting today is still more of an art than a science.

Chapter **14**

The Future of Brand Licensing

B rand licensing is built on a simple idea: Popular brands sell. Consumers naturally trust well-known names, making licensing a smart and cost-effective way for companies to expand their product lines and boost revenue. Instead of spending time and money building a brand from scratch (which can be expensive and risky), businesses can tap into established brands that already have loyal fans. This approach has fueled the rapid growth of licensing — and it's only getting bigger.

So what's next for brand licensing? No one has a crystal ball, but one thing is certain: Change is constant. Licensing has evolved alongside shifts in technology, retail, and consumer habits. As you look ahead, new innovations and emerging trends will drive even more opportunities.

Brand licensing is still going strong, with enormous growth potential ahead. Since 2000, the world has seen digital commerce explode, consumer expectations shift, and technology reshape the way brands connect with their audiences. Licensing is all about tapping into consumer emotions, and as society evolves, so do the brands people love.

In this chapter, we explore the current and emerging trends in brand licensing and how they may shape the field's future.

Learning from the Past to Predict the Future

History often gives the best clues about what's coming next, so studying past trends can help you understand where licensing is headed. The major forces shaping the industry fall into four key categories:

>> **Technology:** The rise of e-commerce, social media, streaming platforms, and digital goods has revolutionized how brands connect with consumers. Licensing is no longer limited to physical products; virtual and interactive brand experiences are taking off.

>> **Regulations and business policies:** Trade agreements, intellectual property (IP) laws, and regulatory shifts like the legalization of cannabis have influenced brand licensing opportunities and restrictions.

>> **Environmental factors:** Sustainability efforts, climate concerns, and supply chain disruptions have forced brands to rethink how they manufacture and distribute licensed products.

>> **Consumer trends and cultural shifts:** Nostalgia-driven products, experiential brands, and the influence of younger generations (Gen Z and millennials) are shaping what consumers want and how they engage with brands.

By keeping an eye on these trends, licensors and licensees can stay ahead of the curve and make informed decisions about the future of brand licensing.

Riding the Technology Wave

Technology is the biggest game-changer in licensing. From the rise of the Internet to artificial intelligence (AI) and digital assets like cryptocurrencies, technology continues to redefine how consumers interact with brands.

Video game technology has also played a major role in shaping licensing opportunities. With advancements in graphics, augmented reality (AR), and virtual reality (VR), gaming has evolved into a powerful platform for branded content. Brands are now integrating their products directly into video games, offering exclusive digital merchandise, character skins, and in-game experiences. Video game sales have now surpassed global movie box office revenues, making gaming one of the most lucrative entertainment industries today.

Major sports leagues like Major League Baseball (MLB) and the National Basketball Association (NBA) have also embraced digital advancements, allowing fans to buy their favorite team's apparel, jerseys, and memorabilia faster than ever through e-commerce and direct-to-consumer (DTC) platforms. Whether it's that championship hat or a game-worn collectible, technology has made sports merchandise more accessible, with faster shipping, exclusive drops, and even blockchain-backed authentication for rare items.

Today, consumers expect instant access to their favorite brands, and licensing thrives in this environment. With just a click, customers can discover, engage with, and purchase branded products. Table 14-1 breaks down the key tech trends shaping licensing today and in the future.

TABLE 14-1   **Technology Trends Impacting Licensing**

Tech Innovation	Examples	Impact on Licensing
AI and machine learning	ChatGPT, CoPilot	AI is transforming licensing by automating research, generating creative assets, and even developing entirely new intellectual properties. AI-driven analytics help brands predict consumer trends, optimize marketing strategies, and streamline content creation, making licensing faster and more cost-effective than ever.
Social media platforms	Facebook, Instagram, TikTok	These platforms have become critical for brand engagement, influencer marketing, and direct commerce. Brands leverage influencers to promote licensed products, run targeted ad campaigns, and drive viral engagement. Social media also allows for interactive experiences, such as AR filters featuring licensed characters or products, enhancing consumer connection.
E-commerce and social commerce	Amazon, Target, Shopify	Online shopping has revolutionized the licensing landscape by making products instantly available to a global audience. Direct-to-consumer models enable brands to bypass traditional retail, while *social commerce* — where consumers buy directly from platforms like Instagram or TikTok — allows for seamless, integrated shopping experiences that boost licensed product sales.
Delivery and transportation services	DoorDash, Uber	Convenience is king, and brands are taking advantage by integrating licensing into food delivery, ride-sharing, and package shipping services. Limited-edition branded packaging, promotional licensing tie-ins, and exclusive product drops through these platforms are creating new revenue streams and enhancing the reach of licensed products.
Gaming and esports	Fortnite, Minecraft	Gaming has emerged as a major licensing frontier, allowing brands to introduce virtual goods, exclusive in-game items, and branded character skins. Esports leagues also offer lucrative licensing deals, with official team jerseys, branded gaming accessories, and live-event merchandise becoming hot commodities for fans and players alike.
Streaming and content platforms	Netflix, Hulu, YouTube	These platforms don't just distribute content; they create new, highly desirable brands that fuel the licensing industry. Hit shows and movies generate demand for merchandise, collectibles, and even experiential licensing opportunities. Streaming services have become incubators for fresh IP, with fan-favorite series spawning licensed apparel, toys, and themed attractions.

Examining Emerging Tech Shaping Licensing

Technology isn't just enhancing licensing; it's redefining it. The next wave of innovation is creating new ways for brands to connect with consumers, from AI-powered virtual influencers to blockchain-backed ownership of digital assets. Here's a deeper dive into the most exciting emerging technologies transforming the licensing industry.

AI-generated brands and IP

Artificial intelligence is no longer just a behind-the-scenes tool; it's creating entirely new brands, products, and intellectual property (IP). AI-generated content, from music to artwork to written stories, is opening up fresh licensing opportunities in entertainment, fashion, and digital media. For example,

>> AI-powered design tools allow companies to generate thousands of product variations instantly, reducing the need for manual design work.

>> AI-driven storytelling tools can produce automated scripts and books, potentially creating new franchise-worthy characters and worlds.

WARNING

Current trademark laws don't protect AI-generated content, meaning that licensing these works to others may present legal challenges until clearer regulations are established.

Blockchain and NFTs: The future of digital ownership

Though the hype around non-fungible tokens (NFTs; see Chapter 4) has cooled, blockchain technology is still revolutionizing licensing by providing a way to authenticate, track, and manage digital ownership. Here are some examples:

>> Brands like Nike (with Cryptokicks) and Adidas (with NFT sneaker drops) are using blockchain to authenticate limited-edition products.

>> Digital artists and content creators are licensing their work as NFTs, ensuring they receive royalties from secondary sales.

>> Video games and sports leagues are integrating blockchain-based collectibles, such as NBA Top Shot and Sorare's licensed fantasy football cards.

REMEMBER

Blockchain provides a secure way to manage IP rights, reduce counterfeiting, and create new revenue streams from digital collectibles.

Virtual goods and the metaverse: Licensing in a digital world

As more people spend time in digital spaces, virtual goods are becoming a massive licensing opportunity. Brands are cashing in by selling virtual clothing, accessories, and collectibles inside metaverse platforms like Roblox, Fortnite, and Decentraland. For example,

>> Luxury brands like Gucci and Balenciaga have launched virtual fashion collections in games and on metaverse platforms.

>> Nike's acquisition of RTFKT shows how major brands are investing in virtual sneakers and apparel.

>> Musicians like Travis Scott and Ariana Grande have hosted concerts inside Fortnite, selling virtual merchandise alongside digital experiences.

Print-on-demand (POD)

Print-on-demand is changing the way brands manufacture products. Instead of producing large quantities of inventory that may not sell, brands can now create customized, on-demand products based on actual consumer purchases. This approach reduces waste, cuts storage costs, and makes licensing more efficient than ever. It's a low risk method to offer licensed products. Here are some retailers getting in on the POD game:

>> **Etsy and Redbubble:** These sites allow artists to license their designs and sell them on a range of products, from T-shirts to coffee mugs.

>> **Amazon Merch and Printful:** These retailers let brands launch apparel and merchandise without upfront investment.

>> **Walmart and Target:** Traditional retailers are adopting POD for exclusive collaborations and seasonal drops.

Smartphones and apps: The mobile licensing revolution

Your smartphone isn't just for making calls. It's a shopping mall, entertainment center, and banking tool all in one. Brands are leveraging apps to drive digital licensing opportunities and engage consumers in new ways:

>> **Retail:** Apps like Nike SNKRS and Adidas's Confirmed offer limited-edition drops and exclusive licensed merchandise.

>> **Streaming:** Apps like Disney+ and HBO Max link directly to e-commerce stores selling show-related licensed products.

>> **Gaming:** Apps like Pokémon GO and Fortnite integrate branded in-app purchases, expanding licensing beyond physical products.

REMEMBER

The future of licensing is in the palm of your hand. Mobile apps are making it easier than ever for consumers to engage with brands and buy licensed products instantly.

Culture Meets Commerce: Seeing How Trends Shape Licensing

Brand licensing doesn't exist in a vacuum. It's shaped by the culture around it. From shifting consumer preferences to evolving shopping habits, cultural trends play a huge role in how brands expand into new markets and create fresh opportunities for licensed products.

In today's hyper-connected world, brands must stay ahead of cultural movements to remain relevant. Whether it's nostalgia for past decades, the rise of socially conscious shopping, or the explosive growth of fan-driven content, cultural trends drive demand for new products, collaborations, and experiences.

To better understand how these shifts impact licensing, we explore two key areas in the following sections: business trends that change how brands operate and cultural trends that influence what consumers want.

TIP

Understanding cultural and business trends helps brands create licensing strategies that feel fresh, relevant, and profitable. Staying ahead of these shifts ensures that brands remain competitive in an ever-evolving marketplace.

Business trends: The changing landscape of licensing

In the past 25 years, brand licensing has seen explosive growth as a result of the Internet, the globalization of brands, e-commerce, and targeted marketing through social media platforms. This growth has spawned the creation of new companies that have expanded the world of licensing by taking advantage of *brand equity* (the commercial value that derives from a brand's name). These companies buy well-known brands that are financially distressed and refocus them to be purely licensed.

Tracking the rise of licensing holding companies

Traditionally, brands manufactured their own products and handled distribution. Today, licensing holding companies like Authentic Brands Group, WHP Global, Marquee Brands, and others acquire multiple brands (intellectual properties) and license them out to third-party manufacturers. This model reduces the risks associated with manufacturing and sales and allows these owners of multiple brands to focus on expanding their licensing programs. By managing well-known names like Reebok, Martha Stewart, and Toys"R"Us, these holding companies play a crucial role in shaping the licensing industry, driving brand expansion, and creating new revenue streams across multiple consumer categories.

Bringing dead brands back to life

Not all brands fade away when they go out of business. Some companies specialize in reviving once-iconic brands that have gone bankrupt and closed their stores. Retailers like Sharper Image, Barneys, and Forever 21 may have disappeared from malls, but their brand names still carry strong recognition. Licensing companies purchase these brands and reintroduce them to the market through new licensing agreements. Instead of operating traditional brick-and-mortar stores, these *zombie* brands (see Chapter 3) live on through e-commerce, specialty retail partnerships, and branded product lines. This strategy not only gives beloved brands a second life but also allows licensors to capitalize on the built-in nostalgia and trust associated with well-known names.

Dealing with direct-to-retail (DTR) partnerships

Many brands are now bypassing traditional licensee manufacturers and forming *direct-to-retail* (DTR) partnerships with major retailers, where the retailer becomes the licensee. This approach gives retailers greater control over product development, pricing, and retail placement while allowing brands to maintain a strong presence in key retail environments.

For example, Better Homes and Gardens has an exclusive DTR deal with Walmart, ensuring a consistent stream of licensed products in stores without relying on third-party intermediaries. Target has built a successful DTR relationship with Magnolia, the lifestyle brand created by Chip and Joanna Gaines, which now boasts over 500 products in home décor, furniture, and accessories. Even grocery retailers are leveraging DTR agreements; Safeway licensed the Looney Tunes characters directly for its Eating Right Kids private-label line of healthy foods.

These DTR partnerships streamline the licensing process, allowing brands and retailers to collaborate more closely on pricing, design, and marketing. More importantly, they provide retailers with exclusive product lines that enhance brand differentiation and drive foot traffic, giving them a competitive edge in an increasingly consolidated retail landscape.

The off-price boom: Licensing for discount retailers

Although some traditional department stores have struggled, off-price retailers like TJX Companies (owner of T.J. Maxx, Marshalls, and HomeGoods) are thriving. With more than 5,000 locations worldwide, these retailers provide a huge marketplace for excess and discounted licensed goods. In times of economic uncertainty, consumers turn to these retailers for branded products at lower prices. This tendency makes off-price channels a major growth area for licensing deals, allowing brands to reach budget-conscious shoppers while clearing out surplus inventory.

Retail consolidation: Working with fewer but bigger players

REMEMBER

As department stores disappear, a handful of mega-retailers dominate the landscape. Walmart, Target, and Amazon now control a significant share of retail sales, limiting the number of potential outlets for licensed products. Brands that once relied on smaller specialty retailers must now adapt their licensing strategies to fit within fewer, but much larger, retail ecosystems. This consolidation forces licensors to negotiate on different terms, sometimes making exclusivity deals with major retailers a necessity.

The sharing economy: Branding beyond products

The traditional retail model is no longer the only way to monetize a brand. Companies like Airbnb, Uber, and WeWork have introduced new business models where branding is about experience rather than product ownership. Airbnb licenses out themed vacation rentals, while Uber collaborates with brands for promotional campaigns.

BRAND RECOGNITION: MACY'S BECOMES A NATIONAL DEPARTMENT STORE CONSOLIDATOR

Macy's has grown ever since the late 1990s from a regional department store to the largest department store in the United States. It did so by acquiring. Here are some of the department store companies Macy's acquired (ask your parents and grandparents whether they remember these stores):

- May
- Famous-Barr
- Kaufmann's
- Meier & Frank
- L.S. Ayres
- Robinsons-May
- Hecht's
- Filene's

- Rich's
- Marshall Field's
- The Jones Store
- Lazarus
- Foley's
- A&S (Abraham & Straus)
- Strawbridge's
- Burdines

The rise of this *sharing economy* is creating new licensing opportunities beyond physical merchandise — think branded co-working spaces, pop-up hospitality experiences, and travel collaborations.

Cultural trends: What consumers want now

The growth of licensing in the last 25 years has been concurrent with the most major cultural shift to happen since the printing press — that is, the shift from an analog to a digital world with the Internet being at the center. This fast-paced shift has caused a great deal of disruption, which, in turn, has led to new technologies and ways to communicate while also creating anxieties among consumers. Added to the technological anxieties are also environmental ones like climate change and a two-year-long global pandemic, which has also destabilized the political landscape of many nations. The result has been a boom for brand licensing. Consumers look to well-known and trusted brands as an anchor in a constant sea change environment.

Beyond just products, consumers today are also seeking ways to experience the brands they know and trust. In other words, the fear and anxiety of so much change is driving consumers to seek out immediate gratification through trusted brand experiences as well as products. The following sections provide some examples of significant growth areas of brand licensing.

Food, health, and lifestyle licensing

Consumers today want more than just a product; they want an experience. This shift has led to a boom in food, health, and lifestyle licensing.

>> **Food and beverage collaborations:** Some of the most viral brand partnerships happen in the food industry. Unexpected mashups like Post Malone X Oreos or Doritos Locos Tacos create buzz, drive sales, and introduce brands to new audiences. These collaborations allow nonfood brands to enter the culinary space in exciting and limited-edition ways.

>> **Fusion cuisine and global flavors:** The rise of hybrid foods — such as sushi burritos, Greek quesadillas, and birria ramen — has transformed the culinary landscape, creating exciting opportunities for restaurant and chef-branded licensing. Consumers are increasingly seeking globally inspired flavors and restaurant-quality experiences at home, driving demand for branded spice blends, meal kits, and frozen food products in grocery stores.

Celebrity chefs and restaurant chains are capitalizing on this trend by partnering with food brands to extend their reach beyond restaurant dining. Notable examples include the following:

- **Zahav,** the acclaimed Philadelphia-based Israeli restaurant founded by chef Michael Solomonov, now sells branded hummus at Whole Foods, bringing its award-winning flavors to a wider audience.

- **Momofuku,** founded by David Chang, has successfully expanded into grocery with a range of branded products, including chili crunch, instant noodles, and seasonings, allowing fans to recreate the restaurant's signature flavors at home.

>> **Health and wellness:** The demand for wellness products is surging, from Wegovy for weight loss to branded dietary supplements. Consumers are more focused than ever on self-care, and brands that emphasize health are seeing massive licensing success. From fitness influencers launching their own protein powders to pharmaceutical brands expanding into wellness, this trend isn't slowing down. For many years, Weight Watchers (now WW) had a licensing program featuring a range of fully branded Weight Watchers food

products. Additionally, brands are leveraging licensing to boost appeal and sales. Nutrabolt's C4 energy drinks have successfully licensed in nostalgic flavors like Popsicle and Jolly Rancher, attracting both fitness enthusiasts and mainstream consumers.

Entertainment and media: From screen to shelf

Hollywood and digital media have always been licensing goldmines, and today's entertainment landscape is bigger than ever. Consider the following:

>> **Franchise films:** Blockbusters like Marvel movies, *Star Wars,* and the *Minions* series drive enormous merchandise sales. Licensing extends beyond toys into apparel, gaming, and even themed travel experiences.

>> **Adult animation:** Shows like *The Simpsons, South Park, and Bob's Burgers* have proven that animated brands can generate billions in licensed merchandise. Collectibles, apparel, and home goods featuring these properties continue to sell well across multiple generations of fans.

>> **Reality TV licensing:** Global hits like *American Ninja Warrior, The Voice,* and *The Real Housewives* shows offer licensing opportunities that extend into fashion, fitness, and home goods. As streaming services launch new reality formats, the demand for show-branded products continues to grow.

>> **Women's pro sports:** The success of the WNBA and NWSL is creating new opportunities in licensed sports apparel and merchandise. As more leagues gain mainstream popularity, the demand for branded gear is rising.

BRINGING AMERICAN NINJA WARRIOR TO FANS

Since 2009, *American Ninja Warrior* has captivated audiences, showcasing thrilling extreme obstacle courses. Recognizing the brand's appeal, Seltzer Licensing Group facilitated a licensing deal with a gym operator, leading to the creation of multiple officially licensed *American Ninja Warrior* adventure parks.

These parks bring the excitement of the show to life, featuring the same challenging obstacles that contestants face on TV. Whether for kids, adults, or aspiring competitors, the parks offer an interactive experience where fans can test their agility, strength, and endurance — just like the warriors on the show.

Fandom and experiential licensing: The age of immersion

Consumers today don't just want to buy a brand; they want to live it. Experiential branding is taking over, driving huge licensing success. Here are some examples:

>> **Experiential licensing:** Pop-up experiences, interactive museum exhibits, and festivals (the FRIENDS Experience, the Firelight Even [a *Gilmore Girls* fan festival], Anime Expo, and New York Comic Con to name just a few) offer fans a chance to immerse themselves in their favorite brands. These events generate significant revenue through ticket sales and exclusive merchandise.

>> **Geek culture and kidults:** Adults have become the biggest buyers of toys, comics, and video game memorabilia, driving the explosive growth of fandom-driven licensing. What was once considered niche geek culture is now firmly mainstream, with demand soaring for collectibles, high-end action figures, themed apparel, and immersive experiences. As franchises expand into streaming, merchandise, and live events, this *kidult* market continues to be a major force in licensing. For a firsthand look at this phenomenon, visit a comic convention like New York Comic Con or San Diego Comic-Con, where more than 200,000 passionate fans gather to celebrate their favorite franchises and experience the latest in pop-culture licensing.

>> **Nostalgia resurgence:** Brands from the 1990s and early 2000s are making a comeback. Rereleased classic toys, vintage logo apparel, and retro food brands are experiencing renewed popularity, proving that nostalgia is a powerful driver of licensing success. This trend is fueled by parents who want to share their favorite childhood brands with their own kids, creating a multigenerational appeal that strengthens brand loyalty and keeps classic franchises relevant for new audiences.

>> **Streetwear and athleisure:** The blending of luxury, sports, and street fashion has created highly lucrative licensing collaborations. Brands like Supreme and Kith regularly partner with musicians, athletes, and entertainment franchises to create must-have limited-edition products.

5

The Part of Tens

IN THIS PART . . .

Avoid rough spots with tips for licensing success.

Check out the licensor side of the coin.

Examine various popular licensing categories.

Chapter **15**

Ten Do's (and Don'ts) for Licensing

Done right, brand licensing can be a powerful tool for growth when. By following these suggestions, you're well on your way to creating successful, profitable licensing partnerships.

REMEMBER

Success in licensing is all about strategy, strong relationships, and delivering lasting value to both the brand and the consumer.

Do Thorough Research on the Brand Opportunity

Before signing any licensing deal, take the time to thoroughly research the brand and its owner (licensor). What does the brand stand for? Who's its target audience? What's its personality? Understanding these core elements helps you maintain brand consistency and authenticity, ensuring your product aligns with the brand's identity and resonates with its existing customer base.

Conduct comprehensive market research before committing to any property. Key questions to consider include the following:

>> **Who else is licensing this brand?** Strong partnerships with reputable licensees can signal a healthy licensing ecosystem.

>> **What retailers currently carry products under this brand?** Established retail relationships can ease the path to market.

>> **Does the brand have a loyal customer base, or is it just riding a fleeting trend?** Sustainable brands have consistent consumer engagement beyond short-lived hype.

Don't get swept away by a flashy presentation or promises of instant success. A slick pitch doesn't guarantee a profitable partnership. Licensing decisions should be based on data and strategic alignment, not just enthusiasm.

Also don't assume that a popular brand automatically guarantees sales. Success comes from thoughtful alignment, not just brand recognition. A mismatched product can confuse consumers, dilute the brand's value, and damage both your and the licensor's reputation.

Do Plan Properly

Effective planning is the foundation of a successful licensing venture. Accurate timelines are critical to ensure smooth product development, timely approvals, efficient manufacturing, and on-schedule distribution. Always factor in buffer time for unexpected delays, especially when dealing with licensors who may have stringent approval processes.

Planning proactively helps you stay ahead of potential roadblocks and ensures your product reaches the market at the right time. Consider key milestones such as these:

>> **Product development:** From initial concepts to final designs, allow time for revisions and adjustments.

>> **Licensor approvals:** Licensors often require multiple review stages, which can significantly extend timelines.

>> **Manufacturing and production:** Lead times vary depending on product complexity and supplier capacity.

>> **Distribution:** Account for shipping, customs, and logistical challenges, especially for international markets.

Don't underestimate how long securing licensor approvals or getting your product onto retail shelves takes. Missed deadlines, particularly for seasonal launches or promotional events, can result in lost sales opportunities and strained relationships with retail partners.

Do Set Realistic Financial Expectations

When entering licensing negotiations, your financial expectations need to be realistic. Know what you're willing to pay for a license and approach negotiations with a focus on value, not just cost savings. Understand the market, the brand's worth, and how the brand aligns with your business goals.

Consider factors such as the brand's market potential, *incremental sales* (in other words, how much adding a brand license will increase the sales of your product versus if your product is generic), and the cost structure involved in bringing the licensed product to market. Having a clear financial plan helps you negotiate effectively without overextending your resources.

REMEMBER

A well-negotiated deal isn't just about the lowest price; it's about creating a win-win scenario that benefits both parties and sets the stage for long-term success.

Do Walk Away from Bad Deals

Not every licensing opportunity is the right fit, no matter how tempting it may seem. If negotiations drag on without progress, or if the terms are unfavorable — such as high minimum guarantees, restrictive territories, or unfavorable manufacturing and distribution clauses — trust your instincts and be prepared to walk away.

Sometimes, the allure of securing a hot property can cloud judgment, especially if you're under pressure from a retail partner eager for the next big thing. However, forcing a deal that doesn't align with your business model can lead to financial pressure, operational headaches, and long-term regret.

Don't get caught up in the hype. No matter how popular a brand is, if the deal requires you to overpay, limits your business flexibility, or imposes unreasonable demands, it's not worth the risk. Licensing is a long game, and other opportunities will always be around the corner. Waiting for a deal that fits your strategic goals is better than compromising on terms that don't serve your business's best interests.

REMEMBER

Walking away from a bad deal is a sign of strength, not failure. It shows you're committed to making smart, sustainable decisions for your company's future.

Do Leverage the Licensor's Marketing Power

One of the biggest advantages of brand licensing is tapping into the licensor's marketing muscle. As we explain in Chapter 12, many licensors have well-established marketing channels, campaigns, and relationships that can give your product a significant boost.

Collaborate with your licensor to amplify your product's visibility by doing things like the following:

>> Participating in co-branded marketing campaigns that showcase your product alongside other licensed goods

>> Taking advantage of the licensor's social media presence to reach a wider audience

>> Using the promotional materials and brand assets the licensor provides, which maintains consistency and credibility

Your licensor wants your product to succeed; after all, it reflects on the brand too. Open communication and joint marketing efforts can create powerful synergies that benefit both parties.

Don't operate in isolation. Ignoring the licensor's marketing opportunities means missing out on valuable brand equity, established consumer trust, and promotional resources that can drive sales. Working together makes your brand licensing efforts stronger, more visible, and ultimately more successful.

Do Build Strong Relationships

Brand licensing is more than just signing contracts. It's about building strong, lasting relationships with licensors, other licensees, and retailers. Robust partnerships are the foundation of long-term success.

Invest time in nurturing these relationships. Regular communication, transparency, and mutual respect go a long way. Build trust by being reliable, responsive, and proactive. When issues arise (and they will), strong relationships help you navigate challenges more effectively.

TIP

Think of licensing as a marathon, not a sprint. The relationships you build today can open doors to new opportunities down the road.

Don't treat licensing as a one-and-done transaction. A short-term, transactional mindset can limit growth and damage future opportunities. Licensing is an ecosystem where collaboration and partnership drive success. Focusing on relationships ensures you're in it for the long haul.

Do Stay Compliant with Licensing Agreements

Compliance isn't optional in brand licensing. Your licensing agreement is more than just a contract; it's a roadmap for maintaining a strong, trustworthy partnership with your licensor. Always adhere to the terms of your licensing agreement, including

>> Submitting products for approval before they hit the market (which we cover in Chapter 7).

>> Reporting sales accurately and paying royalties on time (Chapter 10).

>> Complying with factory audit requirements and providing necessary reports (also Chapter 10).

Following these guidelines not only keeps you in good standing with the licensor but also helps build long-term trust and credibility within the industry.

Don't cut corners on compliance. Late royalty payments, unauthorized product modifications, or ignoring factory audit requirements can damage your reputation, compromise relationships, and even lead to legal trouble. Plus, noncompliance can result in added costs, penalties, or the loss of your licensing rights altogether.

Do Invest in Quality Legal Support

In brand licensing, having the right legal support is critical. Hire experienced intellectual property (IP) attorneys who specialize in licensing deals. Their expertise can help you navigate complex contracts, avoid costly mistakes, and secure favorable terms.

The old adage "You get what you pay for" couldn't be truer. A top-notch IP attorney ensures your licensing agreements are airtight, protecting your interests and minimizing legal risks. They can identify potential pitfalls in contract language that you may not notice otherwise, which saves you from headaches down the line.

Don't skimp on legal fees. Although saving money upfront may be tempting, the right legal advice will pay off in the long run. Poorly negotiated contracts or overlooked details can lead to disputes, financial losses, and even legal battles. Investing in quality legal support ensures your deals are sound, your interests are protected, and your licensing journey is set up for success.

Do Consider Hiring a Licensing Consultant

Working with a trusted licensing consultant (see Chapter 5) can provide valuable insights and strategic guidance. The best consultants have

>> **Extensive industry experience:** A seasoned consultant knows the ins and outs of the licensing landscape, from evaluating brand fit to negotiating favorable terms.

>> **Strong networks:** Your consultant can connect you with key industry players.

>> **A deep understanding of licensing dynamics:** Consultants can offer market insights; recommend licensing strategies; and help you identify the right opportunities, structure deals effectively, and navigate potential challenges.

Don't underestimate the value a knowledgeable consultant can bring to the table. Their fees may seem like an added expense, but the expertise and connections they offer can significantly boost your chances of success. Whether you're new to licensing or looking to expand your portfolio, a skilled consultant can be a game-changer for your business.

Do Consider the Risks

In brand licensing, risk comes with the territory. Consider the financial risks involved, from upfront licensing fees to production, marketing, and distribution costs. Licensing is an investment, and like any investment, it has no guarantees.

WARNING

But here's the flip side: Not taking action is also a risk. Playing it too safe can lead to missed opportunities for growth and innovation. Some of the most successful licensing deals started with calculated risks.

Ask yourself:

>> What's the worst-case scenario, and can my business handle it?

>> Do I have a contingency plan if things don't go as expected?

>> What's the risk of doing nothing and staying in my comfort zone?

Don't ignore risk, but don't let it paralyze you either. Smart licensing is about weighing the risks against the potential rewards and making informed, confident decisions. The goal isn't to eliminate risk; it's to manage the risk wisely.

Chapter **16**

Ten Essential Tips for Licensors

When we set out to write this book, our publisher asked us to focus on one key audience that would benefit the most. We chose licensees because they make up the largest group of new companies entering the licensing world. But to be clear, licensors (brand owners) are just as important! After all, without licensors, licensing wouldn't exist in the first place.

If you're a licensor, this chapter — and the ten suggestions in it — are for you. Although much of this book is aimed at helping licensees succeed, we believe you can gain just as much value. By understanding the needs of your licensees and retailers, you'll be better equipped to create successful partnerships and drive long-term success for everyone involved.

Develop a Strategic Licensing Plan

Jumping into licensing without a well-thought-out strategy is like setting sail without a map. To build a smart, successful, and sustainable licensing program, you need a comprehensive plan that evaluates your brand's strengths, competitive landscape, and retail opportunities.

At my (Stu's) company, Seltzer Licensing Group, we've built a reputation for developing thorough and strategic licensing plans for companies including General Electric, the National Parks, Campbell Soup, Scotts Miracle-Gro, and many others. Our proven approach focuses on two key questions:

>> What products and services can your brand successfully extend into?

>> How much royalty revenue should we expect?

Here's what your licensing strategic plan should include:

>> **Brand analysis:** Assess your brand's equity, brand awareness, and consumer demand.

>> **Competitive analysis:** Research how other brands in your category are leveraging licensing.

>> **Category analysis:** Thoroughly evaluate each product and service category for licensing opportunities. Assess market demand, competitive landscape, pricing trends, and potential challenges to determine where your brand can successfully extend and thrive.

>> **Retailer analysis:** Identify the right retail channels and potential distribution partners.

>> **Revenue projections:** Set realistic expectations for royalty revenue by including both conservative and aggressive projections. A well-balanced forecast helps you plan for steady growth while identifying high-potential opportunities for maximizing royalty income.

>> **Brand impressions:** Many collaboration deals today focus on increasing visibility rather than direct revenue. If brand exposure is a key objective, set clear expectations for how impressions will be tracked and evaluated.

REMEMBER

By developing a strategic, data-driven licensing plan, you position your brand for long-term success, create new consumer touchpoints, and maximize revenue potential.

Invest in Style Guides and Presentation Materials

A successful licensing program requires more than just a strong brand; it also needs the right tools to guarantee consistency, professionalism, and brand integrity across all licensed products. By investing in professional licensing tools, you set up your program for long-term success, ensuring that every licensed product stays true to your brand's identity and meets your quality standards.

One of the most critical tools for licensors is the *style guide,* which provides essential guidelines and resources for licensees to develop products that align with your brand's identity. A style guide serves as a blueprint for brand consistency, detailing everything a licensee needs to know to correctly represent your brand: logo usage, typography, Pantone Matching System (PMS) colors, packaging specifications, and legal disclaimers that must appear on all licensed products. It also provides mechanical artwork and templates to ensure brand assets are reproduced accurately across all materials. Without a detailed style guide, your brand risks inconsistency and misrepresentation in the marketplace.

A licensing *presentation deck* is another important marketing tool designed specifically for meeting with potential licensees. This presentation outlines the brand's story, key assets, consumer reach, and licensing opportunities; it helps prospective partners understand your brand's value and why they should invest in a licensing deal. A well-crafted presentation can make the difference between attracting high-quality licensees and missing out on great opportunities.

Join the Licensing Community

Licensing is a relationship-driven industry, and joining the licensing community is one of the best ways to gain insight, build connections, and stay ahead of industry trends. A great starting point is Licensing International (`licensinginternational.org`), the leading trade association for the licensing industry. Becoming a member provides access to market research, networking events, educational resources, and industry reports that can help you navigate the licensing landscape more effectively.

To stay informed, subscribe to key industry newsletters, including *License Global* (`www.licenseglobal.com`), which offers daily updates on licensing's latest news, trends, and top players.

Another critical step is attending licensing trade shows and networking events. The largest event in the industry, Licensing Expo, takes place in Las Vegas each spring. This global marketplace connects brand owners (licensors), licensing agents, licensees (manufacturers), and retailers looking for new partnerships. If you're serious about licensing, attending Licensing Expo is a must. You can also find regional events such as Brand Licensing Europe (BLE) in London (focused on Europe, the Middle East, and Africa) and Licensing Expo China (catering to the booming Chinese market). We offer a long list of licensing events in Chapter 5.

Additionally, industry organizations like the Society of Product Licensors Committed to Excellence (SPLiCE) offer valuable resources, particularly for corporate brand licensors. The X Tracks Licensing Summits, launched in 2022, provide high-level networking and insights into emerging licensing trends.

Ensure Your Trademarks Are Protected

Before launching a licensing program, one of the most important steps you can take is making sure your trademarks are properly protected. Licensing agreements are built around your intellectual property (IP), so without secure trademarks, your brand may be at risk. Consulting with a qualified trademark attorney ensures that your brand names, logos, and other IP assets are properly filed, registered, and legally protected with the appropriate government agencies.

TIP

Not all IP attorneys have experience with licensing. When hiring a lawyer, look for one with a proven track record in both trademark protection and licensing agreements.

By working with the right trademark attorney, you safeguard your brand, prevent legal disputes, and set the foundation for a strong, sustainable licensing program. Taking these steps upfront protects your most valuable asset — your brand — before you bring it into the licensing marketplace.

Stay on Top of Tracking and Optimizing Licensing Revenue

Licensing isn't a set-it-and-forget-it business. Actively tracking your royalties and financial performance is critical to ensuring a successful program. Most licensing agreements require quarterly royalty reporting, so you need to review these reports diligently to confirm payments are accurate and on time. Keeping an eye on sales trends and licensee projections can help you identify potential growth opportunities and step in with support if sales are underperforming.

TIP

Beyond just tracking revenue, ask your licensees for their retail placements; knowing where your licensed products are being sold provides valuable insight into market performance and brand visibility. If certain products are excelling at specific retailers, you can adjust your strategy to build on that success.

To streamline royalty tracking, consider investing in licensing management software. Platforms like Brand Comply by Octane5, Flowhaven, and Dependable Solutions offer automated tools for tracking royalties, managing approvals, and overseeing contract compliance. These tools help licensors stay organized, improve accuracy, and maximize royalty revenue.

Consider Hiring a Licensing Agency

Building a successful licensing program requires time, expertise, and industry connections. *Licensing agencies* specialize in matching brands with the right partners; they leverage their existing relationships with manufacturers, retailers, and distributors to speed up the process and secure high-quality deals. Hiring a licensing agency can accelerate your success by bringing efficiency, strategic guidance, and direct access to key players in the licensing world.

A great agency acts as an extension of your team, helping to refine your licensing strategy, negotiate agreements, and manage ongoing relationships. It also stays ahead of market trends, ensuring that your licensing program evolves with consumer demand. Additionally, many agencies offer financial management services that track royalty collections, monitor projections, and make sure licensees are reporting and paying accurately. By overseeing the financial side of licensing, agencies help streamline cash flow, reduce administrative burdens, and identify opportunities for revenue growth. Although an agency typically takes a percentage of royalty revenue, its expertise and connections often result in faster deal-making, higher-quality licensing partnerships, and a well-managed financial structure that maximizes long-term earnings.

TIP

However, not all agencies are created equal, so choosing the right one is critical. Consider factors such as their experience with similar brands, industry specialization, global reach, and track record of success. Take the time to interview multiple firms. Ask for (and confirm) their references, and ensure their approaches align with your brand's DNA.

Keep Your Brand Safe and Successful by Managing Licensing Risks

Licensing can be a powerful growth tool, but it also comes with risks. Your brand is your most valuable asset. When you license it to another company, you're trusting that company to uphold your brand's reputation, quality standards, and consumer trust. If a licensee fails to meet expectations — whether through poor product quality, misaligned marketing, or ethical missteps — the damage falls back on your brand.

To mitigate these risks, putting safeguards in place is essential. Start by vetting potential licensees thoroughly, ensuring they align with your brand values and have a proven track record. Hiring an experienced licensing agency (as we discuss in the preceding section) and legal counsel can help negotiate strong contracts, establish brand protections, and enforce compliance. Additionally, implementing a rigorous internal approval process — which may involve your brand team, legal department, and R and D team — makes sure that every licensed product meets your standards before it reaches the market.

REMEMBER

By proactively managing risks, you protect your brand's integrity, strengthen consumer trust, and create a licensing program that enhances (rather than jeopardizes) your brand's long-term success.

Plan for a Long-Term Investment

Licensing takes time. It isn't an instant revenue generator; it requires careful planning, patience, and a long-term vision. Many brand owners expect quick returns, but in reality, the first dollar may not arrive for up to 18 months.

This lag happens because licensing follows a structured process: First, the licensing agreement must be signed. Then the licensee develops the product, presents it at trade shows, secures retail distribution, manufactures the product, and finally ships it to retailers. Each step takes time, and delays can occur due to market conditions, product development cycles, and retail buyer timelines. A well-structured licensing plan accounts for this timeline, ensuring sustainable growth, realistic revenue expectations, and long-term success.

Strengthen Your Partnerships by Hosting a Licensing Summit

Brand owners should consider hosting an annual summit. A *licensing summit* is a powerful way to bring all your licensees together, fostering collaboration, alignment, and brand consistency. These gatherings provide an opportunity to update licensees on new marketing materials, brand initiatives, and upcoming campaigns so you keep everyone on the same page. In-person summits are ideal, but virtual events can also be effective.

A licensing summit also creates valuable networking opportunities. Licensees can meet each other, share best practices, and discuss retail success stories — which often leads to cross-promotional opportunities and a stronger, more unified licensing program. *Remember*: Your licensees are your business partners, and building personal relationships with them helps create trust, loyalty, and a shared commitment to growing the brand. By investing in a regular licensing summit, you reinforce collaboration, strengthen brand messaging, and help licensees succeed; in turn, that benefits your entire licensing program.

Expand Your Licensing Program Globally

Many successful licensors start with a domestic licensing strategy before scaling globally, ensuring they have a strong foundation to build on. If your licensing program is thriving in one region, it may be time to expand into international markets. Expanding globally allows you to tap into new revenue streams, increase brand awareness, and establish a presence in key international markets.

REMEMBER

Expanding globally isn't just about increasing sales; it's about strategically growing your brand's footprint while maintaining quality and integrity. With careful planning, the right partners, and a well-structured licensing strategy, your brand can successfully extend its reach worldwide and unlock new opportunities for long-term growth.

To do so effectively, research which global territories align with your brand's identity and consumer demand. Partnering with regional licensing agents can help you navigate the complexities of international licensing, including cultural preferences, regulatory requirements, and retail distribution strategies. Additionally, work closely with local retailers and manufacturers to ensure brand consistency and compliance across different markets.

IN THIS CHAPTER

» Exploring how licensing expands brand reach

» Considering the most popular types of licensed brands

» Checking out licensing in action in the real world

Chapter **17**

(Nearly) Ten Brand Licensing Areas

From entertainment and fashion to sports, nonprofits, and even museums, licensing is all around you if you just look. Whether you're walking through a department store, attending a sporting event, or scrolling through social media, you're likely encountering licensed products tied to major brands.

In this chapter, we explore the most popular categories of licensed brands. We also help you identify which categories offer the best licensing potential and understand how different industries use licensing to expand their influence.

Entertainment and Character Licensing

Entertainment and character licensing is the largest sector in licensing, generating $147.6 billion in retail sales (a 41.4 percent market share) in 2023. Across Hollywood studios and gaming franchises and beyond, this category drives some of the biggest deals in licensing. It includes areas like the following:

» Movies and TV shows such as *Star Wars,* Marvel movies, and *Harry Potter* properties

>> Video games like Pokémon, Fortnite, and Minecraft

>> Publishing, including iconic authors and book series like Dr. Seuss and the *Harry Potter* novels

If a character or franchise has a fan base, chances are it has a thriving licensing program! Examples of entertainment licensing in action include

>> **Batman X Thermos:** Licensed Batman lunchboxes, letting kids take their favorite superheroes to school

>> **Star Wars X Hasbro:** Licensed action figures, bringing characters like Luke Skywalker and Darth Vader to life

>> **Hello Kitty X J. Franco:** Licensed Hello Kitty bedding, adding cute and colorful designs to kids' rooms

>> **Jurassic Park X Rubie's:** Licensed Jurassic Park Halloween costumes, letting fans dress up as dinosaurs and movie characters

TIP

Visit the International Licensing Expo in Las Vegas, where more than half of the exhibitors showcase entertainment brands.

Corporate Brand Licensing

Corporate brand licensing is the second-largest licensing sector, valued at $90.3 billion (a 25.3 percent market share). Major companies such as the following use licensing to extend their brand into new categories, creating products that reinforce their identity and connect with consumers in new ways:

>> **Food and beverage brands:** Coca-Cola, Starbucks, McDonald's. Nestle is the licensee for Starbucks Coffee sold in supermarkets.

>> **Consumer goods giants:** Procter & Gamble, Unilever. For example, Procter & Gamble licensed its Vicks brand for a Vicks vaporizer. And Unilever's Breyers name appears on licensed hot fudge and ice cream toppings.

>> **Automotive leaders:** Jeep, General Motors, Ferrari. Did you know you can buy Jeep-branded luggage? That's licensing.

>> **Electronics/technology:** Hewlett-Packard (HP), Kodak, Westinghouse. HP has licensed branded printer paper.

Sports Licensing

Sports licensing is a massive industry, representing 11.1 percent of the licensing market with $39.5 billion in retail sales. Fans are loud and proud, making this licensing category one of the most visible. Just walk into a stadium, sports bar, or even your local mall to see jerseys, hats, and team gear everywhere. Fans are willing to spend big to support their teams, and that's why sports licensing is one of the most consistent and visible forms of brand loyalty.

Here are some examples of who's in the game:

>> **National Football League (NFL):** NFL jerseys by Nike; Superbowl championship T-shirts by Fanatics; video games by Electronic Arts

>> **Major League Baseball (MLB):** Caps by New Era; official uniforms by Nike; trading cards by the Topps division of Fanatics

>> **National Basketball Association (NBA):** Jerseys by Nike; trading cards by Panini

>> **National Hockey League (NHL):** Jerseys by Adidas; trading cards by Upper Deck

>> **Major League Soccer (MLS):** *Kits* (that's soccer speak for "jerseys") by Adidas

>> **The United States Olympic Committee (USOC):** Team USA apparel by Ralph Lauren

>> **International football (soccer) clubs:** Manchester United kits by Adidas

Fashion and Apparel Licensing

Fashion licensing has allowed some of the biggest designer brands to expand beyond clothing and into high-margin categories like fragrances, eyewear, footwear, and home décor. Fashion and Apparel licensing accounts for 9 percent of the licensing market ($33 billion). By licensing their names, these fashion houses maintain brand prestige while generating billions in retail sales across multiple product lines. They extend their brand equity into lucrative categories without directly managing manufacturing. Licensing has transformed luxury and lifestyle brands into multicategory powerhouses, making fashion licensing a critical driver of global brand expansion.

You can find designer fragrances, sunglasses, footwear, and more in your local department store that started as licensed extensions of top fashion brands. Examples include the following:

>> **Yves Saint Laurent (YSL):** Fragrances by L'Oréal; eyewear by Luxottica; shoes by Schwartz and Benjamin

>> **Ralph Lauren:** Fragrances by L'Oréal; intimates by Delta Galil; home furniture by Theodore Alexander; underwear by Hanesbrands

>> **Calvin Klein:** Watches by Movado; outerwear by G-III apparel; bedding by Revman

>> **Vera Wang:** Fragrances by Coty; flowers by FTD; jewelry by Zales Corporation

>> **Tommy Hilfiger:** Fragrance by Estee Lauder; eyewear by Safilo; kids' apparel by Centric Brands

Celebrity and Influencer Brand Licensing

In today's market, celebrities and influencers have transformed their personal brands into powerful business empires. With loyal fan bases and significant social media influence, these personalities leverage licensing agreements to expand their reach and offer products that resonate with their audiences. Fans are eager to purchase items associated with their favorite celebrities, creating mutually beneficial partnerships between the personalities and brands.

Who's leading the charge?

>> **Kim Kardashian:** Entrepreneur and media personality with successful ventures in fashion and beauty. Both of her beauty brands, KKW Beauty and Kroma Beauty, are licensed. KKW to Coty and Kroma directly to retailer CVS.

>> **Kylie Jenner:** Influencer and businesswoman known for her impactful beauty and fashion lines. Kylie Jenner X Coty led to Kylie Cosmetics, a beauty brand offering a range of makeup products.

>> **Paris Hilton:** Socialite and entrepreneur with a diverse portfolio of licensed products. Paris Hilton X Parlux Fragrances is a line of perfumes available at major retailers, including Walmart.

>> **Drew Barrymore:** Actress and entrepreneur with a focus on accessible home and kitchen products. Drew Barrymore licensed her brand to Walmart to create the Flower Home Collection.

TIP

Pay close attention to those prominently featured celebrity-branded products in your local retail stores or online marketplaces to see who's turning fame into a thriving business model.

Music Brand Licensing

Music artists aren't just performers; they've evolved into brands with dedicated fan bases. Through strategic licensing, these artists expand (and monetize) their influence beyond music, creating products that resonate with their audiences and reinforce their brand identities. From fashion collaborations to food products, music licensing transforms fan loyalty into tangible lifestyle brands.

These folks are just some of the acts rocking the licensing world:

» **Grateful Dead:** Pioneers in band merchandising, extending their iconic imagery into various products. That includes Ben and Jerry's Cherry Garcia ice cream, a tribute to Jerry Garcia that blends cherry ice cream with cherries and fudge flakes.

» **Taylor Swift:** A modern pop icon known for her strategic brand partnerships and merchandise. Taylor Swift X Stella McCartney was a fashion collaboration inspired by Swift's *Lover* album.

» **KISS:** The kings of rock and roll licensing, turning their image into an empire of branded products. They even licensed KISS-branded coffins and urns, which give fans the ultimate way to rock even in the afterlife.

Art and Museum Licensing

Art and museum licensing brings timeless masterpieces and cultural heritage into everyday life through unique and creative product collaborations. Museums and cultural institutions leverage licensing to expand their influence beyond gift shops, generating revenue while making art more accessible to the public. From high-end collaborations to affordable collectibles, this sector brings history and creativity into everyday life.

Who's showcasing art licensing?

>> **Museum of Modern Art (MoMA):** Partners with brands to create MoMA-inspired home décor, fashion, and games. LEGO X MOMA and Vincent van Gogh, a LEGO set featuring *The Starry Night*, brings fine art to toy shelves.

>> **The Metropolitan Museum of Art (The Met):** Licenses artwork for Samsung's Art Store, allowing users to display famous pieces on Samsung's Frame TVs.

>> **The Louvre:** Partners with luxury brands to create art-inspired fashion and home décor collections. Collaborations include a collection of T-shirts and sweaters with the Japanese clothing chain Uniqlo and home furnishings by Maison Sarah Lavoine.

>> **Smithsonian Institution:** Extends its influence into educational toys, collectibles, and home goods. Retailer Crate & Barrel has licensed the Smithsonian for a line of kids furniture and room décor under their Crate & Kids label.

>> **Victoria and Albert Museum (V&A):** Collaborates with fashion and interior designers to incorporate historical patterns into modern designs. V&A X Wedgwood is a line of tableware inspired by historical ceramics from the museum's collection.

Nonprofits and Licensing

Nonprofit organizations may not be traditional consumer brands, but they have all the characteristics of a solid licensed brand: a powerful mission, strong brand recognition, and an incredibly loyal following. Licensing allows nonprofits to extend their impact, raise awareness, and generate revenue to support their causes. Whether it's disaster relief organizations, environmental groups, or another cause, nonprofits leverage licensing to create meaningful products that resonate with their supporters.

REMEMBER

Consumers who align with a cause are more likely to purchase licensed products that reflect their values and contribute to a mission they believe in. National Park–themed toys, Red Cross safety products, and Girl Scout Cookie–flavored treats are all ways nonprofit licensing turns brand loyalty into real-world impact.

Here are a few nonprofits flexing their licensing muscles:

» **American Red Cross:** A globally recognized disaster relief and humanitarian organization. With Kidde, it licensed smoke detectors, reinforcing the Red Cross's mission of fire safety. American Red Cross X Cascade involves licensed water filtration bottles that promote disaster preparedness.

» **National Park Foundation (NPF):** The official nonprofit partner of the U.S. National Park Service, supporting America's public lands. National Park Foundation X Melissa and Doug includes licensed educational toys inspired by nature and wildlife. NPF has also partnered with Stance to license socks featuring designs from America's most iconic parks.

» **Girl Scouts of the USA:** Leverages its beloved cookie brand and mission-driven programs for fun and engaging licensed products. For example, Breyers sells licensed Thin Mints ice cream, turning the iconic cookie into a delicious frozen treat. Girl Scouts X Chameleon Organic Coffee offers licensed Girl Scout Cookie–inspired cold brew.

Index

NUMBERS

1p (first party) selling options, Amazon, 124–125
3p (third party) selling options, Amazon, 124–125

A

A properties, 89–90, 162
Abloh, Virgil, 19
accounting personnel, 132–133
Acme and the American Red Cross, 32
adult animation, 199
advance payments, licensing agreement, 92
advertising
  brand recognition and, 180
  to consumers, 109–110
  defined, 8
  marketing promotions, 125
  outside agency, 126
  social media marketing
    fan conventions, 177
    fans, 176
    product promotion, 174–175
    recognizing scope of, 175
    social media effect, 176
    superfans, 176–177
  trade advertising, 109
  utilizing partner's existing marketing
    tools, 125–126
  working with licensor partner, 126–127
agents, licensing, 74
agreements. *See* licensing agreement
AI (artificial intelligence)
  AI-generated brands, 192
  brand collaborations, 18
  expanding licensing with, 45–46
  researching licensing opportunities with, 69–70
Air Jordans, 18, 50–51

Airbnb, 196
Amazon Merch and Printful, 193
American Lawn Mower Company, 30
American Ninja Warrior (TV series), 199
American Red Cross, 225
animation, adult, 199
Anime Expo, 75
Anime Japan, 76
Apple, 22–23, 116
art licensing, 44–45, 223–224
artificial intelligence. *See* AI
athleisure, 200
attorney, intellectual property (IP), 86–87
audits of sales and royalties
  attitude toward, 144–145
  common audit issues, 145–148
  handling accounting errors, 148–149
  reasons for, 144
Authentic Brands Group, 36–37
authenticity, 25
auto-renewals, licensing agreement, 92
avatars, 18, 58

B

B properties, 89–90
Balenciaga, 18, 167, 193
Barrymore, Drew, 222
Batali, Mario, 166–167
Batman franchise, 30, 156, 159–160, 220
BAYC (Bored Ape Yacht Club), 55–56
Beatlemaniacs, 50
Beijing International Book Fair, 76
Ben and Jerry's, 223
Better Homes and Gardens, 12, 37, 196
BLE (Brand Licensing Europe), 75, 213
Blippi, 62, 166

blockchain technology, 52, 55, 192–193

Bluestar Alliance, 39

BMW, 29

Bologna Children's Book & Licensing Fair, 76

book fairs, 76

Bored Ape Yacht Club (BAYC), 55–56

brand collaboration
  Air Jordan sneakers, 19
  defined, 18, 47
  Doritos and Taco Bell, 48
  Jurassic Park X Rubie's collaboration, 220
  Kentucky Fried Chicken and Crocs, 47
  Lady Gaga and OREO, 19
  Off-White and American Red Cross, 19
  reasons for, 48–49
  Star Wars and LEGO, 32
  Star Wars X Hasbro, 220
  superfans and, 49–51
  Supreme and Louis Vuitton, 19
  tips for, 49

brand equity, 11–12, 158, 195

brand identity, 22

brand licensing. *See also* celebrity and influencer
    licensing; consumer product licensing;
    digital licensing; licensing process;
    partnerships, licensing
  administrative tasks, 149–150
  art and museum licensing, 223–224
  boosting sales through, 15–16
  brand collaborations, 18–19
  brand equity and, 11–12
  brand licensing ecosystem, 132–133
  building strong relationships, 207
  business trends
    direct-to-retail partnerships, 195–196
    discount retailers, 196
    licensing holding companies, 195
    retail consolidation, 196
    sharing economy, 196–197
    zombie brands, 195
  character licensing, 219–220
  Coca-Cola, 10–11
  for competitive advantage, 32–33

complying with licensing agreements, 207–208

consumer products, 13, 16–17

copyrights, 15

corporate brand licensing, 220

cultural trends
  entertainment and media, 199
  experiential licensing, 200
  fandom, 200
  food, health, and lifestyle licensing, 198–199

elevating product with, 32

entertainment licensing, 40–43,199, 219–220

evaluating risks, 209

experiential licensing, 14, 17, 40–41, 62–63

fashion and apparel licensing, 221–222

hiring licensing consultants, 208–209

investing in legal support, 208

layers of, 153–154

learning from the past, 190

leveraging licensor's marketing power, 206

as marketing powerhouse, 9

music brand licensing, 223

nonprofits and licensing, 224–225

onion metaphor, 154

overview, 8

patents, 15

planning properly, 204–205

power of, 29–31

presentation deck, 213

pure-play licensing, 36

reasons for growth in, 1

researching brand opportunity, 203–204

risk and, 33–34

securing licenses for international markets
  finding global properties, 186
  globalization of retail businesses, 185–186
  intellectual property, 186–188
  sublicensing, 186

setting realistic financial expectations, 205

sports licensing, 221

technology trends impacting
  AI-generated brands and intellectual
    property, 192
  blockchain, 192–193

digital licensing, 193
digital ownership, 192–193
mobile licensing, 194
non-fungible tokens, 192–193
print-on-demand, 193
virtual goods, 193
trademarks, 14
walking away from bad deals, 205–206
Brand Licensing Europe (BLE), 75, 213
brand licensors. *See* licensors
brand loyalty, 23
brand owners. *See* licensors
brand perception, 23
brand promise, 22
brand value, 11–12, 158, 195
branded skins, 18
branding
brand identity, 22
brand loyalty, 23
brand perception, 23
brand promise, 22
defined, 22
emotional branding, 26–27
importance of, 23
purchase pyramid, 28–29
trust in brands, 24–25, 28–29
brick-and-mortar stores, 116, 123–124
Bubba Gump Shrimp Co. cafe, 16
business associations, 72–73
business relationships, building
making good first impression, 78–79
pitching to licensors, 79–80
trust, 78
unique selling proposition, 79
business trends
direct-to-retail partnerships, 195–196
discount retailers, 196
licensing holding companies, 195
retail consolidation, 196
sharing economy, 196–197
zombie brands, 195

C

C properties, 89–90
CAGR (compound annual growth rate), 184
Calvin Klein, 222
campaigns, promotional, 171
cannabis branding and licensing, 60–61
Caterpillar, 11
celebrity and influencer licensing
Alba, Jessica, 62
Barrymore, Drew, 222
Batali, Mario, 166–167
Beyonce, 62
Cyrus, Miley, 165
Deen, Paula, 166–167
Hilton, Paris, 222
Jenner, Kylie, 222
Jordan, Michael, 19, 51
Kardashian, Kim, 222
Kardashian-Jenner empire, 62
Lady Gaga, 165
overview, 222–223
Paltrow, Gwyneth, 62
Rhianna, 62
Scott, Travis, 165
Temple, Shirley, 61–62
West, Kanye, 166–167
YouTube celebrities, 62
Chang, David, 198
channels of distribution, licensing agreement, 91
character licensing, 219–220
ChatGPT, 69, 70
Chevy Corvette, 12
Chief Merchandising Officer (CMO), 117
clearance allowance, 121
Coca-Cola, 220
brand identity, 22, 29
chewing gum, 10–11
collaboration with OREO, 52
fashion and apparel, 10
selecting licensing partners, 10
spending money to make money, 10
trademark, 14

collaboration. *See* brand collaboration

Comic-Con International, 75

common marketing fund percentage, 94

communication. *See also* marketing and
public relations

  in licensing partnerships, 134–137

  public relations, 108–109

  role in building strong relationships, 207

  social media

    connecting with licensors via, 84

    earned social media, 173

    emotional branding and, 25

    fan conventions, 177

    monthly active users, 175

    paid social media, 173

    product promotion, 174–175

    recognizing scope of, 175

    social media effect, 176

    superfans, 176–177

  transparency and, 24

Competitive Advantage (Porter), 32

compound annual growth rate (CAGR), 184

conferences and trade shows

  book fairs, 76

  consumer products and housewares, 76

  expos, 73

  fashion and apparel-related, 75

  food and beverage, 77

  home, lifestyle, and interior design, 77

  industry trade shows, 83–84

  licensing trade shows, 82–83

  licensing-specific, 75

  sports and outdoors, 77

  toys, games, and entertainment, 75–76

consignment, 121

consultants, licensing, 74

Consumer Electronics Show, 76

consumer product licensing

  designing product

    building trust as licensee, 101

    designers, 99–100

    digital/virtual products, 98

    experiential products, 98

    physical products, 98

    product approval, 100–101

    style guide, 98–99

  developing pricing strategy, 107

  entertainment licensing for, 40–41

  finding manufacturer for

    licensor's guidelines, 102–103

    mass-market manufacturing for retail, 103

    print-on demand, 104

    shipping and duty costs, 104–105

  marketing and public relations, 108–110

  matching product to license

    non-exclusive licenses, 72

    overview, 70–71

    retail intelligence, 71

  overview, 13, 16–17

  packaging, 105–106

consumer products and housewares trade shows
and conferences, 76

consumer psychology, 26–27

contracts, smart, 55

copyrights, 15

core product releases, 171

corporate brand licensing, 220

Costco, 182

COVID-19 pandemic

  brand collaborations and, 44, 52

  branded experiences and, 63

  experiential retail and, 116

  impact on Hollywood, 163

creative director, 132

cross-collateralization, 94

cultural trends

  entertainment and media, 199

  fandom, 200

  food, health, and lifestyle licensing,
198–199

culture licensing, 44–45

customers, engaging with. *See* engaging
with customers

Cyrus, Miley, 165

D

deal memo (term sheet), 93
Deen, Paula, 166–167
designing products
  building trust as licensee, 101
  designers, 99–100
  digital/virtual products, 98
  experiential products, 98
  physical products, 98
  product approval, 100–101
  style guide, 98–99
Diamond, Stephanie, 175
digital licensing
  Dodo, 53–54
  emoji company, 53–54
  navigating, 18–19
  non-fungible tokens, 54–56
  online betting, 57
  overview, 14
  phygital products, 56–57
  virtual goods, 193
digital ownership, 192–193
direct-to-consumer (DTC), 191
direct-to-retail (DTR) partnerships, 37, 195–196
discount retailers, 196
Disney, Walt, 41
disposable income, 180
distribution strategy, sales, 155–156
Divisional Merchandise Manager (DMM), 117–118
Dockers, 12
Dodo, The, 53–54
Dotdash Meredith, 37
DTC (direct-to-consumer), 191
DTR (direct-to-retail) partnerships, 37, 195–196
Dunder-Mifflin paper, 114
duty costs, 104–105, 182

E

earned placement, 171
earned social media, 173
Eating Right Kids private-label line, 196

e-commerce
  advantages and disadvantages of, 122–123
  Amazon, 124–125
  hybrid retail, 123–124
Elad, Joel, 84
email marketing, 9
emoji company, 53–54
emotional branding, 26–27
endcap displays, 172
engaging with customers. *See also* marketing and public relations
  branded experiences, 63
  building brand trust by, 25
  digital licensing, 18
  mobile licensing, 194
  online betting, 57
  with social media, 25
entertainment licensing, 40–43, 199, 219–220
equity, brand, 11–12, 158, 195
ESPN, 56
Etsy, 193
event-based marketing, 125
evergreen property, 39
experiential licensing, 14, 17, 40–41, 62–63, 200
experiential retail, 98, 116

F

factory audits, 121
fan conventions, 177
fandom, 49–51, 176–177, 200
fashion and apparel licensing, 221–222
fashion and apparel-related trade shows and conferences, 75
Ferrari, 220
first party (1p) selling options, Amazon, 124–125
Flintstones, The, 42–43
food, health, and lifestyle licensing, 198–199
food and beverage trade shows and conferences, 77
Forrest Gump (movie), 16
franchise films, 199

Frankfurt Book Fair, 76
free-standing inserts (FSIs), 172
FRIENDS Experience, 17

G

Gaines, Chip, 196
Gaines, Joanna, 196
Gamercon, 75
geek culture, 200
Gen Alpha, 17, 60
Gen Z, 17, 60
General Motors, 220
Girl Scouts of the USA, 225
Global Licensing Group, The, 83
globalization of brands
  global market
    responding to global demand for unique
      products, 183
    size and scope of, 184
  securing licenses for international markets
    finding global properties, 186
    globalization of retail businesses, 185–186
    intellectual property, 186–188
    sublicensing, 186
  United States
    advertising and brand recognition, 180
    Hollywood, 180
    top brand licensing companies, 181
Goldner, Brian, 38
Grande, Ariana, 193
Grateful Dead, 12, 223
guaranteed minimum royalty payments
  (GMRPs), 89–90, 92
guaranteed sale (return privilege), 121
Gucci, 193
GUND and Winnie the Pooh, 32

H

Haring, Keith, 12
Harry Potter brand, 40–41
Hasbro, 38, 186

Head of Buying, 117
Hello Kitty, 42, 48, 59, 220
Hewlett-Packard (HP), 220
High Point Market, 77
Hilton, Paris, 222
Hollywood
  brand globalization, 180
  impact of COVID-19 pandemic and writer's
    strike on, 163
home, lifestyle, and interior design trade shows
  and conferences, 77
Hopkins, Samuel, 179
HP (Hewlett-Packard), 220
hybrid retail, 123–124

I

identity, brand, 22
incremental sales, 205
industry bodies, 72–73
industry directories, 84
industry trade groups, 72–73
industry trade shows, 83–84
influencer and celebrity licensing
  Alba, Jessica, 62
  Barrymore, Drew, 222
  Batali, Mario, 166–167
  Beyonce, 62
  Cyrus, Miley, 165
  Deen, Paula, 166–167
  Hilton, Paris, 222
  Jenner, Kylie, 222
  Jordan, Michael, 19, 51
  Kardashian, Kim, 222
  Kardashian-Jenner empire, 62
  Lady Gaga, 165
  overview, 222–223
  Paltrow, Gwyneth, 62
  Rhianna, 62
  Scott, Travis, 165
  Temple, Shirley, 61–62
  West, Kanye, 166–167
  YouTube celebrities, 62

Ingersoll-Waterbury Clock Company, 41
innovation and trends
  business trends
    direct-to-retail partnerships, 195–196
    discount retailers, 196
    licensing holding companies, 195
    retail consolidation, 196
    sharing economy, 196–197
    zombie brands, 195
  cannabis branding and licensing, 60–61
  cultural trends
    entertainment and media, 199
    fandom, 200
    food, health, and lifestyle licensing, 198–199
  experiential licensing, 62–63
  technology trends
    AI-generated brands and intellectual property, 192
    blockchain, 192–193
    digital licensing, 193
    digital ownership, 192–193
    metaverse, 193
    mobile licensing, 194
    non-fungible tokens, 192–193
    print-on-demand, 193
    virtual goods, 193
  YouTube, 61–62
Inspired Home Show, The, 76
insurance, product liability, 121
intellectual property (IP)
  AI-generated brands and, 192
  from international markets, 186–188
  popular trends related to, 188
intellectual property (IP) attorney, 86–87
International Dairy Deli Bakery Association Expo, 77
International football (soccer) clubs, 221
international shipping, 182
IP. See intellectual property
ISPO Munich, 77

J
Jeep, 220
Jenner, Kylie, 222
Jordan, Michael, 19, 50–51
Jurassic Park X Rubie's collaboration, 220

K
Kamen, Herman "Kay," 41
Kardashian, Kim, 166, 222
Kidscreen Summit, 76
kidults, 200
KISS rock band, 223
Kodak, 220

L
Lady Gaga, 165
liability insurance, product, 121
License Global, 35, 68, 84, 181, 213
licensees. *See also* licensing process
  building trust with licensing partner, 78, 101
  crafting and submitting licensing proposal, 87–90
  defined, 8
  following licensor's guidelines, 102–103
  mass-market manufacturing for retail, 103
  matching product to license, 70–72
  of nonprofits, 45
  print-on demand, 104
  shipping and duty costs, 104–105
  for Yves Saint Laurent, 31
licensing agents, 74
licensing agreement
  canceling, 166–167
  discussing additional terms, 94–95
  minimum royalty payment guarantee, 162
  mitigating risk, 162–163
  negotiating basic terms of, 91–93
  term length, 161
  term sheet and, 93
licensing consultants, 74

Licensing Expo, 75, 82–83, 213

Licensing Expo China, 213

licensing holding companies, 195

Licensing International, 69, 84, 99, 183

Licensing Letter, The, 69

licensing managers, 110–111

licensing process

  building business relationships

    making good first impression, 78–79

    pitching to licensor, 79–80

    trust, 78

    unique selling proposition, 79

  licensing consultants, 74

  matching product to license

    non-exclusive licenses, 72

    overview, 70–71

    retail intelligence, 71

  negotiating license deal

    connecting with licensors, 82–84

    crafting and submitting licensing proposal, 87–90

    finding and hiring an intellectual property attorney, 86–87

    knowing when to walk away, 95

    licensing agreement, 90–93

    long-form legal agreement, 95

    using research to your advantage, 84–85

  researching opportunities

    with AI, 69–70

    online publications, 68–69

  SPACE HOLD, 67

  trade associations, 72–73

  trade shows and conferences, 75–77, 82–83

licensing summits, 217

licensors

  Authentic Brands Group, 36–37

  Bluestar Alliance, 39

  communication, 134–137

  connecting with

    with industry directories, 84

    at industry trade shows, 83–84

    at licensing trade shows, 82–83

    via social media, 84

  defined, 8

  Dotdash Meredith, 37

  embracing marketing assistance from, 157

  Hasbro, 38

  investment in marketing, 170–171

  manufacturer expectations, 102–103

  Mattel, 39

  NBC Universal/Universal Products & Experiences, 38

  packaging requirements, 105–106

  Pokémon Company International, 38–39

  respecting the partnership, 136–137

  staying connected with, 134–135

  tapping into retailers' marketing muscle, 171–173

  tips for

    developing strategic licensing plan, 211–212

    expanding licensing program globally, 217

    hiring a licensing agency, 215

    hosting licensing summits, 217

    investing in style guides and presentation materials, 212–213

    joining licensing community, 213–214

    managing risks, 216

    planning for long-term investment, 216

    protecting trademarks, 214

    tracking and optimizing licensing revenue, 214–215

  Walt Disney Company, 36

  Warner Bros./Discovery, 37–38

  WHP Global, 39

LinkedIn, 84

LinkedIn For Dummies (Elad), 84

London Book Fair, 76

long-form legal agreement, 95

Looney Tunes characters, 196

Louvre, The, 224

loyalty, brand, 23

M

Macy's, 123, 196

MAGIC Marketplace, 75

Magnolia, 195

Maison & Objet, 77
Major League Baseball (MLB), 56, 190–191, 221
Major League Soccer (MLS), 221
managers, licensing, 110–111
manufacturers. *See also* licensees
  building trust with licensing partner, 78, 101
  crafting and submitting licensing
    proposal, 87–90
  following licensor's guidelines, 102–103
  mass-market manufacturing for retail, 103
  matching product to license, 70–72
  print-on demand, 104
  shipping and duty costs, 104–105
markdown funds, 121
market challenges
  celebrity licenses, 165–167
  franchise classics, 164–165
  morality clause, 166–167
  timing delays, 164
marketing and public relations
  advertising to consumers, 109–110
  aligning retail distribution and marketing
    strategy, 158–160
  customers, 176–177
  licensor partners
    investment in marketing, 170–171
    tapping into retailers' marketing
      muscle, 171–173
  marketing promotions, 125
  maximizing public relations efforts, 108–109
  outside agency, 126
  social media marketing
    fan conventions, 177
    fans, 176
    product promotion, 174–175
    recognizing scope of, 175
    social media effect, 176
    superfans, 176–177
  trade advertising, 109
  utilizing partner's existing marketing
    tools, 125–126
  working with licensor partner, 126–127
marketing commitments, 94

marketing director, 133
Marketing For Dummies (McMurtry), 109
mass-market manufacturing for retail, 103
master toy license, 186
matching product to license
  non-exclusive licenses, 72
  overview, 70–71
  retail intelligence, 71
Mattel, 39, 106, 171
McCartney, Stella, 223
McDonald's, 14, 22, 220
McMurtry, Jeanette Maw, 109
media franchises, licensing revenue for, 187
Merch and Printful, Amazon, 193
metaverse, 45, 58–60, 193
Metropolitan Museum of Art, The (The Met), 224
Mickey Mouse, 29, 41, 180
Minecraft, 59
Mini Brands toys, 183
minimum royalty payment guarantee, 140, 162
MIPCOM, 76
MLB (Major League Baseball), 32, 56, 190–191, 221
MLS (Major League Soccer), 221
mobile licensing, 194
MoMA (Museum of Modern Art), 224
Momofuku, 198
monthly active users (MSUs), social media, 175
morality clause, 166–167
MrBeast, 62
Ms. Rachel, 62, 166
museum licensing, 223–224
Museum of Modern Art (MoMA), 224
music brand licensing, 223

N

National Basketball Association (NBA),
    190–191, 221
National Football League (NFL), 221
National Hockey League (NHL), 221
National Park Foundation (NPF), 225
National Restaurant Association, 77

Natural Products Expo, 77
NBC Universal/Universal Products & Experiences, 38, 114
negotiating license deal
  connecting with licensors
    with industry directories, 84
    at industry trade shows, 83–84
    at licensing trade shows, 82–83
    via social media, 84
  crafting and submitting licensing proposal
    estimating sales and royalties, 88–89
    guaranteed minimum royalty payment, 89–90
  finding and hiring an intellectual property attorney, 86–87
  knowing when to walk away, 95
  licensing agreement
    discussing additional terms, 94–95
    negotiating basic terms of, 91–93
    term sheet and, 93
  long-form legal agreement, 95
  using research to your advantage, 84–85
Nestle, 220
net operating revenue, 10
Netflix, 118
new content releases, 171
New York Comic-Con, 75
New York Toy Fair, 75
NFL (National Football League), 221
NHL (National Hockey League), 221
Nike, 14, 29, 50, 193
non-exclusive licenses, 72
non-fungible tokens (NFTs), 45, 54–56, 192–193
nonprofits and associations, 45, 224–225
nostalgia products, 42–43, 200
NPF (National Park Foundation), 225
Nutrabolt, 199
NY NOW, 77

O
Office Experience, 17
off-price retailers, 196
omnichannel retail, 39

online betting, 57
online resources
  brand collaborations, 47
  Cheat Sheet for book, 3
  Coca-Cola chewing gum, 11
  License Global, 68, 213
  Licensing Expo, 82
  Licensing International, 99, 184
  Society of Manufacturing Engineers, 102
  USPTO website, 15
online reviews and testimonials, 27
OREO, 19, 26, 44, 52
organization chart, retailers, 117–118
Outdoor Retailer, 76
owners, brand. See licensors

P
packaging products, 105–106
paid social media, 173
Paramount, 38, 157
partnerships, licensing
  brand licensing ecosystem, 132–133
  licensing relationship triangle, 133–134
  licensors
    communication, 134–137
    respecting the partnership, 136–137
    staying connected with, 134–135
    troubleshooting product development obstacles, 135–136
  marriage analogy, 131–132
  troubleshooting product development obstacles, 135–136
patents, 15
payments
  advance, 92
  minimum royalty payment guarantee, 140, 162
perception, brand, 23
phygital products, 56–57
physical products
  designing
    building trust as licensee, 101
    designers, 99–100

product approval, 100–101

style guide, 98–99

developing pricing strategy, 107

entertainment licensing for, 40–41

finding manufacturer for

licensor's guidelines, 102–103

mass-market manufacturing for retail, 103

print-on demand, 104

shipping and duty costs, 104–105

marketing and public relations, 108–110

matching to license

non-exclusive licenses, 72

overview, 70–71

retail intelligence, 71

overview, 13, 16–17

packaging, 105–106

pitching to licensors, 79–80

placement, product, 26, 120–121

POD (print-on-demand), 104, 193

point-of-sales figures, 110

Pokémon, 12, 38–39, 186–187

pop culture, emotional branding with, 26

Porter, Michael, 32

PR (public relations), 9. *See also* marketing and public relations

preferred vendors, 121–122

Première Vision Paris, 75

preselling licensed products, 156–157

presentation deck, 213

print-on-demand (POD), 104, 193

Procter & Gamble, 220

product approvals, 100–101

product liability insurance, 121

product placement, 26, 120–121

product sell-through, 117, 163

promise, brand, 22

promotional campaigns, 171

psychographics, 49

public relations (PR), 9. *See also* marketing and public relations

purchase pyramid, 28–29

pure-play licensing, 36

Q

quality assurance, 25

R

Ralph Lauren, 222

reality TV licensing, 199

Redbubble, 193

Reese's Ice Cream, 32

researching licensing opportunities

with AI, 69–70

online publications, 68–69

using research to your advantage, 84–85

resources, online. *See* online resources

retail and retailers

brick-and-mortar, 116, 123–124

e-commerce

Amazon, 124–125

hybrid retail, 123–124

finding best retailer for product, 116–122

globalization of, 185–186

marketing and public relations

outside agency, 126

utilizing partner's existing marketing tools, 125–126

working with licensor partner, 126–127

mass-market manufacturing for, 103

organization chart, 117–118

overview, 113–114

preferred vendors, 121–122

product placement, 120–121

researching retail partners, 117

retail channels, 115–116

three-star process, 118–120

wholesale versus retail, 115

retail business development

aligning retail distribution and marketing strategy, 158–160

Batman licensing lesson, 159–160

capitalizing on brand value of products, 158

distribution strategy, 155–156

retail business development *(continued)*
  embracing marketing assistance from
    licensor, 157
  preselling licensed products to retail, 156–157
  recognizing strength of existing licensed
    brands, 155
retail channels, 115–116
retail consolidation, 196
retail development experts, 133
retail intelligence, 71
return privilege (guaranteed sale), 121
risk
  brand licensing and, 33–34
  evaluating, 209
  managing proactively, 216
  mitigating, 162–163
  sales projections and, 156
Roblox, 59
Rogers, Will, 78
royalties. *See* sales and royalties
Ryan's World, 166

S

Safeway, 196
sales and royalties
  audits
    attitude toward, 144–145
    common audit issues, 145–148
    handling accounting errors, 148–149
    reasons for, 144
  estimating, 88–89
  licensing agreement
    minimum royalty payment guarantee, 162
    mitigating risk, 162–163
    term length, 161
  market challenges
    celebrity licenses, 165–167
    franchise classics, 164–165
    morality clause, 166–167
    timing delays, 164
  marketing tools that boost retail sales
    licensor partners, 170–173
    social media marketing, 173–175

reporting and paying
  licensors' common complaints about,
    142–143
  sending reports, 140–141
  on time and in full, 141–142
retail business development
  aligning retail distribution and marketing
    strategy, 158–160
  capitalizing on brand value of products, 158
  distribution strategy, 155–156
  embracing marketing assistance from
    licensor, 157
  preselling licensed products to retail, 156–157
  recognizing strength of existing licensed
    brands, 155
  tracking, 110
sales professionals, 132
San Diego Comic-Con, 177
sandbox games, 58–59
Scott, Travis, 165, 193
Scotts brand, 30
Scotts Miracle-Gro, 12
search engine optimization (SEO), 9
sector associations, 72–73
sell-off period, licensing agreement, 92
sell-through numbers, 110
Seltzer Licensing Group, 212
Semantic Web, 52
SEO (search engine optimization), 9
sharing economy, 196–197
Sharjah International Book Fair, 76
shipping and duty costs, 104–105, 182
Shopify, 123
SHOT Show, 77
Signature Foods and Breyers, 32
skins, branded, 18
Singh, Shiv, 175
smart contracts, 55
Smithsonian Institution, 224
sneakerhead culture, 50
soccer (International football) clubs, 221
social media
  connecting with licensors via, 84
  earned social media, 173

emotional branding and, 25

fan conventions, 177

monthly active users, 175

paid social media, 173

product promotion, 174–175

recognizing scope of, 175

social media effect, 176

superfans, 176–177

Social Media Marketing For Dummies (Singh and Diamond), 175

social proof, 25

Society of Manufacturing Engineers, 102

Society of Product Licensors Committed to Excellence (SPLiCE), 214

software, turnkey, 149

Solomonov, Michael, 198

sports and outdoors trade shows and conferences, 77

Sports Licensing and Tailgate Show, 77

sports licensing, 221

Stanton, Daniel, 115

Star Wars, 11

brand longevity, 155

Star Wars and LEGO, 32

Star Wars X Hasbro, 220

sublicensing, 186

Starbucks, 220

stocking shelf fees, 121

store checks, 117

stores, brick-and-mortar, 116, 123–124

storytelling, 25

streetwear, 200

style guide, 213

sublicensing, 143, 186

summits, licensing, 217

superfans, 49–51, 176–177

Supply Chain Management For Dummies (Stanton), 115

supply chain staff, 133

Sweets & Snacks Expo, 77

Swift, Taylor, 223

T

Target, 160, 165, 167, 193, 196

term sheet (deal memo), 93

territory, licensing agreement, 92

third party (3p) selling options, Amazon, 124–125

three-star process, retail, 118–120

Titanic Exhibition, 17

TJX Companies, 196

Tommy Hilfiger, 222

Topps and Major League Baseball (MLB), 32

toys, games, and entertainment trade shows and conferences, 75–76

trade advertising, 109

trade associations (industry trade groups; business associations; sector associations; industry bodies), 72–73

trade shows. See conferences and trade shows

trademarks

defined, 14

protecting, 214

transparency, 24, 173

trends and innovation

business trends

direct-to-retail partnerships, 195–196

discount retailers, 196

licensing holding companies, 195

retail consolidation, 196

sharing economy, 196–197

zombie brands, 195

cannabis branding and licensing, 60–61

cultural trends

entertainment and media, 199

fandom, 200

food, health, and lifestyle licensing, 198–199

experiential licensing, 62–63

technology trends

AI-generated brands and intellectual property, 192

blockchain, 192–193

digital licensing, 193

digital ownership, 192–193

metaverse, 193

trends and innovation *(continued)*
  mobile licensing, 194
  non-fungible tokens, 192–193
  print-on-demand, 193
  virtual goods, 193
  YouTube, 61–62
trust in brands
  building, 24–25, 28–29
  importance of, 24
trust-but-verify reaction, 144
turnkey software, 149

U

Uber, 196
Unilever, 32, 220
unique selling proposition (USP), 79
United States
  advertising and brand recognition, 180
  Hollywood, 180
  top brand licensing companies, 181
United States Olympic Committee (USOC), 221
Universal Pictures, 38, 114, 157
U.S. Patent and Trademark Office (USPTO), 14
user experiences, 25
USP (unique selling proposition), 79

V

value, brand, 11–12, 158, 195
vendors, preferred, 121–122
Victoria and Albert Museum (V&A), 224
video game licensing, 18, 58–60
virtual avatars, 18
virtual licensing, 14, 18, 193

W

Walmart
  Batman products, 160
  Better Homes and Gardens and, 37, 196

brand promise, 22
celebrity and influencer licensing, 165, 222
effect of Mattel's packaging error on, 106
globalization and, 185
hybrid retail, 123
print-on-demand, 193
Walt Disney Company,The, 36, 157
Warner Bros., 30, 37–38, 40–41, 156, 160, 171
Web3, 52–53
Weight Watchers (WW), 198–199
West, Kanye, 166–167
Westinghouse, 220
WeWork, 196
wholesaling, 115
WHP Global, 39
women's pro sports, 199
Writers Guild of America, 163
WW (Weight Watchers), 198–199

X

X Tracks Licensing Summit, 76, 214

Y

YouTube celebrities, 62
Yves Saint Laurent (YSL), 12, 29, 31, 222

Z

Zahav, 198
zombie brands, 46, 195
ZURU toy company, 183

About the Authors

Steven Ekstract is the founder of Global Licensing Advisors, a boutique consultancy that connects brands for collaborations and licensing. He's also founder and chief content curator of X Tracks Licensing Summits, executive-level licensing conferences focused on the latest trends in licensing started in 2022. From October 1997 to September 2020, he was the founder and longtime publisher of *License Global* magazine and various other publications for the licensing industry. He also served as the brand director for the Global Licensing Group of Informa Markets, providing oversight, content, and direction for its world-class licensing expositions in the United States, Europe, Japan, and China. In addition, he speaks extensively on licensing at conferences around the world. He serves on the Trend Committee for Spielwarenmesse's Nuremberg Toy Fair, the largest toy fair in the world.

Stu Seltzer is the president of Seltzer Licensing Group, a global agency he has guided for more than 25 years; it's renowned for its comprehensive expertise in brand licensing, partnership marketing, and strategic alliances. His understanding of the licensing field and adept negotiation skills were honed through pivotal roles at organizations such as Yves Saint Laurent and the DC Comics division at Warner Bros. His strategic insights have driven substantial returns on marketing investments for clients such as Unilever, Scotts Miracle-Gro, and the American Red Cross.

In academia, Stu has contributed significantly as an award-winning professor at New York University, where he has taught a pioneering course on brand licensing to undergraduates for more than 20 years. He's also a sought-after speaker who has delivered compelling seminars at various global conferences for decades. Stu's boundless enthusiasm is evident in his presence at industry trade shows, where he's known for his tireless energy and his company's entertaining video recaps. His passion for life and community involvement shine through in everything he does. This spirited approach inspires those around him, contributing further to his respected status in the industry.

Dedication

The authors would like to dedicate this book to Dan Romanelli, the first president of Warner Brothers Consumer Products and a true mentor, who so generously shared his wisdom and counsel with so many licensing colleagues.

Authors' Acknowledgments

The authors would like to thank the incredible *For Dummies* team for the guidance throughout this project — especially Steve Hayes, our acquisitions editor, who kept the faith; Traci Cumbay, Leah Michael, and Megan Knoll for their editing skills; and Chrissy Guthrie for her patience and insight. In particular, we wish to thank our intrepid literary agent, Marc Mikulich, who not only shepherded the project but also is passionate about the topic.

Publisher's Acknowledgments

Executive Editor: Steve Hayes

Development Editor: Christina Guthrie

Copy Editor: Megan Knoll

Senior Managing Editor: Kristie Pyles

Cover Image: © 2025 Peanuts Worldwide LLC